Touching Cloudbase

The Complete Guide to Paragliding

Ian Currer

6th Edition

Published by :

Air Supplies Publishing
Skywalk House
South Rd
Kirkby Stephen
Cumbria
CA17 4SY

First edition Published by Leading edge press Ltd 1991   ISBN 0-948135-27-1

Second edition published by Leading edge press Ltd 1992   ISBN 0 -948135-41-7

Third edition published by Air Supplies Publishing 1996   ISBN 0 9528862-0-0

Fourth edition published by Air Supplies Publishing 2003   ISBN 0 9528862-1-9

Fifth edition published by Air Supplies Publishing 2011   ISBN 978 0 9528862-2-8

Copyright: Ian Currer.

British Library Cataloguing in Publishing Data

A catalogue record for this book is available from the British Library

ISBN: 978-0-9528862-3-5

Text: Ian Currer

Illustrations: David Barber and Kathy Underwood

Page design and layout: Neil Cruickshank and Simon Mayoh

Cartoons: Bill Lehan

Printed and Bound: Cerberus Printing, Kirkby Stephen, England.

Contents

Ch.		Page
	Contents	3
	Acknowledgements	4
	Foreword	5
1	Introduction	6
2	History of Paragliding	7
3	Health and Safety	12
4	Introduction to the Equipment	16
5	How the canopy flies	22
6	Terms	27
7	The BHPA and the UK Pilot Rating System	33
8	Site Assessment	46
9	Weather Assessment	54
10	Parachute landing falls	57
11	Pre-Flight Checks	60
12	The Forward or Alpine launch technique	64
13	Reverse launches	67
14	Launch problems	74
15	First flights	77
16	Landing	85
17	After the Elementary/Parapro 2 stage	91
18	Other equipment	96
19	Buying a paraglider	111
20	Packing & Care of your equipment	118
21	Soaring flight	122
22	Accelerator systems	127
23	Site discipline & Rules of the air	130
24	Air Law	135
25	Meteorology	146
26	Cross Country	158
27	The Polar Curve	168
28	Instability and recovery	170
29	Emergency Procedures	178
30	Human Factors	185
31	Tow launching & Launching from Skis	189
32	Tandem Flying	193
33	Flying in new environments	200
34	Competitions	204
35	Becoming an instructor or coach	207
36	Paramotoring	209
37	Passing your Exams	229
38	Paragliding Equipment Design & Testing	232
39	Pushing the Limits	239
40	The Future	250
41	Information	252
	Glossary of terms	261
	Index	264

Acknowledgements

I am very grateful for the help and encouragement of many people and companies in producing this book.

In particular:

The late Bernard Kane and Stan Abbot for their encouragement back in 1990 in helping me get the first edition written.

Neil Cruckshank for the help, input and work in knocking subsequent editions into shape.

All the staff and instructors at Northern Paragliding Ltd and Sunsoar Paragliding Ltd. Especially Ian Brown.

The illustrations which are so important in this type of book are the work of David Barber and Kathy Underwood. Several are based on original drawings by Rob Cruickshank.

Photo credits are included in the book but special thanks are due to Ozone gliders, Red Bull, Skywalk gliders, Swing, U-Turn gliders, Gin gliders, Sup'Air SARL and Jerome Maupoint. (Whose inspirational 'photo graces the front cover).

And of course all the readers who have bought, read and given me feedback on previous editions.

Any mistakes are my own.

Finally thanks to Jackie for putting up with my flying obsession all these years.

Ian Currer May 2015

Foreword

Welcome to the absorbing world of paragliding. With this new edition of Touching Cloudbase as your guide you will progress with confidence in this wonderful aerial sport. Ian Currer has been right at the front of paragliding training throughout its development, and would appear on any list of the most respected instructors in the business.

The techniques revealed in this book have evolved from Ian's many years of experience as a BHPA Examiner and member of the Safety Panel. Read everything with care. Paragliding is not just another sport to play at. It is real flying and you have to learn to be a pilot. Once you have developed the mental outlook that being a safe pilot demands, and have mastered the basic flying techniques under good instruction, the sky really is the limit!

With a good instructor and benign weather, the early stages of learning to handle a paraglider can be very easy. In a few hours you will be able to skim down the training hill and land under control. Those flights will probably be as exhilarating as anything else you have ever done, but they are simply a beginning. It is vital that all the different skills and knowledge essential to piloting are built up steadily, together. Launching and guiding the wing are a very small part of an overall picture which includes terrain, weather, air law, glider choice, site discipline and advanced cross-country flying. Here, Ian leads you expertly through all the steps in an easy and understandable way.

In the many years since the first edition of this book appeared, paragliders have developed amazingly in both performance and safety. This new version will enable anyone to be up-to-date with the best-proven practices, drawn from worldwide experience. It is far more than simply a book for novices. I am sure that paraglider pilots in many countries will make Touching Cloudbase an essential source book for guidance through to the highest stages of qualification. I have every confidence in recommending it.

Noel Whittall

Noel has been Chairman of the British Hang Gliding Association, Secretary of the Hang Gliding and Paragliding Commission of the FAI and is author of several excellent books about flying for sport.

Introduction

Welcome to amazing world of paragliding.

If you are thinking about starting the sport or are already partway through your training you will soon find that your dreams of floating above the earth and soaring like a bird will be a reality.

There will be plenty of challenges, and it takes some time and effort to master the skills you will need. It takes some patience, especially if you are not lucky with the weather, but it is worth it for the rare experience of being one of the few who enjoy truly free flight.

Throughout this book both pilots and instructors are referred to as "he". This is only for the sake of writing style; paragliding is in many ways an ideal sport for women, and is certainly one on which women can participate on equal terms.

This book is meant as an aid to learning, and can be referred to throughout your training and flying career, but it is not a "teach yourself" manual. Paragliding is perhaps the simplest and easiest form of aviation, Thousands of people of all ages and backgrounds can become pilots, but like all adventurous sports there is an element of risk that can never be entirely eliminated. Paragliding can result in injury or death, especially if the pilot is poorly trained or flying in unsuitable weather conditions.

THE ONLY WAY TO LEARN SAFELY IS TO BE TRAINED BY A PROFESSIONAL QUALIFIED INSTRUCTOR.

If you have any questions on any topic in this book, or anything to do with flying, do not hesitate to ask your instructor. There is no substitute for experience and he or she will be happy to help.

It is not possible to make the sport completely safe, but by arming yourself with sufficient knowledge about your equipment and flying environment, you can make better informed decisions about your flying and be a more capable and safer pilot.

The aim of this book is help you towards that goal.

Ian Currer
January 2015.

Air Supplies Publishing
Skywalk House
South Rd
Kirkby Stephen
Cumbria
CA17 4SY

iancurrer@gmail.com

History of Paragliding

Back in the 1940's on the east coast of America, just down the road from the site of the Wright brothers' first successful flights, another aviation pioneer was conducting experiments with kites and gliding parachutes, made initially from pieces of glazed curtain material. His name was Dr. Francis Rogallo and, after much persuasion, his work was eventually followed up by his employers: NASA

It was 1948 when he filed for a patent for his flexible delta designs. From Dr. Rogallo's work came a whole mountain of research, testing and flexible wing (flex-wing) construction technology.

This resulted in both the Ryan Aircraft Company's bizarre looking aerial cargo-delivery wings – which used a folding kite wing – and most notably the steerable recovery parachutes used by the Gemini series in the US space programme.

But by far the most important offshoot of this research (as far as we are concerned), is that the Rogallo wing was utilised by several latterday aviation pioneers as an excellent way of getting off the ground. This occurred either by means of a tow-launch behind a boat or a car, or by foot launching. Some of the earliest exponents of hang-gliding (so called because, in those days, you literally had to hang on by your armpits), made their wings from bamboo, polythene and sticky tape. Not surprisingly, the golden rule was never to fly higher than you would care to fall.

Very soon, the machines were being made of stronger stuff and, as early as 1961, Tom Purcell Junior was tow launched on a Rogallo wing in the USA. Barry Palmer also had great success with a rogallo based design, though at his stage the pilot was still hanging on with parallel bars under the armpits. The following year John Dickenson, a water skier and pioneer of early hang-glider flight developed and flew a Rogallo wing with a triangular control frame and a swing seat, a design that Is the basis of all flexwing weight shift hang-gliders to this day. It was he who introduced the idea to two men whose names are recognised by hang

The amazing Ryan aircraft

L to R: Dr Francis Rogallo, Rick Ware, Ian Currer (author), Mark Dale. This photo was taken in 1985
(Photo: Northern Paragliding)

An early Rogallo hang-glider

Parascender

glider pilots world wide – Bill Moyes and Bill Bennett. These two dominated the early development of the sport of hang-gliding as we know it today.

Meanwhile, in the UK, Walter Neumark was flying new types of parachute designed by Lemoigne and Pioneer, which were capable of far superior performance and control than the existing types. Even back in 1961, Neumark, a sailplane pilot, could envisage a self-inflating parachute being used for soaring flight. Shortly afterwards, he wrote a manual, "Operational Procedures for Ascending Parachutes", and training began in what was to become known as parascending.

In 1968 Dan Poynter recorded in an article for Parachutist magazine that canopies were foot launched at Lake Placid in the USA during the annual parachute competition. In 1973 the British Association of Parascending Clubs was formed. At first the association was concerned only with towed operations,

but in 1989 changed its name to the British Association of Paragliding Clubs, reflecting its interest in a range of related pursuits from over-water towing operations, towed parascending and, especially foot launched paragliding.

It was not until about 1980 that parachutes were foot launched regularly from hills. At first it was a small minority of pilots, mostly in the French and Swiss Alps, who began to emulate the hang-glider pilots by launching from the steep slopes with their ram-air "rigs", but the sport was to grow with surprising speed. In the UK there was Gerald Williams, a lone hang glider pilot who could be seen drifting to earth beneath his canopy in the Peak District while his fellows shook their heads and muttered that it would never catch on.

In the intervening years the sport of hang-gliding itself had become firmly established: the brightly coloured wings were to be seen on mountainsides on every continent but Antarctica.

Agreements were made with landowners for the use of their hills, training procedures were established and a great deal was learned about the performance and stability of these extraordinary aircraft. Cross-country flights of hundreds of miles were made; even club pilots regularly used thermal and wave lift to gain thousands of feet of altitude.

As the performance of the craft improved, so too did the expense and time required to learn to fly them. Despite the lure of being able to soar like a bird, the sport has always been for the few who had the considerable determination to carry the 70lb craft up the hill time and time again during their training and the courage to attempt what can appear a frightening or dangerous activity (although, of course, with current equipment and training techniques, hang-gliding is in reality nowhere near as dangerous as many people might imagine).

In the early 1980s everything was in place for the birth of foot launch paragliding as we know it today – the expertise and example of the hang-gliding fraternity and the improving performance ram-air canopies.

The canopies being used were initially jump chutes designed to withstand the stress of opening in free-fall. It very soon became apparent that these stresses were not present with the less abrupt inflation of self-launch, and very soon manufacturers sprang up producing wings made from non-porous materials. Such fabrics would probably cause a modern paraglider to explode if it was opened by a free-falling skydiver at terminal velocity, but it offered a major performance advantage. Jump chutes also had to inflate evenly and rapidly and, as competitions often involve a near vertical descent to achieve target accuracy, these design criteria led to the evolution of

One of the first true paragliders, an Off-Chute Mirage, circa 1989

square canopies with very large cell entries and docile behaviour in the stall.

The foot launch paragliding manufacturers, however, had different criteria. They were looking for a very slow rate of descent and a good gliding performance and, as the wing was inflated before launch, they could afford to be less particular about instant opening. Very soon paragliders diverged totally from their jump chute roots. They utilised high-lift airfoils, narrow cell entries and long, slender wings, more akin to the shape of a hang glider.

In terms of aircraft development, the evolution of the hang-glider had been remarkable. There had been precious little research done on the behaviour of

aerofoils at speeds below 40mph but, even so, every year the designers and manufacturers came up with significant improvements in performance and stability.

There had, of course, been a number of failures, some of them fatal, and the national associations of the major hang-gliding nations had introduced test facilities so that each new design could be thoroughly checked before being given a certificate of airworthiness.

If the development of hang-gliders had been remarkable, that of paragliders was positively meteoric, with new and improved designs appearing on an almost monthly basis, although there has now been a significant slowdown in terms of

Ian Brown flying a Harley Elite overlooking Ullswater Cumbria circa 1990

A modern performance wing Pic Jerome Maupoint Gin Gliders

performance gain, mirroring the hang-gliders development curve of the 1970s and 1980s.

Fortunately, because the national association in most countries is the same for both sports, the procedures and equipment for testing were already in place and in virtually all European countries at least, there is a mandatory test programme for new designs.

At the time of writing (Autumn 2014), the distance record for a paraglider is 502km, achieved by circling and climbing in thermals and hopping from one cloud to the next, in the same way as hang-gliders and sailplanes have been doing for years. Perhaps more significant than this, though, is the sheer number of people attracted to the sport. In Alpine countries they number tens of thousands, and the sport is still finding new enthusiasts all over the world.

In 1992 The British Association of Paragliding Clubs. And the British Hang-gliding Association amalgamated into one body: The British Hang-Gliding and Paragliding Association (BHPA).

Similar associations exist in most countries where flying takes place, and whilst this book is based on the practices in the UK, similar procedures (though sometimes less effectively regulated) are common worldwide.

Presently there are good training systems in many countries and all major manufacturers are supporting the airworthiness programmes for equipment. The accident rate for pilots is on a reassuringly downward slope. The sport now has a 35 year track record, and whilst we are still relatively young and are still learning, paragliding has become a well-established activity.

Health and Safety 3

Paragliding is not suitable for everyone, there are few medical, legal and other restrictions on a person's suitability to be a paraglider pilot.

Before you start a paragliding course, the school will probably ask you to sign a form attesting that you will not be under the influence of alcohol or drugs, and also that you are of reasonably sound body (they seldom enquire after your mind!). Flying itself actually requires very little physical effort in most circumstances. However, to fly well does require reasonable reactions and, certainly during the training period, you do need to be able to climb a fairly steep hill several times.

People of a wide variety of ages and occupations enjoy paragliding, but if you are daunted at the prospect of walking up a steep hill or have a history of epilepsy, heart complaints or other medical conditions, you should consult the school before signing up.

As a general rule the school will, in such instances, ask you to produce a doctor's note certifying that you are fit to fly. Many schools require a similar declaration for pupils aged 60 or more.

Recent research has shown that more than 50% of women over the age of 40 exhibit signs of osteoporosis (loss of bone density) which may significantly increase the risk of sustaining a fracture in an impact situation. This is an important consideration in a sport like paragliding.

The Air Navigation Order states that you may not be the solo pilot of an aircraft below the age of 14. Those aged 18 or less must have written consent from a parent or guardian. You will also probably find somewhere on your booking conditions that the chief instructor reserves the right to refuse to train anyone he considers unfit or ill-prepared to fly. The reasons are self-evident. The schools' primary concern is safety.

Partial deafness is usually no problem, provided the instructor is informed (in one instance a student pilot did not mention the fact that he was deaf in one ear – unfortunately the radio system being used at the time only had a speaker on that side of the helmet. This was only noticed when the radio check was being done!).

Flying requires good visual awareness, both for setting up a landing at the correct position and altitude, and also for knowing where other pilots are when you are flying: it becomes second nature to keep a kind of visual map of the position of other fliers which is constantly updated by glimpses as you turn, and through your peripheral vision.

If your sight is OK with glasses, that is fine, as you can wear them with no difficulty (though some people use a cord or elastic to make sure they stay in place). Contact lenses are less practical as they could fall out, and a heather covered hillside is not a good place to look for them. Any permanent visual impairment may make you unfit to fly, and again the instructor should ask for a doctor's certificate before accepting your booking.

Schools are sometimes asked by doctors for details of what is involved before issuing such a certificate. The standard reply is that the person must have a sound musculature and skeletal system, and have no problems with balance, co-ordination or visual perception. He must have a sound heart and respiratory system and be able to exert himself without ill effects. In practice the potential pilot should be able to run 50 metres, jump over a 0.5 metre obstacle, be able to walk up a steep hillside, and be capable of falling over from a standing position without ill effect.

If you take up paragliding you are likely to be flying in close proximity to others, and whilst 99% of the time it is all fairly routine, at some point you may have to react very quickly and if you do not respond in a decisive and co-ordinated way you may seriously injure yourself and possibly others. There are a significant number of people who can (say) drive a car in reasonable safety but whose reactions are simply not sufficiently sharp to deal with the kind of situations that can occur in crowded airspace where others may be coming at you from any direction or where you may suddenly lose 50ft of altitude.

At any stage, if you are not sure that this is the sport for you then it is important to have a frank discussion with your instructor, particularly before progressing on to the soaring stage, where your actions might affect other pilots as well as yourself.

This subject is discussed in more detail in the chapter "Human Factors".

Responsibility

There has been an ever-growing trend over the last few years in our society to hold someone responsible for any mishap that occurs. It is of course only proper that a negligent individual or company is called to account for their actions, but unfortunately the reverse of this coin is that there is a tendency (fuelled by the legal profession!) for individuals to abdicate taking responsibility for themselves.

Flying generally and paragliding particularly is very unforgiving of poor judgement; it is reliant on the vagaries of the wind and weather, which are not always predictable.

Being a pilot requires patience. parawaiting

There have been instances of pupils who expect both to be paraglider pilots and to have their safety absolutely guaranteed. This is not possible. Even when learning you will probably be flying solo; the instructor is powerless to assist you other than by briefings and by advice on a radio. For this reason it is important that every potential pilot understands that he needs to accept the risks and take responsibility for himself. You must feel confident that you can cope with the exercise being attempted, and because the risks of an adventure sport like paragliding cannot be totally eradicated, you must be prepared to accept those risks.

Paragliding is not exactly a natural activity for a ground dwelling species like us, and it is normal to feel nervous. Every pilot up to and including world champions have felt a surge of adrenaline when they hit a spot of turbulence or find themselves uncomfortably close to another pilot. A certain amount of fear is a good thing, and helps keep you alive, but if it turns to panic or the pilot should freeze in a high-stress situation it can be a serious problem.

Insurance

In the UK and some other countries the national association's insurers cover individual qualified pilots for their third party liability, but it does not have any personal accident element. It is strongly recommended that anyone taking up the sport should ensure (for their own sake and that of their dependants) that they have suitable cover.

Permanent health insurance that covers you for any illness or accident is available from a variety of general insurance companies and for qualified pilots who are association members there is very often no additional loading of premiums, (though there may well be a 'no cover' period of weeks or months to minimise short term claims).

For paragliding-only cover it is also possible to get a short term policy. Whilst the scope is more limited than a regular permanent health policy it has the advantage of being instant and a "one off" premium and so is very convenient for those attending a course.

Third party cover is also available from most other national associations, but do check your situation if you are flying abroad. For British pilots used to free

*Flying suits are a convenient wind-proof layer
(Photo: Sup'Air SARL)*

NHS treatments the cost of medical expenses can be very high in many countries. It is vital you get suitable medical and repatriation travel cover before flying abroad.

The other insurance worth mentioning is the commercial liability cover of schools. Due to a number of claims over the years it is becoming more difficult to obtain suitable commercial cover and the situation may soon exist where none is available. In such a case it is clearly more vital than ever that each student carries suitable personal injury cover.

Clothing

In the summer months or in warm climates it is not unusual to see pilots flying in shorts and T-shirts. However, until you have amassed a good deal of experience it is better to wear something that offers more protection – it is quite possible that you will be falling over, or even being dragged along the ground. During your course you may well be required to roll about on the ground as part of your training, so do not wear anything that is too fragile or expensive! Gloves are invaluable as, even in summer, a good breeze on a hill-top can be cold, and when you are flying your hands are always in the airflow. A good wind-proof jacket is also essential in all but the best weather. If you are flying in winter, wear plenty of layers: it is easy to take things off if you have brought too much, and it can spoil your enjoyment and affect your concentration if you are shivering. If you take the sport up and fly regularly, you will soon find that temperature drops sharply with altitude, and the wind always finds the gaps between jackets and trousers. Many trousers have pockets that are difficult to get at when in a harness,

for these reasons most pilots who fly regularly invest in a purpose built flying suit.

These suits have insulation in the front where it is most needed, zips to allow them to be put on and off without removing your boots, and are designed with pockets for radios etc in the right positions. All good flying centres will stock flying suits.

Footwear

Good footwear is essential: during training you will be walking up hills and a good grip is necessary. If your landings are less than perfect, the ankles are the first set of shock absorbers available so something offering good support is a good idea. Hiking or fell boots are fine. In any event, bring spare shoes, as your flying gear may get wet. If you are serious about taking up the sport then there are some ideal boots that are light, waterproof and have good ankle support and grip, which are made especially for paragliding and most centres stock them.

Good boots are essential
(Photo: UK Airsports)

Introduction to the Equipment

4

The canopy

A paraglider is a simple aircraft, but in common with all other aircraft it is in fact the result of complex and painstaking design. Small changes in the line lengths or subtle alteration of the cut of the fabric can make the difference between a sweet responsive wing and one with poor characteristics.

The canopy is constructed of a top and bottom surface joined by a number of (usually) vertical segments. The resulting chambers are called cells. They have an opening at the front – the leading edge. Larger entries generally indicate a slower and more stable aircraft; narrow or valved

Inside an inflated cell

entries are found on craft with the aim of maximising performance. Each cell is separated from its neighbours by an

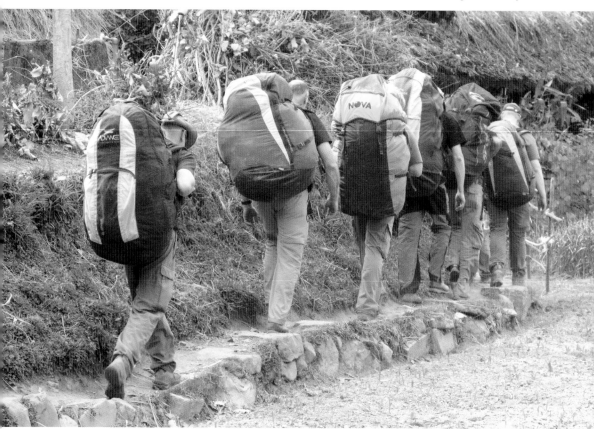

An aircraft that fits into a rucksack.

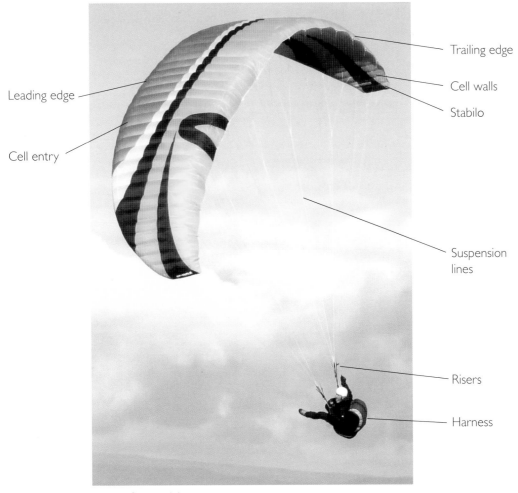

Leading edge

Cell entry

Trailing edge

Cell walls

Stabilo

Suspension lines

Risers

Harness

Layout of a paraglider

inter-cell wall. These define the shape of the wing section: the more inter-cell walls, the more accurate the control of the section of the wing, and the better the performance.

These walls feature several holes, or ports, so that air can pass from one cell to the next, helping to keep the internal pressure balanced and the wing evenly inflated. The front part of the cell walls is often reinforced with heavier fabric such as mylar, or with thin fibre glass rods to give additional stiffness. This helps the cells stay open for easier inflation and stability, and spreads the load from the lines.

When it is fully inflated, the cell takes up an aerofoil shape with a flattish lower surface and a curved, or cambered, top surface. The point of maximum thickness usually occurs between 15 and 30% of the way back from the leading edge.

The rear of the wing is called the trailing edge. On a typical canopy there may be anything from 30 to 100 cells. Those in the centre will be longer than those at the tips, giving the canopy a tapered or elliptical shape; this shape, when viewed from above, is called the planform. Many canopies may have small vertical areas at the tips, known as stabilos or "ears".

Their function is to provide stability; they stretch the wing as they are forced outwards and reduce induced drag.

On many designs the leading edge is a combination of open and sealed (closed) cells. The sealed cells are reliant on the internal pressure of the wing to remain inflated, and have the advantage of forming a well-defined airfoil section. They also resist deflation in the case of a tuck as the air cannot easily escape; however, they can take longer to inflate initially or after a collapse. The designer's skill is in combining the different elements of cell entry shape, sealed or sometimes valved cells and internal airflow, to maximise performance and minimise instability.

Paragliders use non-porous coated fabrics (either nylon or polyester), and some of these may have an additional finishing coat to further protect against ultraviolet degradation.

The lines

The lines are made of very strong materials so that they can be kept thin to minimise drag and weight. There are two main types: Kevlar, which is a polyaramid (carbon fibre) material, usually encased in an outer sheath of Dacron (terylene) or something similar; and polyethylene, usually known as Dyneema or Technora (Spectra in the USA). Polyaramid material is extremely strong and has excellent resistance to stretching or shrinking. It is not temperature sensitive. However, it requires regular checking as kinking or knotting around a small radius can easily damage it. This is most commonly used for the major suspension lines where retaining an accurate length is critical.

Polyethylene (Dyneema) is also very strong and it is more flexible too, which tends to prolong its life, especially with hard use. Because it much more resistant to being knotted and pulled through pulleys etc, it is commonly used for the brake lines. However, it is more likely to stretch or shrink and is fairly temperature sensitive, so lines of this material should be protected from high temperatures (being left in a car in full sun for example). Some gliders have used dyneema for main suspension lines, but for the reasons mentioned above this material proved to have problems in retaining an accurate length. The golden rule with all line material is to check it regularly for stretch, shrinkage and strength.

For more details on the properties of line materials see Chapter 20.

In order to minimise drag and make the whole construction less complex, the lines branch into two (or more) about halfway up their length. Lines are referred to by their position on the canopy, A-lines being those at the leading edge and C- or D-lines being those at the rear. The control lines are attached to the trailing edge terminating in a handle on the rear riser and are often produced in a distinctive colour to make them easy to locate.

The risers

The risers connect the canopy to the harness. Usually made of one inch or 25mm webbing, they transfer the loads from the harness through the lines. There is usually one attachment point on each side of the harness to which the bottom of the risers are connected with a maillion or carabiner. The tops of the risers (there may be three or four per side) terminate in small steel maillions or links to which the lines are attached. The risers give the pilot a convenient point to hold when launching and make it simple to swap one harness with another.

The rear risers also feature small rings or pulleys, known as keepers, through which the control lines pass. These, as the name suggests, prevent the control lines flying away out of reach in the wind. The control handles themselves, attached to these lines, are usually fastened to the riser by some easy release system such as a magnetic clasp or a popper. Virtually all modern canopies have an accelerator system attached, operated by a foot stirrup (These are discussed in more detail in Chapter 22).

The front (A) riser is frequently divided into two, or has a smaller branch attached. The outer portion supports just one or two lines. The reason for this is to make the "big ears" manoeuvre easier to perform and it also helps with certain aspects of ground handling.

A few models also feature trimmers so that the length of the rear riser can be adjusted in flight. These are most commonly found on tandem wings (where a foot operated accelerator is not practical) or on some high performance wings whose pilots are likely to require trim alterations in flight.

Magnetic brake connectors

A modern harness with airbag protection and foot-stirrup

The harness

Paragliding harnesses follow the same basic pattern – a solid seat plate, usually made of plywood, fibreglass or a carbon composite, a webbing structure that includes the leg and waist straps and which also continues around the pilot's back and under the seat, and a fabric shell. The fabric is primarily for comfort, for providing storage space and a reserve parachute compartment, and to house any protective padding. There are a host of other features that may be included, such as attachments for accelerator systems, foot stirrups, compartments for radios or ballast, and various passive protection systems.

All harnesses include adjusters so you can refine the size and adjust the shape and flying position. There are a great variety of harnesses to choose from, varying from superlight versions for mountaineering (some without seat plates), to those with sophisticated protection systems and racing harnesses designed for minimum drag. These types are covered in greater detail in Chapter 19.

Helmets

In a training environment you will probably be using an open face or adjustable helmet. It is important that your hearing is not impaired, as judging your airspeed is very much a function of hearing the airflow moving past your ears; and of course your instructor may be giving you commands by radio.

Open face helmets are light and airy.

The lightweight adjustable types are good for walking up the hill – something you will be doing quite a bit of for the first few days, but when you come to purchase your first helmet there are a number of other factors to consider. Primarily you need protection – there is a CE certification standard for airsports helmets – fit, warmth, and of course, style!

Helmets are covered in more detail in Chapter 19.

Full face helmets offer better protection (Photo: Chris Fountain)

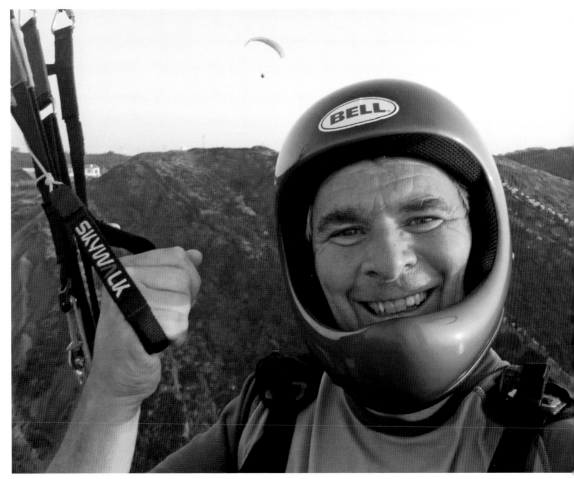

Photo: Iain Bell

How the canopy flies 5

When any object is dropped, it will fall towards the surface of the earth. We cannot prevent this happening, but we can use a couple of techniques (and the atmosphere) to minimise the impact! One technique is to make the drag of the object very large in relation to its weight, so that it will fall slowly. And the second is to deflect or vector the force of gravity, so that we fall off to one side rather than straight down. Paragliders use a combination of both approaches. Clearly they are relatively large, and we can use the air to help us vector the force of gravity by using an aerofoil; which is essentially a shape that will slide sideways through the air in a stable and efficient way.

Size is clearly important! The higher the loading on the wing the higher the sinking rate and as a general rule a more heavily loaded wing will fly at a faster airspeed. This can be an adavnage of course and many pilots chose to fly "speedwings, which are very small and heavily loaded paragliders."

When a paraglider is fully inflated, it forms a solid wing with an aerofoil section that creates lift in the same way as that of a conventional aircraft. In order to fly, it must create enough lift to carry its own weight and that of its pilot, and it achieves this with gliding flight. The wing is constantly flying forwards and downwards through the air and in doing so causes the airflow over the wing section.

So how does an aerofoil work? Look at *Fig 5.1*. As the wing glides forwards and down, the molecules of air that hit the leading edge are divided into two streams, -those over and those under the canopy. Those below it are contacting the lower surface at a shallow angle and creating a high-pressure area. About one third of the aerofoils' lift is derived from this "push" or deflection. The molecules that pass over the top surface, however, are obliged to follow a longer path as they are forced upwards over the cambered top surface. As the curve continues, the flow is deflected further upwards, while at the same time the air above the aerofoil is doing its level best to remain undisturbed and not alter its position (or alter course if it is moving). This process is strengthened by the natural tendency of the air to try and drift away from the

Fig 5.1: Airflow around a wing section

Photograph taken in a smoke tunnel showing the airflow over an aerofoil section. The pulsed smoke streams in this 'photo clearly shows the acceleration of the airflow over the upper surface. (Photo: Shell UK)

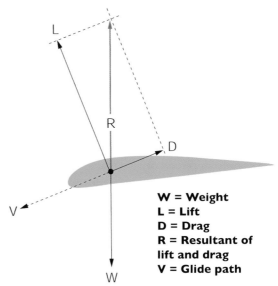

W = Weight
L = Lift
D = Drag
R = Resultant of lift and drag
V = Glide path

Fig 5.2: Forces on an aerofoil

curved surface, rather like a car going around a bend at speed. The result of this is that the air flowing over the top of the section is squeezed between the physical barrier of the wing below it and the inertia of the "normal" air above it.

It behaves exactly like water being squeezed through a narrow space (like the end of a hosepipe) by accelerating, so the air is travelling more quickly over the top surface. At this point the physics becomes a little more complex, but the result of this acceleration is that the pressure reduces (Bernoulli's theorem). This low-pressure area generates a pulling force and contributes about two thirds of the lifting force of the wing. A lifting surface does not have to be an aerofoil, even a flat piece of paper will glide if the correct angle is maintained, but the aerofoil in its various forms is the most efficient and stable shape to achieve good lifting and therefore gliding performance.

So far, we have established two forces acting on the canopy, gravity, which is acting to pull us down, and lift, acting upwards and slightly forwards. There is a third force as well; drag. This acts opposite to our direction of travel and reduces the speed and efficiency on the

wing. The lift and drag combined are shown in Fig 5.2 as R-the resultant. (Drag is mentioned in more detail in chapter 5, Terms). When all these forces are in equilibrium, the wing will glide at a specific rate. This glide path is the actual direction of travel through the air. (V) – See *Fig 5.2*.

Providing the canopy is flying with sufficient airspeed and at a suitable angle of attack, it will continue to glide correctly. But what happens if we disturb this equilibrium?

Firstly, let us suppose that the angle of attack becomes too low. This is not readily achievable in normal flight as, at high speeds, the drag created becomes too great to permit any further acceleration. However, if too low an angle is achieved, the soft aerofoil ceases to inflate properly and begins to deform, internal pressure drops, and as the cell entries cannot work and the load is removed from the front lines, the wing will collapse at the front. This is known as a "tuck" and is quite easy to bring about if the pilot is stationary on the ground.

In the air, the pilot tends automatically to swing under the canopy to the correct position, but a tuck can happen in flight if the pilot has induced a low angle of attack in recovering from a stall for example, or in turbulent air.

Without pilot input a paraglider is generally fixed in its angle of attack (this is determined by the line lengths chosen by the designer. But the pilot can alter the angle of attack by use of the controls. (including speed or trimmer systems) There is a ratio between the lift and the drag generated, and by adding more drag (usually by braking) we can alter that ratio. This means that the wing is now moving forwards less rapidly and the airflow is at a higher angle of attack. (If you look up as you add brake, you can see the leading edge of the canopy move back slightly as it takes up a more rearward position).

Trailing edge deflection at launch

The initial result of this is an increase in the amount of lift – the greater the pressure difference between the top and bottom surfaces, the greater the lift. The point of maximum lift is known as the minimum sink rate. However, if the angle is increased too much, the air is unable to flow smoothly over the curve, and at the point at which the previously smooth laminar airflow breaks away from the top surface (which in normal flight is next

Photograph taken in a smoke tunnel showing the airflow over a stalled aerofoil section. (Photo: Shell UK)

Fig 5.3: A stalled wing section caused by too high an angle of attack, A

to the trailing edge), rushes forwards across the aerofoil until almost all the top surface is covered in a turbulent airflow. The low- pressure area is broken up and the aerofoil ceases to work efficiently. This situation is a stall – see *Fig 5.3*.

Some canopies in certain circumstances will find a point of equilibrium even with an angle of attack that is too high. The wing remains at least partially inflated but, because it has little or no forward speed, it is unable to generate sufficient lift and sinks very rapidly. This state is known as a "deep" or "parachutal" stall. If forward motion is lost altogether, by a sharp application of maximum brake for example, the internal pressure will drop and the cells will deflate. The aerofoil section itself is then lost. This is a "dynamic" or a "full" stall. Both deep and dynamic stalls can be recovered from easily, though this may involve considerable altitude loss – see Chapter 28, Instability & Recovery. For this reason, a paraglider – like any aircraft – should be flown at slightly above the absolute minimum speed to ensure a margin for error.

The controls and how they work

Paragliders can be steered by weight shift and most models have foot operated accelerator systems to add extra speed, but all of them rely principally upon the control lines. The term "controls" is used rather than the common name of brakes because, in addition to their function in controlling speed, they are also used for steering and to stabilise the canopy in the event of a collapse. Each control is a single line, usually colour coded to prevent confusion with the suspension lines. Unlike them, it is not attached to

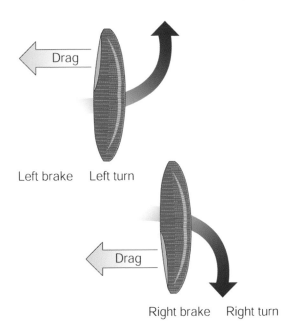

Fig 5.4: The mechanics of inducing a turn

the riser directly but runs through a ring or pulley known as a "keeper" attached to the rear riser, and ends in a handle. The top of the control line is divided into a "cascade" or "fan" of smaller lines which attach to the trailing edge at several points.

When a pilot pulls down one of the control handles, the trailing edge of the canopy on that side is deflected downwards into the airflow. *(See photo opposite)*. This has two effects – the first is to increase the angle of attack of that side of the canopy slightly and to increase the lift generated. The second effect is to massively increase the drag and reduce the airspeed of that side. These two effects work against each other, one trying to turn the canopy one way and one the other. On most conventional aircraft this creates the problem known as adverse yaw, which is usually overcome with the addition of a rudder. But, on a canopy, the drag created in this way is far more

View from below, clearly showing the deflection of the trailing edge during a right turn

effective than any opposing effect of lift and the craft will always turn towards the deflected side. If both controls are applied at the same time, the wing will slow down uniformly and may also create slightly more lift. The further the controls are depressed the more drag is created and the slower the wing will fly until, eventually, the canopy will have such a high angle of attack that the wing will stall.

Obviously, if the canopy is being flown slowly and one control is raised, this will also produce a turn. The steepest turns are achieved by simultaneously raising one side and depressing the other.

CAUTION – it is possible to stall one half of the wing in this way and enter a spin.

The controls also have three other uses: the first is on the ground during ground handling or a reverse launch where they can be used to manipulate the wing to change the height and position of the "wall". The second is to collapse the canopy after landing or if you are being dragged (see Chapter 16, Landing). The third use is to aid recovery from various unstable situations – tucks etc. – see chapter 28, Instability & Recovery.

The controls are the equivalent of brakes and steering wheel on a car combined. It is vital that they are in good order and free of hitches or wear. They are also the easiest part of the canopy to get into a tangle – always use the poppers or magnets provided to attach the controls to the riser after every landing.

Terms 6

In many specialised areas of knowledge and activities people use technical language or jargon to describe a thing or concept. Paragliding is no different, and the language around pilots and in the training school is sometimes not all that clear to the newcomer. Paragliding uses regular aviation terms and of course quite a few of our own.

Below is a guide to the more commonly used and useful terms and what they mean.

Centre of pressure

Different areas of the aerofoil and the span of the canopy produce varying amounts of lift. For the purpose of showing this force, the term "centre of pressure" is often used. More accurately this is the centre of pressure difference, a theoretical balance point through which the lift can be said to act. This point does move back and forth as the angle of attack is altered. This knowledge is not relevant to the pilot in normal flight, but during the design and development phase the behaviour of the centre of pressure is critical, as it determines the recovery characteristics of the wing.

Drag

The term has already been mentioned a couple of times. What is drag? This is the thing that holds us back! It is the resistance of the air to anything passing through it, and it can be divided into two major categories.

Parasitic drag

Friction caused by any surface or obstruction (pilot, lines etc.) The faster you travel through the air the more parasitic drag you create. Doubling your speed quadruples the parasitic drag. Parasitic drag can be sub-divided again into components such as skin friction, form drag and profile drag. (The latter relates to the turbulence caused, for example, by moving any non-lifting surface through the air).

Induced drag

The action of an aerofoil disturbs the air as it passes through and this creates induced drag. There is always a little drag induced at the trailing edge where the airflow from above and below the aerofoil meet again at slightly different speeds. The majority of the induced drag, however, is normally created at the wing tips. The area of low pressure above the wing is "attractive" to the air at a higher pressure below the wing. But at the wingtips, it is easier for the air to flow around the end of the wing, and this is what happens. The result is a vortex at each tip – see *Fig 6.1* and photo below.

Photograph taken in a wind-tunnel illustrating the formation of wing-tip vortices (Photo: Shell UK)

Fig 6.1: Wing tip vortices; at the tips, the pressure difference between the upper and lower surfaces is equalised by the air flowing up and around the end of the wing..As the canopy moves forwards it leaves a trail of rotating air behind each tip. This is the prime cause of induced drag. (And the cause of "wake turbulence" often encountered downwind of an aircraft.)

Some designs feature "stabilos" or "ears" at the tips and one of their intended functions is to try and minimise this problem, The high aspect ratio (long slim) wings that are becoming more common reduce this problem in the same way as hang-gliders, sailplanes and albatrosses – simply by having a relatively smaller area of wing tip. The High arch design of competition paragliders use a combination of both approaches to minimise drag and maximise performance.

As can be seen on the graph *(Fig 6.2)*, induced drag reduces with speed, and parasitic drag increases with speed, so there is a certain point at which parasitic and induced drag combined give a minimum total figure. This is the speed at which the "lift/ drag ratio" is best. Note that the graph lines stop at about 13kph; at this airspeed the angle of attack is usually so high that the craft stalls. When this occurs the whole drag profile changes dramatically; the airfoil no longer works and the drag is now simply a huge parasitic force operating vertically. At speeds over about 60kph the parasitic drag becomes too great for the weight to overcome and the wing cannot achieve any higher airspeed.

Fig 6.2: Graphical illustration speed v drag

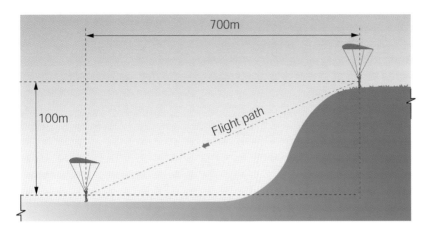

Fig 6.3: Lift to drag ratio and glide angle. The pilot launches in still air and flies 700m horizontally for a total height loss of 100m. His glide ratio, or lift to drag ratio in this case is 7:1

L/D (Lift/Drag) Ratio & Glide angle

L = lift and D = total drag, so the L/D ratio measures the gliding efficiency of the wing. The best L/D ratio occurs when the lift is greatest relative to the drag. See *Fig 6.2.* (The effect of speed on drag).

In practice this is when the canopy is flown at the speed where it will cover the most distance from a given height. For example, if a paraglider has an L/D ratio that allows it to glide 700 metres along for every100 metres of altitude lost, this is referred to as glide angle of 7:1 *(see Fig 6.3)* This figure can only really be used as a comparative guide to the performance of the canopy. When you are actually in the air, any wind or any lifting or sinking air will distort the performance by several hundred percent in either direction.

Sink rate

If you read manufacturers' information sheets, another figure you may see quoted is minimum sink rate. This refers to the slowest rate at which the canopy will descend through still air. If your minimum sink rate is, say, 1.2 metres per second, then the canopy will always be descending through the air at at least that rate. To soar, i.e to maintain or gain height the trick is to find some air that is rising faster than you are sinking.

The minimum sink rate is frequently rather poorly identified by inexperienced pilots. Because adding some brake increases the angle of attack, it slows the wing down and the wing briefly generates more lift. The pilot feels the resulting climb, and a variometer may even chirp briefly to register this as a better sink rate.

Very soon the pilot "learns" that adding a bit of brake seems to reduce the sink rate, and thereafter always flies with some brake in order to sink as slowly as possible.

However the "surge" that is felt is often the conversion of stored energy into a short-lived climb (such as on launch), or a small defined patch of lifting air.

In fact a paraglider's brakes add so much drag that the increased lift caused by the altered angle of attack is invariably cancelled out by the added drag, and performance is actually reduced. Many new pilots fly too slowly as a result, and cannot understand why their sink rate is not as good as someone else's.

In consistently smooth air (including lift) the best sink rate is generally found at the glider's trim (hands off) speed. We are talking here about the actual aerodynamic sink rate which is not necessarily your most efficient speed to fly. In practice there may be very valid reasons for flying a bit more slowly. If you are going though a lifting patch of air, for example, a less efficient but slower airspeed may keep you in the lift longer and so, on balance, you win. Or if it is rough, keeping some brake applied helps to stabilise the wing and reduce the chance of a collapse.

A high aspect ratio glider
(Photo: Ozone Gliders, Nick Greece).

While we are on the subject, there is a way of increasing the angle of attack whilst avoiding much of the drag penalty of brakes, and that is by using trim devices, which tilt the whole wing. These are much more efficient, but because they fix the wing at a different angle of attack, they can unfortunately make managing and recovering from unstable situations like stalls and collapses more demanding. For this reason, trimmers are usually found only on high-performance or tandem wings.

Aspect ratio

The aspect ratio is a measure of the canopy's shape. When a paraglider is laid out flat, the planform (the shape viewed from above) can give us clues about the

A low aspect ratio paraglider

characteristics and likely performance of the wing. A high aspect ratio wing is long and slim, which probably means high performance and lower stability, though of course all manufacturers are struggling to improve the first without compromising the second. An albatross or a sailplane will have a very high aspect ratio, whereas a paraglider or a songbird will have a low one.

Aspect ratio is calculated by dividing the square of the span by the area of fabric. For example, a canopy with a span of 10.5 metres and an area of 25 square metres would work out as 10.5 x 10.5 = 110.25 divided by 25 = an aspect ratio of 4.41. This is a mid-range wing, and is likely to have average performance and good stability.

There are two different aspect ratio figures that you may come across; one is the "flat" aspect ratio as described above. The other is the projected aspect ratio. This is always slightly lower, as it is calculated not by the "actual" area of the wing but by the projected area i.e the area of the shadow of the wing when the wing is inflated and in flight. Because the canopy takes up a curved shape, the projected area is always lower.

This figure is given because different designs have different degrees of curvature and so this figure give a more accurate comparison in terms of flight behaviour.

CAVOK

This is a piece of aviation weather jargon; it is actually derived from the abbreviation of "Ceiling And Visibility OK" and its definition is that there is no cloud below 5,000ft, visibility is at least 10km and there is no precipitation reaching the ground.

Windspeed, groundspeed and airspeed

Windspeed is simply the speed of the wind over the ground.

Groundspeed is the speed of the aircraft relative to the ground.

Airspeed is the speed of the airflow over the aerofoil.

A point worth noting is that, in flight, some pilots have trouble distinguishing between airspeed and groundspeed. Take a look at *Fig 6.4*.

A. The pilot is standing on top of a hill with an inflated canopy. The windspeed is 10mph, the groundspeed is 0mph and his airspeed is therefore 10mph.

B. Now he has taken off. The windspeed is still 10mph and his groundspeed is now 15mph. As he is flying into wind, the airspeed over the canopy must be 25mph. So far so good.

C. Now our pilot has encountered a 20mph windspeed; his airspeed is still 25mph. His groundspeed has now dropped to 5mph.

D. As he is a long way from the hill, he decides to turn round and come back. He does not alter his airspeed, which remains at 25 mph, and the windspeed is still 20mph. His flight path is now downwind and his groundspeed is now 45 mph. The sudden increase in speed over the ground can be disconcerting if the pilot is not prepared, particularly as he may now be heading straight towards the hill. Pilots have been known to slow down at this point by braking hard; the result is, of course, a stall, which can mean losing control and hitting the hill, with painful consequences. It is easy to avoid this mistake by knowing what to expect

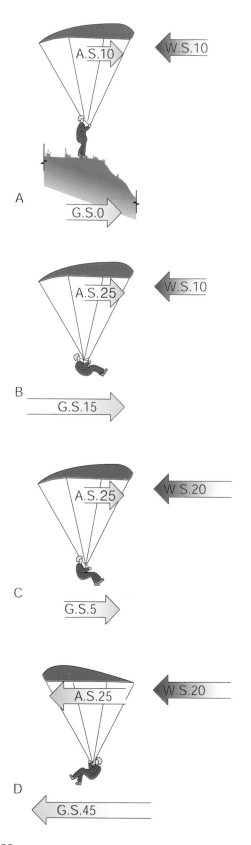

A.S.10
W.S.10
G.S.0

A

A.S.25
W.S.10
G.S.15

B

A.S.25
W.S.20
G.S.5

C

A.S.25
W.S.20
G.S.45

D

and by judging your airspeed not by the ground, but by the feel of the airflow in your face and the position of the controls.

In a school situation the instructor can mention these figures, but to really appreciate the acceleration in groundspeed you need to experience a downwind turn. Just for comparison, a 180° turn on a typical paraglider takes around one second to complete, so your increase in groundspeed in the illustration above would be some 40mph in one second…. Unless you happen to be a racing driver, chances are this makes your car look a bit flat!

If the wind is not blowing directly onto the hill, the same thing occurs to a lesser degree as you soar along it. One "beat" will be slow relative to the ground as you pull into wind and the other very fast. Be careful to maintain airspeed on the fast leg! There are some other terms that are used in the sport and in this handbook – refer to the glossary at the end.

Fig 6.4: The interaction between windspeed, groundspeed and airspeed

The BHPA and the UK Pilot Rating System

7

The British Hang-Gliding and Paragliding association is the governing body of the sport in the UK. The Civil Aviation Authority, which controls all non-military flying in Britain, has allowed the BHPA to shoulder the responsibility of ensuring adequate training, pilot and instructor qualifications, aircraft airworthiness and accident investigation. In addition to this the BHPA liaises with other air-users' associations and with landowners, the government and the general public. It arranges insurance cover for members and publishes regular bulletins detailing safety notices and other information in the monthly magazine, Skywings. Together, these tasks represent a major undertaking, with a good deal of the work being done by unpaid voluntary officers.

We shall only retain our enviable freedom to fly in the UK if the BHPA and its members can act, and be seen to act, responsibly. Most nations where paragliding is established have a similar association. Membership is mandatory for anyone learning to paraglide at a registered school in the UK. There are three basic types of membership.

Full membership

This gives all benefits, including 3rd party and public liability insurance of five million pounds (at present). Membership incudes a subscription to the magazine Skywings, which is published monthly. Full members may also hold ratings, and have voting rights etc. This is renewable annually If more than one member

of your family flies you can get family membership, which simply removes the duplication of copies of the magazine. There are concessions available for those in full time education.

Training membership

This offers the same insurance cover and benefits such as Skywings magazine, but does not carry any voting rights. This membership option is designed for those who are still trying the sport out and have not yet decided it is for them. It is valid for 3 months. This period is designed to allow sufficient time for a course to be completed. You cannot hold a rating or licence with this type of membership, so when you have completed CP (Novice) level you will need to renew or upgrade to full member status.

Day membership

This is simply an 'insurance only' package for one day, and is designed to cover those who are having an air experience flight or "taster" day.

BHPA membership also confers a number of benefits that are less immediately obvious. The instructors who teach you have been through BHPA training courses and are examined for their licences. BHPA schools have regular inspections. Officers and volunteers in the association investigate and report on any accidents or incidents to try and learn how best to keep the sport safe, and there is the inevitable administration work of dealing with insurers, producing exams and club bulletins, arranging competitions and events and dealing with government departments.

Outside the UK

You may be reading this book in a country other than the UK and using a somewhat different training regime. The exercises outlined below are designed primarily for the dynamic hill soaring conditions common in Britain. For mountainous terrain there is far less emphasis on techniques for dealing with strong winds and far more on thermalling technique and other factors. However, the outline of the system below is broadly relevant to most new pilots.

In fact Training by Uk schools is now very commonly conducted in other countries to take advantage of more reliable weather, so it is quite likely that even with a BHPA school you will be training outside the UK. This is covered in more detail towards the end of this chapter

Training overview

This section is an explanation of the process of learning to fly a paraglider.

It is essentially an overview of the British Hang-Gliding and Paragliding Association's training programme, including a brief look at the alternative options adopted by other paragliding training systems.

In the UK it is usual to begin the day early by ringing your school to check on weather conditions, and, in some cases, the meeting place. If you do not ring in, or if the school does not offer this facility, you run a far greater risk of a fruitless journey.

Once you have arrived to start your course, the instructor will begin by answering any questions and giving an introductory talk on the sport. (see below) He or she will check that everyone is in good health and fit to fly, and ask if anyone has had any previous experience in flying that could be useful.

You will be encouraged to ask questions. It is not the sort of class where you can sit quietly at the back and nod even if you do not understand something – your safety can depend on your knowing what is going on so that you can decide what to do next.

You will be required to join the national association – this is mandatory in the UK and in several other countries. Membership confers third party insurance, which is necessary before you fly. Some schools will also provide you with a theory book or notes for you to use as a back up to your instructor's lessons.

A few words on starting paragliding

If you choose to enroll on a course, your instructor will very likely begin with an introductory chat about the sport and what you can expect. However, by that time you will probably have already paid for a course and it is a bit late to back out! The school has an interest in attracting you, and the instructors are all enthusiasts themselves, so all brochures and conversations tend to be on the optimistic side. (There are no pictures of rainy days on the website!)

The reality is that paragliding is a great sport, but the weather is fickle and you will almost certainly waste a lot of time and fuel trying to ensure you are at the right site on the right days. Each year many students are disappointed that they cannot complete their course during their holiday week, or on the days they have put aside. When training in the UK most schools will say somewhere in their literature that you are purchasing a course of instruction, not a specific weeks holiday.

If you are unlucky and it rains or blows all week, you can expect to be able to re-book for a later date, but you cannot expect a refund.

Paragliding is potentially dangerous. No matter how well you are trained and how good your gear is, you cannot entirely escape the risk of injury or even being killed.

Anyone can make a mistake, and the environment we fly in is not always completely predictable. However good your instructor may be, he cannot make you a more decisive person or help you (other than by advice) if you get into trouble.

Before you even pick up the phone to book your course you do need to understand and accept these facts.

Paragliding can be successfully done by a wide range of people, and this is one of its greatest appeals.

Fitness and co-ordination

Many "adventure" or "extreme" sports require a good deal of physical fitness or high levels of skill and technique to master. Some, like leading difficult rock climbs, or carve-gybing a windsurfer at high speed, are quite simply beyond the capabilities of many people.

By contrast, launching, flying and even thermalling a paraglider from a high

mountain is really quite easy. Students taking the controls of a tandem wing can quite easily circle up to cloudbase on a good day, even if they have never been near a paraglider or flown anything prior to that flight. In this respect paragliding is quite often technically undemanding. (Many flights are not much more energetic than playing a piano).

The structured training programme possible in UK, starting with small flights on shallow slopes in good weather, and gradually increasing the height and demands on the pilot, is designed to get as many people through the course as safely as possible. However, it is possible to get a slightly unrealistic sense of security from this type of approach.

If you should make a mistake whilst flying and misjudge your landing pattern for example, you could find yourself trying to manoeuvre into a small or hazardous area. Hit some turbulent air, and the whole picture can change dramatically; the paraglider can collapse, drop dozens or even hundreds of feet, and be difficult or impossible to control within a very short time. These situations are not common, and can usually be minimised with good planning, and can generally be dealt with, but the experience can most definitely be an extreme one! If you keep flying long enough, it is inevitable that eventually you will experience an "event" of this type.

You may, like many of us who fly, consider the risks worthwhile, and be happy to take responsibility for your own safety. But just because paragliding is easy to do does not necessarily mean it is any more suitable for those who are less capable of dealing with the physical and mental demands it can make in certain situations.

With the extremely rare exception of an equipment malfunction, the primary causes of accidents and injuries in paragliding (and quite a few other activities) are pilot error, and almost all of them have their root in one of two situations:

1. Underconfidence

Especially being indecisive, or, at worst, "frozen" by fear.

2. Overconfidence

Thinking, "I will be OK flying this Deathship Mk 3 prototype" or (more commonly!), "I am sure I can deal with these conditions, I am just as good as that pilot up there."

The ideal student pilot is confident, but just a little bit wary as well.

If you have any flying experience, this is very useful, and you should tell your instructor. Initially, even pilots with thousands of hours on other aircraft are just as challenged by the alien skills of launching and ground handling an inflatable wing, (kite flying is the closest related skill here). But, when you reach the approach planning stage, the pilots have an advantage.

Though it seems easy, when flying, especially in close proximity to the ground, your brain is making decisions in three dimensions, and although we are all used to judging speed and direction, most people have little practice at judging altitude loss. Pilots – especially Hang-glider or other slope soaring pilots – find this easier and may benefit from reduced training requirements.

The good news for non-pilots is you soon pick up the trick of judging approaches in just a few flights. Though if your concentration is broken, or you are tired for example, it is easy to misjudge your height.

Before you venture onto the slopes, your instructor may well ask you about your medical fitness etc (see Chapter 3, Health and Safety). He or she may also tell you about special rules for the site; what paths to use, toilet facilities (if you are very lucky) and advice, such as no smoking upwind of the gliders.

On arrival at the flying site, your first lessons will be in assessing the site and the weather and an introduction to the equipment; these subjects are covered in subsequent chapters.

The BHPA Progressive training system

This is a brief introduction to the training system used at all approved schools in the UK. There will be some variation in style from school to school, of course, and in some countries the reverse launch that is used in windy conditions is not as critical. This syllabus refers to foot launching. There are some other disciplines to be mastered if you are launching from skis or being towed aloft.

The section below gives an overall view of the system and then a blow-by-blow explanation of each exercise.

The previous chapter mentioned how easy paragliding can be, and it is probably true that you could throw ten students off the top of a mountain and seven or eight of them would have mastered the basics pretty well by the time they landed an hour later. Unfortunately these odds are not quite good enough, and next of kin of the remaining 2 or 3 who do not make it might take rather a dim view of this arrangement.

It seems fairly obvious how to teach someone to fly a paraglider: simply start low down or with a tandem flight and work your way up steadily. That way you can catch any problems close to the ground and the instructor can assess each pupil's progress before going on the next task. That, in a nutshell, is how it is done.

Over many years, the BHPA has monitored training and the best practice has been gradually refined to concentrate on common problems, increase standards, and ensure vital elements are all included.

The most recent revision of the training system is very comprehensive, and specifies all the exercises that a student needs to complete, and the briefings required to ensure everyone coming though the system has had a solid grounding in all the skills and knowledge they will need. This is laid out in a logical manner. You must have a lecture on the rules of the air before you fly with others, for example. In the BHPA model the pupils and instructors jointly "sign off" the exercises as they are completed.

It is always subject to revision, but the present (2015) system is reproduced below. The version shown is for Hill launched paragliding; there are other variants for Tow-launched training.

On your first lesson you will be allocated a Student pilot training booklet. This is a vital log of all the training exercises, and you and your instructor(s) will work through each exercise and sign them off as you go.

The first page is a risk warning and a record of your BHPA membership type.

The risk warning is an important element. In the past, students have stated that they did not appreciate that there were risks involved in paragliding. This warning is included in order to ensure that no-one is misled into the mistaken belief that paragliding is totally safe.

The membership type is for administrative use so that your instructor can check at a glance if your membership is still current. The training pack is issued by the BHPA to those who have annual or training membership. It includes a copy of Training wings magazine and literature on the association. Some schools add their own elements, such as details of holidays or feedback questionnaires on your course.

The notes on each task are fairly self-explanatory., and it is well worth taking the time to read them before attempting the exercise. An instructor could, in some circumstances, be training as many as six pupils, and to some extent may rely on the students themselves agreeing that they are confident at a specific exercise. If you do not think you are ready to move on then do not sign the task, but discuss it with your instructor.

Phase 1: Ground Training

This covers the basic theory of launching and landing into wind, and how the airflow determines the flying environment. It is often covered on site. You then move on to looking at the equipment and being shown how to unpack and lay out the glider and harness. If the weather is suitable the instructor may well demonstrate a launch and a quick flight. This shows the class what to expect and also serves to allow a check of the conditions.

The next element in the ground training is pre-flight checking the equipment. The checks will be demonstrated and explained by the instructor before you have a chance to unpack more gliders and practice your own checks. Demonstration is an essential teaching technique, but there is no substitute for doing it yourself when learning a new skill.

You should now have the site, weather and equipment all checked and be ready to start flying. But before getting airborne the instructor is required to run through additional safety checks, most notably the parachute landing fall drill.

About Parachute Landing Falls (PLFs)

You cannot realistically learn a perfect PLF technique in a very short time, but the aim of this exercise to ensure that you have grasped the basics of dealing with a hard landing.

PLF's are, in fact, of no use in normal flying and you may well fly for many years without the need to employ this technique. So it is not realistic to spend a lot of time on it. However, if you do find yourself descending vertically or near vertically after a low level collapse for example, or under a reserve parachute, then knowing about the correct position to adopt and rolling with the impact can help prevent a number of potential injuries.

This training also has a number of other purposes: if a potential student has a problem with quite gentle impacts or difficulty with co-ordination, then this exercise "flags up" such a problem to the instructor before he become airborne. If you cannot fall on the ground from a standing position without problems, then paragliding is not for you.

There is a mental preparation angle too. Paragliding can be very easy, and is of course great fun, but it is possible for students to forget that it carries very real risks. Starting a course by discussing the possibility of getting injured, and the steps to reduce this risk, is a reminder that proper training is a serious business,

and that the instructor or school always has safety as the main priority.

Phase 2: Ground handling

Flying a paraglider is very easy, but getting airborne can be quite difficult! However, if you want to be a solo pilot, you have to learn ground handling and launch techniques before you can fly. This phase covers the vital pre-flight checks, including the site, weather and equipment, and gives the opportunity to get to grips with the power of a paraglider and familiarise yourself with the controls before becoming airborne.

The instructor will usually help quite a bit at first, but the eventual aim is to get each pupil to be able to check, inflate and be ready to launch the paraglider himself. This section includes steering, "flaring" the wing to collapse it, gathering up the wing to carry it "posy" fashion and laying it out again ready for the next launch. This will include a lot of running down a gentle slope and walking back again. Do not be discouraged if this seems to be taking a long while to master, this is normal!

Phase 3: First hops

When your launch technique is good enough you may find that you are either "moon walking" (ie have only a part of your bodyweight on your feet) and can take huge strides with the wing supporting much of your weight through the harness, or possibly that you are leaving the ground completely and making small flights just a few feet above the ground.

The aim at this stage is to maintain a consistent airspeed and hold a course.

As your instructor sees you progressing he may move you to a steeper slope or perhaps help by adding a little extra airspeed with a well placed hand on the back! As the flights get longer, you will find it easier to judge your speed and direction and make course corrections and gentle landings.

These first three phases are a fair indicator of what can be achieved on your first day if the wind is OK and no-one has any serious problems.

Phase 4: Flight Exercises

This begins with the eventualities briefing. What should you do if you start to drift to the left? What if you unexpectedly get lifted up 20m? It is important to start considering the different options you have, as from this point on you will be the master of your own destiny, and though the instructor can advise you, he cannot directly affect your decisions by taking control, so you need to understand and accept this responsibility.

Some schools use radio communications, and some use visual signals, such as bats in the landing field. Whatever the system employed, you do need a check to ensure that they are working and that you understand the signals or commands.

The first flights should be quite low, although they can be quite long if the site is gently sloping. The first aim is just a continuation of the hops, to hold a course and speed. You must complete at least four good flights like this.

The natural next step is to introduce gentle turns. To do this you will need a little more room, and you may be flying with up to 40m ground clearance. Again, at least four good flights with turns of up to 90° is the standard.

Phase 5: Theory & Examination

By now you will have been flying for two or three days, and unless you are very fit you will be getting a bit tired with all the walking back up the hill. Usually on day 2 or day 3 the instructor will call a break or two to discuss some of the theory of paragliding with you (and let you have a rest!). The subjects to cover include basic meteorology and airflow over hills, the principles of flight and how your craft works, and the rules of the air (anti-collision rules) and the laws that govern our activity.

The remaining time on your Elementary course is taken up with polishing the basic skills. I.e achieving more consistent self launches, planning and executing flights with good airspeed and smooth turns of up to 180°, and setting up and completing controlled and reasonably accurate landings. For your higher flights you will be launching from a take-off area at the top of the flying site and flying down to a landing area, your ground clearance could be anything from 60m to 600m depending on where you are learning, some students may encounter lifting air, but the EP standard is essentially top to bottom flights conducted in smooth conditions.

You will need to take and pass the BHPA EP exam, which is a multiple choice paper covering basic principles of flight, the weather and very basic air law including the anti-collision rules of the air.

The Exam is only partially a test of you. It is also final check for the instructor: if half the class gets question 6 wrong something has obviously been missed and needs re-visiting.

Final assessment (EP)

The final assessment is signed by a senior instructor to confirm that you are ready to start on the Club Pilot syllabus. In practice the progression can be fairly seamless; for example you may have already done some of the theory or have good enough reverse launches to have these CP tasks signed off before you complete the EP level.

The main reasons for having an EP then CP level are really to do with people moving schools, or doing half the course then having a break before continuing. It is just a convenient level to draw a line. It marks a national standard, and allows schools to market the course in two halves, as taking one week at a time off work, and paying in two parts, is more practical for many students. The EP is also a natural point to sort those who just want to try the sport out from those who are considering taking it up and perhaps buying equipment.

The school may have some CP gear, but it is quite common for students to buy their own at this stage and continue their training (perhaps at a reduced cost) on their own glider.

Achieving the elementary level usually takes about 4 to 5 flying days. This level means that the holder is ready to start on the Club Pilot course and soaring flight. It does not confer any kind of licence or insurance cover for flying without instructor supervision. EP level students are not registered as qualified pilots with the association.

This is an important point, as there have been cases of EP holders buying gear and flying without the supervison of an instructor, and this situation may well be viewed by the authorities (and life insurance companies) as negligent behaviour. In the worst case the air navigation order makes it an offence to operate any aircraft in a negligent manner. Negligent could quite easily be defined as "without a suitable licence".

Club Pilot (Novice) stage

It is not unusual for the Club Pilot level to be done at a different venue from the EP level or with another instructor, or with the same school but in a different venue, or some weeks or months later. In such cases the instructor will need to refer back to the student's record book, and a refresher of some of the high flights and briefings may be needed to ensure that the student is ready to attempt the next stages. It is also quite likely that a new glider may be introduced at this stage, so a repeat of a couple of previous flight plans on the new equipment is a sensible precaution.

Accidents are very often the result of too many new things at once: new glider, new site and new task after a break of a few weeks is a classic recipe....

Phase 6: Pre-soaring

The pre-soaring flights will involve 180° turns, ie quartering the same area of ground in both directions and making planned approaches to a defined landing area. This skill is vital in using lift effectively and gaining height. Semi-soaring flights (ie following a soaring pattern but descending because there is not sufficient lift or your outside the lifting area,) are an excellent exercise for improving control, and once you are in a good lift band, the task of staying up will be comparatively easy.

You will be required to demonstrate a number of accurate landings. Accurate landings and approaches not only show that the pilot can land where he wants but are a very useful task in learning about the handling and turn radius of the glider. Once soaring you will extend the range of places you can fly to in order to land, so it makes sense to ensure this skill is of a reasonable standard before you start using lift to extend your flights.

Phase 7: Soaring (Dynamic lift)

Ridge soaring is not a new skill; it is simply a question of making controlled turns in the right place and taking advantage of the fact that the air is rising in this area faster than your canopy is sinking. The key skills, therefore, are an ability to read the site and anticipate the areas of useful lift, and having good enough control to make the most of it.

This is often made both easier and harder by the presence of other pilots: easier in that you can see where the lift extends to and is strongest or most consistent, and harder in that you will need to have part of your brain working on keeping track of the other gliders' positions.

If there are too many other pilots airborne for you to be able to process this information then it may not be suitable for your first soaring flight. Your soaring flight must demonstrate that you are not only able to use lift effectively but also to fly safely with other air users and know the rules of the air.

Your first flights will be with radio contact from your instructor. Hopefully he will be prompting you by saying things like "as you get towards that end of the ridge, check over your shoulder for traffic; if it is clear, turn when you feel the lift is strongest"

This kind of prompting ensures that you know what to do, but allows you the freedom to make your own decisions.

After a couple of successful beats, if you have joined the pattern and are managing well, your instructor will probably leave you get on with it for a while and make your own decisions.

To complete this exercise you need to make at least five good soaring flights and these must be on more than one site or day. By this time you should be comfortable flying in dynamic ridge lift in good conditions, your airtime should now be counted in hours rather than minutes!

As you are staying up, it seems rather pointless landing at the bottom and having to walk up, so if the site is suitable the next task is top landing.

Again, with gradually reducing input from your instructor, you need to make at least four good top landings. These must be well planned and executed, – being blown backwards, or inadvertently drifting sideways onto the top is not acceptable as a top landing!

Top landing is not always possible, especially if learning on mountain sites, so the practical portion of this exercise can be waived by the instructor, if the terrain makes it unsafe, but only when they are satisfied that you have the requisite glider control skills and knowledge to do this safely when conditions permit.

Phase 8: Improving skills

Soaring flight is a key goal for most new pilots; however, learning to soar is only one of the skills you will need to fly safely.

Phase 8 includes showing a familiarity with your glider's speed range, using the accelerator system and knowing its limitations, and maximising your performance by making coordinated turns. This phase also includes a specific requirement to show competence, both forward and reverse launching (just in case you have managed to get this far without mastering one or other of these techniques).

Also mentioned in this phase are cross-wind or side-slope landings. This is not a mandatory task, but is a very useful skill for many flying sites in the UK.

360° turns are not specifically mentioned in the task book, as they could be difficult to achieve at some sites and could cause long delays in completing the CP for some pilots. However, for schools with access to bigger hills or mountains, the 360° turn is a very useful skill to master and is commonly included.

A key skill in paragliding is controlling your wing well on the ground, new pilots are of course keen to get airborne, and that urge, combined with the frustrating nature of ground-handling can lead some pilots to neglect this skill. The BHPA training system addresses this in two ways. Firstly by giving an instructor the option to sign a pupil off to go and practice their ground handling without supervision, this is very helpful to many pupils as they are now insured to practice way from the school. However it does put the emphasis on you the student pilot to be careful in selecting a safe environment and weather conditions.

Secondly ground handling is recognised as an exercise in its own right and like the other exercises needs to be signed off as adequate by the instructor before you can obtain a CP qualification.

Phase 9: Instability & Emergencies

Keep flying long enough and you will come across a situation that requires specific knowledge to deal with it. This section covers the commonest of these and your instructor will discuss all the calamities that may befall the unwary pilot and ask you to try out some of the techniques to cope with them.

Rear riser and weight shift steering mimics a situation where a brake line has broken or become tangled. Active flying is simply dealing with the air when it is not very smooth and so minimising the effects of turbulence.

Big ears is an invaluable technique in the dynamic conditions of the UK, as it is a relatively straightforward way of combating strong lift.

Dealing with small asymmetric tucks is equally vital and all these things will be discussed and practiced.

The more serious instability situations that can occur, such as spins and stalls, are not practiced at CP level for obvious safety reasons. In fact, if properly understood, these events should never occur at all. (Both situations are only possible in very severe turbulence or as a result of gross pilot input). This exercise is to impart the knowledge of how they can be avoided and to discuss what actions should be taken in each case.

The use of a reserve parachute should be properly understood so that, should the case ever arise where it was appropriate, the pilot would be prepared to use it

Phase 10: Theory & Examination

This consists of the further theory and subsequent exam. Your instructor may give separate lectures to CP level, he may combine them with the EP level theory session, or he may provide material (such as this book) for you to improve your knowledge yourself.

Exercise 40: A talk on human factors is of particular note. Human factors such as drugs, (including hangovers), tiredness and stress (including fear), have been implicated in several reportable incidents.

Much emphasis is placed on pre-flight checks and annual inspections of your gear. The test authorities and manufacturers spend a huge amount of time and effort improving the standard of equipment. But if the pilot decides to fly after a drink, or fly anyway when it looks a bit rough to impress his new girlfriend, it all goes out of the window!

Paragliding itself is reasonably safe, but unfortunately the same cannot always be said of all paraglider pilots.

Human factors are addressed in more detail elsewhere in this book.

Final Assessment (CP)

Just getting all the exercises signed off as complete and passing your exam is not the whole story. Your instructor must then sign you off as having the right attitude and standard of airmanship. What does this mean?

It means different things to different instructors no doubt, but a pretty good definition might be the answer "Yes" to the question, "Would I be happy knowing this pilot is out flying tomorrow on a new site?" If this is the case, then you will get the signature and will become qualified as a Club Pilot, ready to fly with just the informal advice or coaching of more experienced pilots. Many clubs have designated coaches who have been selected and had some training to offer support to new members.

Your record book is kept by the school. If you need it for any reason (such as going on a foreign trip with another school, or to transcribe information into your personal log book) they can usually supply a copy, but they are constrained to keep the original.

Different training systems

The method of training employed is determined to a great extent by the geography and weather of the region. The BHPA system has been refined in windy conditions where shallow slopes are common and walking back up is practical.

In many countries paragliding is a true mountain sport and the tuition is quite different.

In place of many short low-level flights, the initial training may be carried out on a flat or almost flat field. However, if there are no low hills, the next move is to fly from a large mountain.

In fact this is much easier in some respects, as there is plenty of time to think and space to get it slightly wrong and make a correction. Because the weather in mountainous regions is determined as much by the topography as the weather patterns, it is frequently possible to fly in zero wind, especially early and late in the day.

Whilst zero wind launches do require a committed run, the actual flights are very smooth and easy to control. Most instruction is by radio, and though the risk of the pupil finding himself in the wrong place at the wrong altitude is significantly greater than on smaller hills, the advantage is that a pupil may make dozens of flight path corrections or turns on one flight and so progress very much more quickly.

Manoeuvres like the 360° turn are introduced almost immediately, as there is a lot of room and little wind drift. Students learning in an alpine environment typically progress in their airborne canopy control skills very quickly.

Mountain flying does carry a significantly higher risk of accidents, primarily because of pupils having trouble judging their position when 1,000 metres above the landing field, and because the landing area is often quite restricted. In Ski resorts for example, the cables of the ski-lifts that make the sport possible, are themselves an additional hazard.

In spring and summer the thermal activity and valley winds in mountainous regions mean that flying for beginners is strictly a morning and evening activity. As the students progress the window of flyable weather becomes wider, but so do the challenges posed by turbulence and wind. A common problem is for pupils who have learnt in one environment switching to another. British pilots flying in the Alps for the first time find phenomena such as valley winds and lee-side thermals quite alien to their experience. Conversely, Alpine pilots may struggle to ground handle, reverse launch, and top land in strong dynamic conditions.

Tandem flights with an instructor are a much more common feature of mountain flying. However, in non-thermic conditions the flight generally ends up at the bottom of a mountain, requiring a long drive or cable car ride to get back up. As the instructor can only take one person at a time, the cost of training this way can become very expensive.

The commercial pressure of earning money from taking members of the public for an experience flight, rather than flying students on courses, means that in some popular resorts, the instructors and tandem wings are often employed full time for tourists, something student hoping to learn in some areas have found a frustrating experience.

Many countries with dry consistent climates and mountainous terrain are great for flying, but of course do not have the soil and grass cover found in the UK and the resulting slopes are rocky and often covered in scrub. Whilst the local pilots may clear launch areas, flying and landing in such regions requires good planning (and good boots). Launching from uncleared areas, or side slope landing below launch in places like Morocco, Greece or Spain is not recommended.

Other regions are covered in trees and flying tree-covered slopes has a significant effect on the airflow; again, conservative flight planning in such areas is vital.

Coastal soaring in sea breezes and landing on beaches is a worldwide phenomenon and many pilots with low airtime flying abroad would do well to explore the coastal sites available.

It is possible to learn many of the skills of paragliding without any hills. Tow launching is a popular option in some countries and regions where the right sites are not readily available. The BHPA have a slightly different syllabus and task book for tow launch training, including such vital areas as signalling, emergency release procedures, and flying a circuit over an airfield, which may be in use by other aircraft.

Tow launching requires a team to operate the winch or tow vehicle, lay out the lines and signal the launch. It is a great group or club activity but does mean you cannot suddenly decide to go and have a fly when you wish. In the busy skies of the UK a tow permit from the Civil Aviation Authority (CAA) is required before towing above 60m is allowed.

Towing does have the advantage of not requiring any walking up hills. Given a reasonable field you can often fly no matter what the wind direction.

The downside is that with a minimum sink rate of around 1.2m/sec your flight from a 300m tow will only last 4 minutes or so. You would need to be very lucky indeed to contact a good thermal in the first couple of minutes in order to get a longer flight. Flying from a mountain or a hill with ridge lift generally gives you far more airtime to play with.

The International Para-Pro System

Most paragliding countries with an association operate their own training systems, and instructors in each tend to be reasonably conversant with those of their near neighbours, making cross-over ratings fairly easy. The closest thing to an internationally recognised standard is the FAI Para-Pro system.

The Para-Pro system recognises 5 stages and many associations affiliated to the FAI can "convert" your national rating to the appropriate Para-Pro level. This may make acceptance or conversion to a different standard simpler for those pilots who may wish to fly in a number of different countries.

The Levels are:

Stage 1: Ground Skimming

Stage 2: Altitude Gliding

Stage 3: Ridge Soaring

Stage 4: Thermal Soaring

Stage 5: Cross- Country

Comparison of this system with the BHPA PRS would put a Student pilot at about half way between stage 1 and stage 2, and a Club pilot at just slightly short of Stage 3 (which requires 10 hours experience).

The BHPA Pilot and Advanced Pilot levels equate quite well with Stages 4 and 5.

The full text and detailed requirements for the International Para-Pro system can be found at **http://www.fai.org/ hang_ gliding/ documents/parapro.asp**

An International Para-Pro licence card (IPPI card) is available, and even if your association is not using this system, it is usually possible to obtain one on the strength of your national rating. This is the case in the UK and in a number of other countries.

There is a small fee for issuing these cards.

Site Assessment

To assess when and where to fly safely you need to be able to understand the factors affecting a site. Foremost of these factors is being able to visualise how the air is behaving: where the good lift will be, where the wind will be stronger or lighter, what the likelihood of turbulence is.

In order to understand its' behaviour we need to know a little bit about the air. We do not take much notice of the air in our daily lives unless the wind is very strong, but when flying, its behaviour is of crucial importance and great interest.

Air is composed of molecules that are bouncing around all over the place, constantly colliding with each other and any nearby object. It has mass and weight, which is handy as it keeps the air stuck to the planet! The air is gaseous, but it in many important ways its behaviour is similar to a liquid, so perhaps the easiest way to visualise its movement is by imagining it as water flowing over the landscape. Obviously there are some differences. For example, air can climb slopes more easily than water, but it gives you the general idea.

When you stand on a hilltop with the air moving along as wind, it is helpful to visualise the flow as broad river flowing towards and around the landscape. Ask yourself where you would see rough or white water. This is likely to be in and around woods and buildings, in the lee of hills, or wherever an obstacle interrupts the flow *(see Fig 8.1)*. We have immediately established the major areas of turbulence. The reason why air (like water) has a turbulent flow is because it cannot make sharp changes of direction. Its mass and inertia keep it moving one way. This analogy also explains some other characteristics of airflow that are important to us. A small or conical hill cannot generate as much lift as a straight ridge, as the air will flow round rather than over it if it can just like a rock in a stream.

If you do have a long ridge but it has a gully or pass in it, *(see Fig 8.2)* the air will accelerate through the gap, and so this area should be treated with caution. One pilot flying along a line of hotels on top of a coastal ridge in Israel flew too close to such a gap and described the experience as being "hoovered" backwards through the space. He ended up on the roof of a house (fortunately they are flat in that part of the world).

Fig 8.1: Mechanical turbulence

Fig 8.2: Airflow in a gully

The same phenomenon is found at the end of a ridge (see Fig 8.3). The last few metres are often of no use, in generating lift, as the wind is escaping around the end of the ridge rather than being pushed over the top as lift.

In very mountainous areas, or those with narrow valleys, you may find that the airflow is affected more by the shape of the land than by the prevailing wind direction. Even in a light westerly breeze the wind in the bottom of a deep north-south valley is likely to be northerly or southerly. Even in quite small sites with a concave aspect like a bowl, the airflow is distorted by the terrain (Fig 8.4).

Fig 8.3: Airflow on a cliff and ridge end

If the wind is forced to change direction suddenly by flowing over a cliff for example, the result of its inertia is for the airmass to "overshoot" in the same way as a waterfall in a fast flowing river, and to leave an area of relatively low pressure behind the obstacle. The air then curls back on itself to fill the space and the result is a rotating airflow or "rotor". Figs 8.1, 8.3, 8.5 and 8.6 show such common areas of turbulence. The water analogy does become less applicable when dealing with vertical obstacles as, unlike water, air will flow up a cliff, for example, causing a rotor over the top edge. (Fig 8.5)

Fig 8.4: Airflow in a bowl

A "spine-back" ridge has an even greater effect on the airflow with a very large area of descending and potentially tumbling and chaotic air on the lee side. (Fig 8.6)

However, the advantages of the inertia of an airmass is significant to the soaring pilot. When wind comes into contact with a slope, it is forced upwards, and the flow has a vertical component we call lift.

Fig 8.5: Airflow up a cliff showing lift band and dangerous areas affected by rotor

47

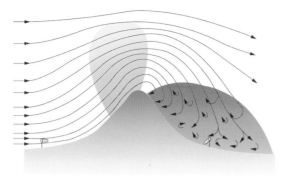

Fig 8.6: Airflow over a spine-backed ridge showing lift band and area affected by rotor

The steeper the angle the air climbs at, the better the lift. A shallow slope with a given wind speed will always create less lift than a steep slope in same wind speed, as the vertical component is less *(see Fig 8.7)*.

We also need to take into account the wind strength and direction. Is it too strong? Is there enough wind to soar? Is it blowing directly onto the hill? Very often the wind does not meet the hill at a right angle. If it is, say, 30° "off" the slope, less lift will be produced, as the air will climb the hill at a shallower angle. In this case a slope that looks like the steeper example in *Fig 8.7* will actually behave more like the shallower example in terms of the lift produced.

If the wind is "off" it also means that when you are soaring in the rising air in front of the slope, you will, on alternate beats, be flying on a downwind leg – this situation is addressed in the section on airspeed, groundspeed and windspeed. You must decide whether it is worth flying or moving to another hill, or not to fly at all. This kind of judgement can only be made with experience. If in doubt, do not fly.

As well as the shape and aspect (direction) of a site, a further variable is size. Bigger sites are better at producing lift as a larger body of air is being deflected upwards. This means that the "new" upward direction of the air mass is more established and the lift band will be higher and broader. The size criterion does not only apply to the actual ridge or hill itself; the upwind terrain also has a bearing on the effectiveness of the site at generating lift. A small ridge that is located downwind of gradually upward sloping ground will produce more lift than the same sized site with flat or undulating ground upwind of it.

Many apparently "perfect" ridges are in fact the sides of valleys, with another slope facing the opposite way just upwind. Such sites demand great caution,

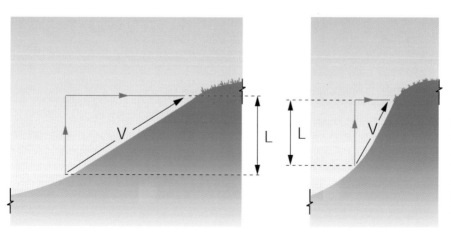

Fig 8.7: Steep and shallow slopes and the different amounts of lift (L) produced from the same wind speed (V)

Lots of hazards here

as many are dangerous to fly, or can only be used in very light winds, due to the downslope winds or rotors affecting the lift band of the potential site. If there is any doubt about such a site it is better to be left unflown until it has been checked out by highly experienced flyers. (In the UK most possible flying sites have already been investigated.)

A site will often have bowls or spurs that face in slightly differing directions; parts of the ridge may be higher than others and parts will be steeper; one section may have a nasty rotor behind the edge, and the shape of the lip may give a strong venturi effect at another point. If you have a basic understanding of airflow and lift production you should be able to predict where the site is safe to launch and land, where the best lift will be in a given direction and if there are any areas that should be avoided or need extra height to cross.

While assessing the site there are other factors to consider. There may be hazards such as trees or power lines. The landing area should be large enough for your level

of experience, and if you are planning to soar and top-land there must be a suitable area for this. The aspect of a site is very important, ie what is it facing? If the area immediately upwind is rough or down-sloping, or has high buildings, this will adversely affect the airflow. If it is has green fields the chances of thermals are less, and if it has a dry or rocky landscape the chances are much greater. Sites facing the sea often benefit from very smooth airflow and are often very suitable for early soaring flights.

Putting all this information together we can look at a site such as in *Fig 8.8 (overleaf)*. With the wind coming from the north (a northerly) the ridge is pretty straightforward and looks easy to soar. Because it has a south-easterly face as well, it would be dangerous to drift too far back, so caution is required in stronger winds. The rocky gulley may be a good source of thermals, but it may also "trap" you in the venturi effect if the wind is strong. This is doubly dangerous, as the power lines are immediately behind this point.

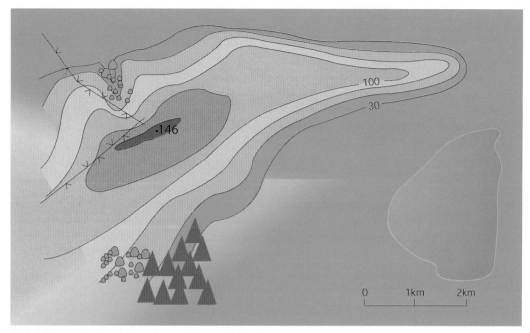

Fig 8.8: Topographic (map) view of a possible paragliding site

If you fly beyond the gulley, the lift will weaken very quickly if there is any easterly component to the wind, as the wind flows around the face rather than along it. You may lose height and find it hard to get back, especially with the power lines between you and the landing area. Until you have a good deal of experience, the whole western end of the ridge beyond the trig point on top is best left alone.

In a south-easterly wind the ridge is longer and perhaps a little easier to use. The area of rocks that are sheltered from the wind by the trees and facing directly into the sun are a very strong trigger point for thermals to be formed. However, as the ridge gets shallower here, the ridge lift will be weak, and the best option may be to work up some height first, then go and loiter for a while in that area, before coming back to the main ridge if you do not find a good area of lift.

The lake is a good indictaor of the wind that is approaching the ridge, and ruffles or calm patches seen on the surface can help you "see" the approach of gusts or of thermals. Because the ridge is a spur, if you do gain say 500m of height above take-off in a thermal and follow it downwind, when you fly out into the flatlands behind it you will immediately "gain" another 150m of altitude, making this an easy site to fly cross-country from. This can all be assessed simply from the map; when you can see the terrain and sky for yourself, there are many more clues you can glean as to how the lift will behave at a specific site.

A thorough site and weather assessment should give you enough information to decide if it is suitable for you to fly.

Wind gradient

Air is affected by friction as it moves over the landscape; all the grass and trees, bushes and buildings obstruct the flow, preventing the airmass from travelling the way it wants and slowing it down,

Wind speed

Fig 8.9: Wind gradient

so at ground level, where there is a lot of friction, the air is moving relatively slowly. A few metres above the surface, there is far less friction, though due to its inherent viscosity, the air will still be slowed to some extent by the slower-moving layer beneath. The higher you go, the less restricted and therefore the faster the wind will be.

The first 10 metres or so above ground level can exhibit an increase of 100% in the windspeed. At 200-300 metres or so above the terrain the relative drag decreases more slowly in most circumstances, and the effect becomes less apparent (though different meteorological conditions can have a marked effect on this pattern). See *Fig 8.9*.

Wind gradient is an effect of parasitic drag, and as the windspeed doubles, so the drag generated is squared. This means that in a light wind the gradient is barely noticeable, but as the wind gets stronger so the gradient becomes more marked. A wind of 5kph in the landing field may indicate a wind of 7kph at the launch site 200m higher. A wind of 20kph in the same spot is likely to mean 40kph or more at launch on the same site.

This gradient in wind speed is particularly noticeable on the hills we fly; the "normal" gradient of say 10kph in the landing field and 15-20kph at 100metres above it is exaggerated by a related phenomenon – the "venturi" zone *(Fig 8.10)*.

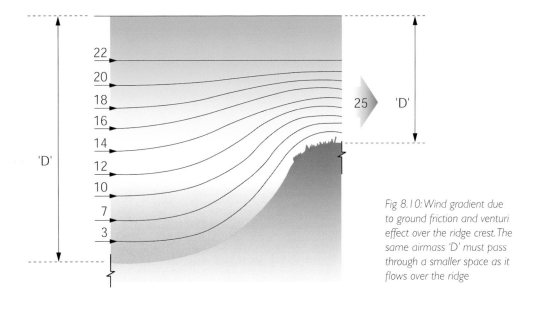

Fig 8.10: Wind gradient due to ground friction and venturi effect over the ridge crest. The same airmass 'D' must pass through a smaller space as it flows over the ridge

Paraglider pilots choose to fly ridges that offer the best lift, that is to say hills which the wind is forced to flow over. And in addition to the wind gradient, the airflow is accelerated over the crest of the hill by being constricted between the ground and the weight and inertia of the horizontal wind above it. The effect is the same as airflow over a wing, -the less space there is, the faster the flow must be. The result of this is that the wind speed at launch may be two to three times the wind strength in the landing field.

It is vital to appreciate this for two reasons in particular. Firstly, if you launch from below the top of a hill, you must assume that the wind will be much stronger above you and that if you ascend into this stronger zone you could have a problem. The second is to do with flight planning. You may suddenly find that you are approaching the bottom landing area more quickly than you anticipated, and with less headwind to reduce your groundspeed, your glide performance can improve dramatically. If you can

Ideal launch area,
ideal landing area

anticipate this situation it is much easier to avoid an inadvertent stall caused by misjudging your speed, or an overshoot of your intended target.

Pilots who habitually fly dynamic soaring sites soon become used to the increase of wind strength with height, but can be caught out when flying big Alpine sites where the phenomenon of valley winds can make the wind strength in the landing area stronger than at take-off. This is also caused by the venturi effect, but in the case of a deep valley which is narrower at the bottom than the top the constriction and subsequent acceleration of the airflow is most in evidence at the valley floor. This situation is covered in Chapter 33, Flying in new environments.

In addition to assessing the airflow patterns and dynamic lift characteristics of a site, there are some other factors that we also need to consider.

The surface of the slope can have significant effects on the way a site is flown. The first is physical: a rocky slope will be less forgiving of an inadvertent touch-down or a slope landing, and so will demand a wider margin between your feet (and wing-tips) than, say, a grass-covered slope. Trees also dictate a larger margin for error, for obvious reasons.

Flying sites are often the venues for transmission ariels and these may be supported with bracing wires. More than one pilot has caught a thermal and circled up the slope, to find their track is leading them straight at a mast. Such obstacles demand a wide margin, particularly as the cables are often almost invisible from certain angles.

In addition to the risks of actually touching your site, the physical properties of the surface can significantly affect the

Rough ground typical of mediterranean contries

air. When snow covers the mountains and hills, the smooth surface and uniform temperature can offer some glassy smooth flying conditions.

However, a rocky slope facing south will soon start to heat up in direct sun, and powerful thermals will give good lift but turbulent air.

When flying over trees at a good height they are just like grass or bushes on a bigger scale and do little to change the airflow pattern, but if you get low, particularly on slopes with a "shoulder" or ledges, the trees can cause areas of sinking air or turbulence in their lee. It is very unwise to try and soar a ridge or work a thermal if that involves flying behind trees.

One very pleasant side effect of tree-covered sites is that, if they have been in sun for a few hours, and the wind drops in the evening, they may gradually release the warm air as the day cools, in a kind of huge, long-lived, slow motion thermal allowing an extended late evening flight, where you seem to be staying up as if by magic. Pilots therefore sometimes know this phenomenon as "magic lift".

A summary of site assessment is to check for: **Shape, Size, Steepness, Surface, Aspect, Access, and Rules.**

Weather Assessment

Adequate visibility is vital

In addition to the properties of the site, we also need to know that the weather is suitable. The weather is a huge subject and there are some excellent books that are definitely worth reading if you wish to know more. To confine ourselves here to the fundamentals, we have three basic requirements.

Good visibility

It is self evident that it is dangerous to fly if there is low cloud or mist obscuring the hill. Even if you can see parts of the

slope or the landing area, there is a very real danger of it thickening quickly, particularly if the temperature is falling, and you can quickly become totally disorientated. If you are in cloud but well clear of the surface, you still run the risk of encountering another aircraft. In thermal generated cumulus clouds (especially near popular flying sites) there may be another glider taking the same gamble. Even far from flying sites you may encounter both civil and military traffic flying on instruments.

At dusk (or dawn if you are really keen!) the visibility may also be poor and make judging distances and altitude very difficult. Obstacles like power lines may be completely invisible. It is worth noting that if you are flying above a hill or mountain it remains light much longer than in the valley or landing field. More than one pilot has been caught out setting up a landing in a dark field late in the evening.

For all these reasons it is illegal to fly in poor visibility, whether caused by cloud or darkness (see chapter 24, Air Law). The actual legal minima for flying an unpowered aircraft in the UK is a visibility of 1500m.

Rain and snow

Flying in light rain or drizzle is miserable, but it is not dangerous for short periods as long as the visibility is OK. It is often easier and quicker to fly down than walk if the weather turns poor. If it means getting a nice dry canopy wet, remember it may be a long job to dry it out again.

If there is heavy rain or snow, it becomes dangerous to fly. The water or snow is carried into the canopy with the airflow and cannot escape. It will build up in the trailing edge and eventually it will distort the canopy and disturb the flight characteristics. If sufficient weight builds up you could enter a stall from which you cannot recover. More than one pilot has been killed in this way flying in snow. Heavy rain is often associated with squally or turbulent air, and this is another reason to avoid flying in very wet conditions.

Paraglider airworthiness certification and recovery characteristics are tested in dry conditions, a wet canopy is likely to be significantly poorer at recovery from instability situations like a collapse or stall, as wet fabric is heavier and more likely to stick to itself and to the lines.

Wind

We require a reasonably smooth breeze to fly. For training, it can be anywhere between zero and about 20kph (though not too gusty). For ridge soaring we need at least 10 to12 kph, but no more than about 25kph. We can check the wind strength and how smooth it is in several ways. The first and most important is by feel and experience. Standing on the edge of the hill for five minutes before deciding whether or not to fly is never a wasted exercise. If you think it is near the top limit for you this is particularly true: you would not wish to launch only to find that you had taken off during a temporary lull. You can confirm your impressions with a wind speed indicator. These come in several forms and give you an accurate readout of the wind speed. They can only tell you what the wind is doing on the spot where you are holding them, so it is worth walking to the edge of the slope and angling them into the airflow to obtain the highest reading you can. The maximum reading will be the most accurate. They can also assist in deciding just how gusty it is.

Gusts are the thing to watch out for: it is safer to fly in a steady wind of, say, 24kph (providing the site is suitable) than in one that is varying between 10kph and 20kph

There are also visual clues to the wind's behaviour. Among the most obvious are windsocks or streamers (most flying sites should have one, and it is worth having a small windsock of your own). The motion of trees and grass and of course the flight patterns of other pilots are all very useful.

You may be sharing the site with hang-glider pilots whose craft have a greater resistance to turbulence. If they are getting pushed about it may be a good idea to wait a while. The best plan of action is always to ask those who have just flown. They are usually happy to give you their impressions. Model aircraft and birds can also be useful indicators.

An electronic wind speed indicator (WSI)

Clouds offer perhaps the best way to assess the wind from the ground. Look first at how quickly they are travelling; if there seems to be just a light breeze on the surface, but the clouds are hurtling by only a few hundred metres above your head, some further investigation is required before you consider flying. The other way in which clouds can help you assess conditions is that each cloud type is an indicator of the air's behaviour. Thermals – rising columns of warm air that create lift and associated turbulence – are frequently marked by cumulus (cotton wool) clouds, formed when the moisture in the air condenses when it cools. The taller and darker the cumulus clouds the more powerful the thermals feeding them and the rougher the air will feel.

Lenticular clouds are indicators of atmospheric waves set up by the flow of the air over the hill or mountain ranges. Such waves are a source of both lift and, at their fringes, turbulent air. Perhaps the most noticeable of all clouds are cumulo-nimbus (cu-nim for short) which are associated with heavy rain and storms and in which the turbulence has been known to tear the wings off sailplanes. Thermals and wave lift are discussed in chapter 26, Cross Country.

The greatest single cause of accidents is flying in poor or unsuitable weather conditions (especially strong winds). If in doubt, always ask for advice. Remember, the mountains will still be there tomorrow.

A change in the weather such as this building thunderstorm can easily catch you out. You must allow a good amount of time to make a controlled descent and landing

Parachute landing falls 10

A paraglider is unlike any other aircraft in that it offers no protection at all to the pilot in the event of a hard landing or a crash. If you do approach the ground too fast or in the wrong direction, it is certain that you are going to be the thing that hits hardest.

There are a couple of things that we can do to protect ourselves: the first is always to wear sensible clothing, boots and a helmet, and to have a spinal foam pad or airbag of some type incorporated in the harness.

The second is to become proficient at the parachute landing fall. The PLF, as it is usually known, was developed in the UK by the military when the number of injuries sustained by paratroops on landing was becoming a cause for serious concern. There is no doubt that the technique has subsequently saved many potential injuries in the parachuting world. Whilst the horizontal component of a paragliders landing approach makes it less applicable in most cases, there are a number of situations in which it works equally well for us

A good technique and airbag combined can do a lot to minimise injury (Photo: Gus Hurst)

(a low level collapse, being "dumped" by turbulence or deploying a reserve for example); and for this reason it is a mandatory part of the BHPA's training programme.

The PLF works by reducing the shock to any one part of the body by ensuring that the shock is absorbed over a large area. A PLF cannot be learnt from a book, but the basic position and the roll are illustrated here.

The important points to remember are:

- Tuck in your elbows and chin.
- Bend your knees and keep them together.
- Bend slightly at the waist.
- Twist away from the direction of travel (45° or so is best).
- Try to go "floppy" (blowing out your air and "deflating" may help).
- PRACTICE – It's no good if you can't remember what to do when the ground is coming up too fast.

Common faults when practicing PLFs include:

- **Not bending at the waist enough** (the feet do not end up going the right way if you do this).

- **Not turning as you flop:** the sides of your knees, not the front of them, should touch the ground.

- **Being too stiff;** try to "crumble" into the ground, not fall over like a felled tree. The calves should touch first.

- **Legs coming apart as you roll** – don't let them – gripping something like a glove between the knees may help you practice.

In conclusion, the PLF is rarely used in a real situation, but when it has been, it has certainly prevented injury. It should be practiced regularly. If you cannot remember anything else, always twist away from the ground, so you do not hit head-on, and bend -the foetal position will do the job. Shouting something just before contact (you can choose your own word!) is helpful as it empties the lungs and helps you "deflate", but do remember to keep your tongue in and your mouth shut as you impact!

Pre-Flight Checks

Like any aircraft, a paraglider must be pre-flighted before launch. The reason is very simple: the air itself is not inherently dangerous, but it is an environment that is very unforgiving of mistakes.

The consequences of (say) failing to do up a buckle are liable to be a lot more serious than falling off a windsurfer.

Pre-flight checks fall into three categories:

Canopy inspection

To be carried out at least once a year or after any damage. This should be an exhaustive check of all the fabric for tears and excessive wear, all the lines of stitching, and all the lines, including attachment points. It is normal to measure a selection of lines to ensure they conform to the original specification. Ideally, the fabric should be tested for its

air impermeability (porosity) and a line broken to check the reduction in breaking strain. If the canopy is faded, it may be suffering from ultra-violet degradation, particularly in hot climates.

The annual check should be carried out by a professional dealer or manufacturer. The LTF & CEN airworthiness certification and most glider manufacturers specify that an annual check by a professionally authorised person is a requirement of the certification and the warranty.

Porosity check during a paraglider's anual inspection

A professional repair facility carrying out a glider inspection

It is worth reiterating this point as it quite often overlooked by pilots. If you have a certified wing and you miss out your annual service/ check then the wing becomes uncertified. A fact that can have serious implications either because your kit may have a problem hat you have not picked up, or in the sense that insurance companies could very easily may decide that you are flying an uncertified craft and are therefore operating outside the terms of their cover.

Daily inspection (DI)

These are visual checks that are to be carried out each day before flight.

Helmet – Correct size, on and done up?

Harness – Check stitching. Check for wear, especially where any metal touches webbing. Ensure buckles are functioning correctly – there have been cases of quick lock buckles popping open especially in sandy or snowy conditions. Ensure that any protective padding is correctly installed. Check that the reserve parachute locking pins are securely in place.

Maillons/Carabiners – All should be fully done up (large and small). Note that all riser/ line maillons should have the gates exposed. If they are "turned over" and hidden inside webbing loops they can be unscrewed by the motion of the risers.

Risers – Check stitching, especially where it is "bar-tacked", as this is very prone to abrasion. Magnetic keepers and poppers are also often a bit unreliable as wings get older.

Control lines – Are they secured correctly to the handles? Do the lower two metres show signs of wear?- this can happen as they run through the keepers/ pulleys. Make sure they are free running and not wrapped around the risers.

Checking the glider and lines (above) and the risers (below) during the Daily Inspection

Lines – Check for damage and tangles, vegetation and rubbish can easily get caught in your lines and cause a problem. If you run them through your hands you can both see and feel for lumps or thin spots where the line may be damaged inside the outer sheath.

When checking your lines, make sure the tip lines do not cross over any others, if they do, it is a sign that perhaps a line is caught over the canopy fabric, (a line over) which will inevitably mean an aborted launch.

Canopy – Check the fabric for signs of wear and tear. Any rips or punctures? Check stitching, especially around the highly stressed leading edge. Make sure there are no obvious internal ruptures and that there are no objects in the envelope (stones, sandwiches etc, one of my students once found a missing SLR camera in his glider!)

Instruments – Is your battery life OK? Are all attachments secure? Have you set your altimeter?

Line damage

The famous launch site of Col de La Forclaz overlooking Lake Annecy in France. Gliders laid out, inspected and ready. You may have to wait a while if you fluff your first attempt!

Pre-launch inspection

To be completed before committing yourself to each flight:

1. Wind and weather

- Is the strength and direction still OK?
- How is the sky looking?
- Is visibility good?
- What is on the horizon? (Upwind weather)
- How are other pilots doing?

2. Kit

- Harness: On correctly? Leg and chest strap(s) done up? Both carabiners locked?
- Reserve pins securely seated.
- Is my helmet correctly fitted and done up?
- All canopy cells fully open?
- Lines all clear? No tangles, no line-overs?
- No riser twists, Check which way you will rotate for reverse launches.
- Controls lines. No twists or tangles. Are the lines free running?
- Instuments/ Radios On?

3. Airspace

Is the space you are about to launch into clear of all other aircraft and hazards? Check in front, above and behind.

4. Pilot

- Are you feeling OK? Confident and focused?
- Have you got an outline flight plan?
- Have you remembered your PFUP? (Pre-flight urination procedure)

Many pilots use mnemonics to help them recall all the main points of their pre-launch check. Common ones include :

Will **G**eordie **H**ave **H**is **C**at **A**board

Wind & weather
Glider
Helmet
Harness
Controls
All clear

Another is : **S.H.O.W.B.I.Z.**

Straps and buckles.
Helmet
Observation
Wind
Brakes
I'm OK
Z There is no "Z"

Or feel free to make up your own!

This is an actual problem discovered during a a Pre-flight check

12 The Forward or Alpine launch technique

Introduction

This method is used if there is a light (less than 10kph) wind, or no wind at all. As the name suggests, it is commonly used in alpine countries where the majority of launches are on slopes with little wind. It can be used in stronger winds if an anchor-man is used to help hold the pilot while the canopy rotates up.

Preparation

Do your pre-flight checks. In zero wind with a short running space,or if your glider is laying in an area of wind shadow, you may find it helpful for a fellow pilot to hold up the centre of the leading edge. Make sure you have enough room to have a good run.

Committed alpine launch

The launch procedure

1. Lay out the canopy flat on its back (top surface) with the trailing edge into wind. The canopy should be arranged in a curve or crescent shape, This is so that so that the tips do not inflate before the centre,- in fact in no wind at all, is it better to make the curve slightly more pronounced so that the centre cells inflate just before the tips..

2. Stand with your back to the canopy, facing into wind.

3. Hold the control handles as you would in flight and allow all the risers to drape over your forearms. (You usually need to identify and pick up the front (A) risers in your hand at this point.).

4. Step forward until the "A" lines are fully stretched and evenly tensioned; check the air to make sure that it is clear. Note :several glider models with "split" A risers may launch more easily if you ignore the outer A's and hold only the inner front risers.

5. If there is any breeze you may be able to pull the risers a little to create a "wall" and ensure the cells are inflating evenly.

6. Rock back on your heels, but do not step backwards, than lean forwards and run strongly and smoothly forward – keep your head down and keep leaning forwards. At the point of maximum rearward pressure you may need to check your forward motion to allow the wing to "catch up" and rotate up above your head; however as the pressure reduces you will need to continue your forward run, releasing the front risers when the canopy is almost overhead (you can feel the rearwards pressure reducing). You may very well need to add some brake at this point to stabilise the canopy in the correct position above your head.

Leaning forwards helps your hands follow the natural arc of the front risers – do not pull them down or push them forward. The power should come from your run, not from your arms.

7. If you have sufficient space, Turn your head to one side then the other to check the canopy – cells open? Lines clear? Try not to break stride or slow down as you do this: the more pressure and speed you maintain the better. If a cell or two are collapsed on one side, give a firm pump with the control on that side to re-inflate them, do not launch with collapsed cells.

8. If you have time, you can double check that the controls are running freely. Apply pressure to the controls smoothly and evenly as you clear the edge of the hill. Do not be tempted to jump!

In stronger winds some pilots still prefer to use this launch method, where there is very restricted space, for example. In this situation an experienced helper is useful to prevent the pilot being pulled backwards during inflation.

Reverse launches | 3

Introduction

The reverse launch is generally used when there is a breeze that can support the inflated canopy without the pilot needing to continuously move forward. This is usually the case when attempting to ridge soar on hills rather than mountains. There are a few more elements than with a forward launch, and therefore more to go wrong, but with some breeze there is also more time to play with, and you can inspect the inflated canopy at leisure before deciding whether to fly. It is far easier to inflate and pull the canopy up without being pulled over by the wind when you are facing it, so this type of launch allows you to manage alone in a wind that would require help if you were forward launching.

However, if you have any doubt about your ability to control the canopy in a good breeze it may be appropriate to ask an experienced pilot to act as your anchor man and hold you while you inflate your paraglider. Though if the wind is simply too strong for you to managed an unassisted launch then it is likely to be too strong to fly safely.

Preparation

Do your pre-flight checks. Make sure there is plenty of slack in the lines as you prepare and put on the harness – it could be embarrassing and painful for the canopy to start inflating and for you to be dragged along with only one leg clipped in.

A well executed reverse launch demonstrates great glider control. (Photo: U-Turn)

1   Lay the canopy out flat on its back in a gentle arc with the trailing edge into wind.

2   Stand with your back to the wind, facing the canopy. To do this you will have to lift one complete set of risers over your head. You should now have the risers crossed in front of you. See Fig 13.1- look carefully at which way they are crossed. When you come to turn back again (the rotation) you will need to "follow" the lower set of risers around. If you decide at the start of your flying career which way you will turn, and do it the same way every time, you are less likely to get it wrong.

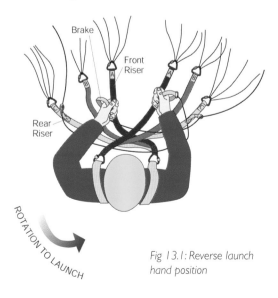

Fig 13.1: Reverse launch hand position

3   If it is windy, grasp at least a metre of control line above the keeper or pulley in each hand (do not cross your arms, just take the line that is controlling the same side as your hand). There should still be no tension on the rest of the lines at this point., if you now lean or move backward the wall should inflate.

4   Or if the wind is not too strong, take the control handles and the corresponding front riser in each hand as well.

5   By pulling on the front risers, inflate the cells to form a "wall"; if it is uneven or tries to lift too soon, you can alter its shape, or lower it, by pulling on the trailing edge with the control lines. If you need to lower the wall quickly, walk towards it at the same time. Ideally, the centre of the wall should be higher than the tips. A low wall of 2-3ft (60-90cm) high is adequate in most conditions. If the cells are squashed on one side it means the wind is coming from that direction and you need to move yourself and the wall round a few degrees until it is inflated evenly.

6 Once the wall is prepared you can set up the launch. There are a few variations on the exact method and each has some strengths. However, the commonest is the "continuous control method" or "crossed brakes" technique outlined below.

7 Now you need to collect the brakes – there shouldn't be too much tension on lines while you do this; step forward if you need to. Look down at the crossed riser sets. Visualise how you want your controls to be when the glider has come up and you have turned. You will need to reach under the crossed set of risers and take the control handle from the lower set. This is the "shortest route" and seems quite natural as your hand is just following the riser.

8 The other arm follows the "longest route" and reaches over the top of everything then around the back of the riser set to take the other control handle. Do not be tempted to put your hand between the risers or you will get tangled as you rotate. This control handle can now be brought back over to a more comfortable position with your arms uncrossed. You will see that the control line you have just collected is now wrapped around the riser set and looks a mess, do not worry, this is normal and it will unwind as you rotate later.

9 You can now re-take the front A riser on each side. There is no need to cross your arms – simply grasp the riser on the right side with your right hand and vice-versa. Each hand is now controlling one front riser and the brake for the opposite side.

10 Complete your pre-launch checks by seeing if your airspace is all clear. If all is well you can fully inflate the wing by pulling on the front risers.

11 As the wing reaches the flying position you may need to add a dab of brake to stabilise it in the correct position. You now have time to check that the canopy is fully inflated and has no tangles. When happy, you can then simply pivot on one foot and rotate under the wing to face forward for your launch.

12 If the wing begins to "fall" one way you can correct this very simply by stepping sideways towards the centre of the canopy and simultaneously applying brake with the hand on the same side (this will of course apply brake to the "high " side of the wing). i.e, if the wing is slipping right, you step right and brake with your right arm. This seems a little strange for the first few attempts, but quickly becomes a normal reaction.

13 If the pull-up has been too weak, the canopy will simply fall backwards and you can re-start. If it is coming up too fast, you can apply brake as it climbs. A big advantage of this technique is that you can apply brake and steer at any point during the launch, as you always have the controls in your hands..

14 When the canopy is stable above you, check for full inflation, clear lines, etc. You can then either turn and launch immediately, or remain facing the canopy while you feel the wind, or wait for an opportune moment to turn and launch.

15 Turn to face into wind. Take care not to reduce the pressure on the canopy – it is common to collapse it at this stage by stepping back under the wing as you turn. An effective technique is to reach out behind you with one leg as you rotate so keeping your movement constantly into wind, and the canopy evenly loaded. Before you turn, check the risers again: you need to follow the lower (obscured) one around. Apply pressure smoothly and evenly to the controls as you clear the edge of the hill.

NOTE – If you find that you have turned the wrong way, the risers will now have a 360° twist in them. If you are on the ground, you can simply go around the other way. If you have been lifted off, as can happen on slopes, do not worry. Simply continue to use the controls to fly the canopy away from the hill until you are well clear., the risers will naturally untwist themselves. Once sorted out, fly off as if that was what you meant to do all the time.

Other reverse launch variations

The cosss-brake launch outlined above became widely popular in the early 90's when canopies became fast enough to require continuous brake throughout the launch procedure. Prior to that, pilots would often pull up the risers with the controls from the same riser in their hands.

That system has a big disadvantage, in that you must drop at least one control handle at some point, or pass it from one hand to another whilst you rotate.

It was not uncommon for pilots to find themselves airborne without one (or both) control handles in their hands, or if they dropped one under some pressure the handle could fly up and hitch itself around the control line.

However, this technique is very good for extended ground-handling, as there is no line wrapped around the risers (which can cause damage and excess wear)

Reverse launch variation (Photo: Sup'Air)

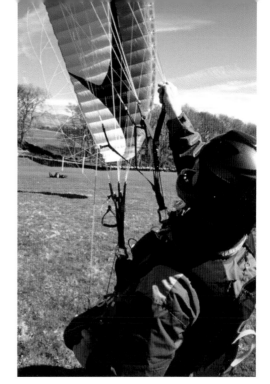

One handed variation

and the natural tendency of the risers to untwist is reduced. For this reason, using the "uncrossed" technique, in which the right hand controls the right tip while the wing is facing you (exactly like kite flying), is very good for extended ground handling practice and for walking an inflated glider back up a slope, for example.

Certain older pilots are reluctant to change from this original technique, as it very familiar to them.

Inflating the canopy with one hand controlling a front riser while the other hand controls the brake on the same side is a very useful technique in strong winds.

In this variation, the pilot stands slightly to one side of the canopy which is laid out at a fairly acute angle to the wind. As it is pulled up into the airflow gradually, and one tip first, the canopy generates much less pressure as it flies up the side of the "window", so it is easier to control without you getting dragged. Once in the stable position, the controls do have to be located after the rotation as above.

This technique is very good for strong conditions, or pilots without great physical strength or body weight, and is rightly popular with tandem pilots who are handling a larger wing for the same reasons. This technique is sometimes referred to as a "Cobra" launch as some pilots like to pause with one tip sitting up in the air while the other is still safely on the ground, and in this position the flying tip often dips and weaves looking very like the snake..

Essentially, all ground control is concerned with modifying the speed of the wing and its direction. It is possible to do this with almost any combination of brakes and risers, you can hold both brakes in one hand and both front risers; in another – though this technique offers very little lateral control and needs fast footwork to stay under the centre of the wing at all times.

You can simply hold both rear risers and steer with those, but because you cannot speed the wing up in this situation, but is easy to stall and drop it, this technique is well suited to use on a steeper slope where the wing is always trying to fly (useful when walking up a steeper slope for example)

There is no "right" way to control a paraglider on the ground and it is very useful and informative to try out a few of these variations when you have an opportunity.

Both front risers in one hand and both brakes in the other hand variation

A soarable breeze ideal for reverse launching

14 Launch problems

Some common launch problems and how to deal with them:

Problem!

The canopy will not climb overhead.

- Too much wind? If the problem is that you are being pulled backwards as the wing comes up during an alpine launch, try switching to a reverse launch.

- Not enough wind? If you are having to walk backwards towards the wind when reverse launching, try an alpine launch.

- Have you remembered to drop/ fully extend the control lines before reverse launching?

- Not physically strong enough to pull the wing up? Try the "One side, or Cobra" technique mentioned in Chap 13.

- Some outside factor, such as sand or snow or other debris in your wing,

- Is your paraglider wet?

- Are you running on completely flat ground, uphill or in turbulent air? It may help to begin closer to the edge if this is safe.

- How old is your wing? A sign of increased porosity is increased difficulty in launching. If your canopy often seems to "hang-back", it is well worth having it professionally checked, particularly if it getting old or the colour is fading.

Problem!

Canopy tucks (collapses forwards).

- Is there enough wind? Try an alpine launch or if already forward launching, run faster.

You may need to be adding brake if the canopy is overflying you. Try the continuous control method.

Are you pulling on the front risers too hard or for too long? Or are you shortening them by pulling them down? (This is quite a common problem and can be hard for an instructor, to spot unless he is holding the risers with you). Are you "punching" and pushing them in front of your body? Guide the risers up with open hands.

Are you stepping back towards the canopy when rotating, thereby reducing pressure? (This is probably the favourite method of cocking up a reverse launch!). Try squatting slightly to load the harness through the seat and help control the power, and prevent you being pulled or lifted by the canopy. Before you rotate, consciously reach back with your foot towards the edge of the slope/into wind, before putting it down and pivoting on it.

If the canopy is climbing too fast for you, try pulling it up holding the A and B risers together in your hands. Stepping towards it as it comes up also helps to de-power it to some extent, but this must be done as it is part way up, not as it reaches the zenith position or it will collapse.

Problem!

Canopy slews to one side.

Turbulence in launch area?

Canopy not laid out neatly?

Canopy not laid out into wind, or pilot not running into wind?

Uncommitted launch – insufficient pressure.

Are you standing on the centre line of the canopy compared to the wind. Many new pilots react to a drift off line by the canopy by walking away from it and trying to pull it back. In fact most off centre launches can be fixed by the pilot quickly repositioning themselves under the centre of the wing whilst also correcting with the controls.

Problem!

Canopy collapses in the centre (claps hands).

Poorly laid out? Try laying it in a tighter arc.

Uneven ground? Try using a helper to hold up the centre of the leading edge.

If you have split A risers, launch with just the middle A's.

This can happen on snow or other slippery surfaces, where the tips of the inflated wing start to slide away from you the moment you relax pressure on the controls. You can dump a few handfuls of snow or sand on the trailing edge to pin it down until you are ready.

Ground handling

Many pilots find that the hardest part of paragliding is controlling the machine while still on the ground. The reason for this is that when flying, your weight will automatically swing below the canopy, and, except in turbulent conditions, there will always be a load on the lines. On the ground however, the canopy can slide over to one side of you or the other; it can drop behind or in front of you and the load can vary from moment to moment. The more you can minimise these variations, the better the canopy will behave.

To keep the paraglider above your head in the proper position you will often need to use the controls and sometimes the risers as well. And crucially by being prepared to move your feet! A lot of problems can be eliminated by good preparation, making sure the canopy is into wind, knowing which way you will need to turn during a reverse launch, etc. If you give it the opportunity, your canopy will try and drag you through the nearest cow pat or fence! You must stay in charge and not allow yourself to be pulled around. If this proves to be impossible, collapse it immediately and start again. If this is not possible to control effectively, it may simply be too windy for you to fly.

Remember that until the wing is flying correctly above your head the controls will serve only to pull it down further, not as effective steering devices. If it is well off to one side you will need to walk back under the centre as you brake, or use the brake and front riser from the high side to pull it back up to the correct position.

The other way you can help yourself is by keeping the load constant. This often means that you must correct and check your canopy while running or walking (often backwards) to maintain pressure through the lines. Take care not to walk backwards over the edge of the hill by mistake!

Many people actually find it easier not to look at the canopy once they have rotated and are facing forward ready for launch. Try to develop control just by feeling what your wing is doing above you.

Inevitably sometimes you will lose the battle and the canopy will end up in a heap on one side or on top of you, and you will have to lay it out again. In a breeze you may find that a little careful manipulation of the brakes and risers can do this without the need to go and move the canopy by hand. An example of this is when the canopy has dived over and is "nose down" with the leading edge and the cell entries pointing into the ground. It is often possible to lean back a little on the risers to give a pivot point, and with a long pull on one brake handle, make the canopy fly back over into the correct starting position.

Ground handling skills are very useful and are something that many pilots, eager to fly, often spend too little time perfecting.

Ground handling practice (Photo: www.sunsoar-paragliding.com)

First flights | 5

By about the second or third day of training you will have completed several low level flights or "hops". You should have mastered use of the controls, and hopefully your instructor will have sorted out any bad habits (looking at the canopy as you fly along is a favourite one). It is likely that you have been responding to radio commands from an instructor or to "bat" signals from him as he stands in the landing area. Now you are ready for your first high flights.

Flight planning

The higher you are, the larger the radius of the circle within which your possible landing sites will lie. Unless you are very lucky this means that you are now able to reach stone walls, barbed wire fences or the field with the bull in it. You can no longer wait for the ground to simply come up and meet you – this is where you really start to pilot the aircraft and make decisions for yourself. Your instructor may well be on the radio, but he will only be a back-up and he certainly won't be able to do anything if you do the wrong thing. The secret

of being a good pilot is to think ahead.

A fairly experienced pilot has been heard to say, *"Well, I can console myself with the thought that the best pilot in the world could not have avoided crashing."* This was in a deep valley with trees, a river, a railway line and no obvious landing area. (He landed in the river) – The answer, of course, is that a good pilot would never have put themselves in that situation.

Pic Jerome Maupoint Gin

Preparing for the first high flight.

The first point, then, about flight planning is that it includes planning not to fly. The next point is that you should think about any hazards and how you can avoid them before you take off (see Chapter 8, Site assessment). This reduces your mental workload when airborne.

"...a huge field with one tree in it..."

Bill Lehan

A third and slightly contradictory element of flying un-powered aircraft, is that you must be prepared to revise your flight plan as you go along. If you decide to fly over that wall, and you start to sink low as you approach it, do not blindly follow your plan (or even your instructor's). Decide on an alternative and do it. It is far easier if you think of these alternative flight plans, along with your intended plan, before you launch. The worst thing you can do is still be trying to make up your mind when you get there. Pilots have been seen to approach a huge field with one obstacle such as a tree in it. They veer left as they come in, then right, then left again and end up narrowly missing it simply through indecisiveness.

The first high flights

Usually done with radio contact from an instructor, the aim is to achieve a good clean launch, fly at a suitable airspeed, and be able to initiate a number of turns in order to follow a basic flight plan and arrive in the right position for a straightforward landing approach and a reasonably accurate and well controlled landing.

The flights may be made from a smaller slope with some lift, or may be from a higher hill or mountain. The bigger the "jump" in altitude the more preparatory hops are required first.

The progressive nature of flying training means that the first few flights may be lower and contain as few as two turns, and later flights may require many turns to arrive in the right place at the right height. Simply being in the air, and making the control inputs to follow your flight plans teaches you to anticipate your

"...your instructor may well be on the radio..."

wing's responses and gets you used to the sensation of gliding flight. Because the paraglider is trimmed to fly straight and at a suitable speed if left alone, it is often a good policy to do less rather than more on the early flights. You may have slightly elevated adrenaline levels in your bloodstream on early high flights, but try and remember that effective piloting is more about technique and progressive input than about strength!

First high mountain flights – this is North Cyprus. (Photo: Gus Hurst)

79

Pic: Iain Bell

As the "I am really flying" sensation hits you and the ear to ear grins start appearing, it is worth remembering that actually flying in smooth air is very easy; it is launch and flight planning elements that need the most work, so your instructor may be keen for you to complete several lower flights, whilst pupils are often keen to go higher and have longer flights as soon as possible.

As you become more confident, new elements like larger turns are introduced, and planning your approaches becomes more critical. Your instructor may well give you rather less input as you start making decisions for yourself, and new exercises such as slope landings and weight shift steering may be added to your flight plans. Some of the useful exercises are included below and many form a part of your training syllabus.

Exercises

People take part in paragliding courses for different reasons. It's certainly a more memorable way of spending the day than staying at home to wash the car. However, if you are interested in becoming a pilot, the best way to progress is to learn as much as you can from each flight. It is easy to waste a lot of time (and money) by undertaking training flights with no eventual aim. There are several exercises you can set yourself, or your instructor can set for you, to make the most of each day.

Ground handling

If the weather is poor – mist on the hill, for example, or strong winds at launch – you can still learn a good deal by practicing your ground handling and emergency collapses. PLF's can be done without even getting your paraglider out.

Launch practice

Almost everyone finds flying easier than launching. You can practice this on a small slope and fit in as many launches in an hour as you would get in a day on a large hill.

The first low hops are all followed by the walk back..

Short field landings

This is an excellent one to practice – imagine an obstacle such as a fence across your usual landing area. Try to plan your flight to land short of it. When you have done it with an imaginary fence a few times, a small field with a real fence is far less of a problem.

Spot landings

As above, but try to hit a specific target – you learn a lot about yourself as well as about the capabilities of your wing. Don't forget, it is an exercise – it's not much use claiming from your hospital bed that you were the closest.

Soaring beats

This is perhaps the most valuable of all the exercises. In order to prepare yourself for soaring flight, try to fly parallel to the ridge, execute an efficient 180° turn and fly back over the same ground in the opposite direction. If you can do this in light winds near the hill, or in stronger winds further out beyond the lift band, you will find that doing it when there is lift is far easier.

Some of these exercises are listed in the BHPA Pilots training record (Phase 8 improving skills)and your instructor will help you work your way through each one.

Exploring the speed range

Try to make changes to your airspeed as you fly. Stalls are dangerous, so discuss this with your instructor before you try it.

Accelerator systems

This is also an exercise in the training syllabus, but too many students try it once or twice in order to get signed off and then never use their accelerator system again until they find they are pinned by strong winds. By using it from time to time in smooth air you become much more familiar with locating and activating the foot stirrup and with the effect it has on your speed and stability.

Weightshift and pitch roll co-ordination in turns

Even on quite early flights the roll (turn) response of the wing can be improved by weight shifting; ie leaning your body weight into the turn. This is normally done by moving the C of G to one side with a simple leaning motion, or (for maximum effect) by lifting one buttock from the seat and leaning the outside leg over the inner one, to load the inner wing. Because the wing is being banked

Always fly with your accelerator connected, you never know when you may need it

Weight shift steering; note how the wing is deformed (Photo: UK Airsports)

some airspeed in hand; then slowing down again as the wings level on the new course. This process converts some of your speed back into height and so regains some of the altitude lost in the original speeding up and turn.

Done properly, a well co-ordinated turn can be noticeably more efficient than just pulling on one brake line as a way of changing direction or reversing course, and is therefore particularly useful when you are trying to remain in (or get back into) a defined patch of lifting air with minimum height loss.

Cross wind and side slope landings

You may need to land on a slope one day, and it is often a useful technique when you do not want to end up with a very long walk. This involves landing cross-wind – which is likely to mean faster – so start on a gentle incline and work your way up. There is usually one beat that is more upwind and therefore means a lower groundspeed than the other way. Always choose the upwind beat for slide landings.

and loaded due to weightshift, less brake input is needed to complete the turn, and as braking is inefficient (as it works by adding drag to one wing) the turn efficiency is improved.

Pitch- rolling means allowing the glider to speed up slightly, which in turn will improve the roll response of the canopy; then initiating the turn, which can be a little tighter than normal if done with

Do not try to land on rough or rocky terrain. on a slope of more than about 45°, or in a strong wind. You could partly collapse or stall the canopy, then find yourself airborne again.

360° turns

If you have plenty of altitude and space, 360° turns are a very useful tool, both for re-positioning yourself, prior to starting a landing approach for example, and for using lift. Efficient and co-ordinated 360° turns are vital for using thermal lift. The term 360° turn is used, as that is how many degrees you turn through, but it is rather misleading as it implies that you are flying in a circle. While this may be true in still air; because you need to fly downwind during a 360, you will drift with the wind, and so your actual ground track looks more like a fishhook! If there is a breeze you will need to ensure you are well away from the hillside before trying this manoeuvre. As always, check with your instructor before trying this task.

Instability exercises

Generally these are part of the later syllabus, and are tackled when you are soaring. However, in some training systems (from high mountains etc), they are added at an early stage in the training.

Asymmetric tuck practice is an important safety skill, but must be carried out under direct radio supervision of an instructor. This is usually covered in the later stages of training. If you fly long enough, you will experience an unexpected tuck, and if you are properly trained and react quickly and appropriately, most tucks can be dealt with easily and with little disruption to your flight plan. Dealing with more major collapses is covered in the instability section.

Rear riser steering

This is also an exercise in the BHPA PRS. The purpose is to simulate a control line tangle or break. If you have lost a control handle it is possible to control the canopy quite well using weight shift, and holding and pulling slightly on a rear riser on the side of the missing handle can help you to turn the wing.

DO NOT PULL DOWN STRONGLY OR ON BOTH REAR RISERS AT ONCE – YOU CAN ENTER A DEEP STALL.

See Chapter 28, Instability and Recovery.

Note that you cannot control pitch or speed very well, or recover from a tuck without your controls, and therefore it is not advised to attempt this exercise in rough conditions.

Active flying

Active flying is a term used to mean making small control inputs in order to "smooth out" the bumps in the air. The canopy only flies at its best when it is directly above you, so by braking to slow it down if it pitches forwards, or by adding speed if it drops back, you can minimise the effects of rough air. The small adjustments are similar to the subtle inputs made on a car steering wheel when driving down a straight road. A small input at the right time may avoid the need for a big one later. Active flying is something that becomes automatic with practice and is directly linked to the time spent airborne.

Rapid descent techniques

Big ears, Spiral Dives and B line stalls should all be carried out under the supervision of an instructor. Big ears in particular is a useful skill that is part of the BHPA Pilot Rating System, but it does have some associated hazards. See chapter 28 for more information on these manoeuvres.

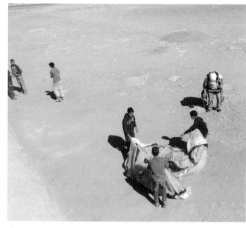

Obstacles in the landing area

Always stay within range of a suitable landing area

Landing 16

Preparation

First you must decide where to land. The earlier you think about this, the more options will be open to you. The landing field should, preferably, be a flat area with no obstacles, clear of any turbulent airflow from upwind obstacles such as woods or buildings or other hills. The bigger the landing field, the better. Other factors to consider are animals or people in the area and how easy it will be to get out of (is there a gate?) Are there any power or telephone lines to avoid?

Approach

Having followed your flight plan, you need to decide what kind of approach to make. There are several options.

All landing approaches are basically a question of arriving near your chosen spot with excess height and burning it off in a controlled manner to leave you in the right position for an into wind glide to touchdown. *Fig 16.1* illustrates how you can judge whether you will clear an obstacle or not when on final glide.

If high or if there is little wind you can opt for the classic aircraft approach. This usually starts upwind of your intended area and consists of a circuit, with downwind leg off to one side of your touch down point, a cross-wind base leg and a final approach into wind. This option is designed to allow an aircraft to join a pattern at an airfield with other craft launching, and with a high base leg it can take advantage of changes in your approach speed or descent rate to give an accurate touch down. This is well suited to aircraft with power or aerodynamic controls such as airbrakes that can be used to degrade the glide angle on approach. The system can work well for paragliders, particularly for outlandings from cross-country flights, or flights from big mountains in little wind.

If there is much wind (or you do not know how strong it is), the lack of penetration into wind can make loitering downwind of the landing spot impractical.

Starting from high downwind and using linked S turns or beats to lose height is very effective, and is the system used by most new pilots from a training hill where landing areas are typically huge. However, it is difficult to be accurate with

A   B   C

Fig 16.1: Relative motion; Flight A-B-C will clear the wires and land on the target. Flight C_B_A will land short

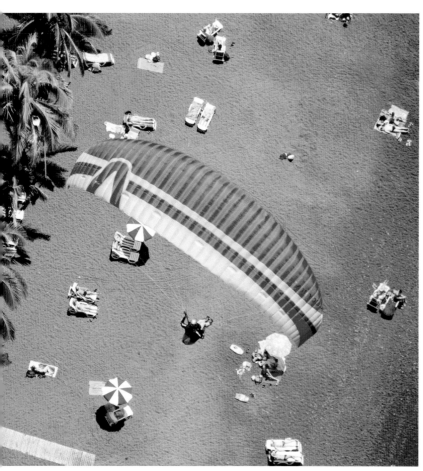

Making a landing approach to avoid hazards. (Photo: Skywalk GMBH)

instructor had kindly placed pretty much where your glider wanted to land anyway.

Once you start playing with lifting air, or bigger flying sites where a short landing is required, you must refine your technique.

When you look down and sideways at your intended field or landing spot you should be able to judge the glide you need to reach it. Of course you should be too high to fly straight in at this point (or you will need a closer field!) You must then fly past or parallel to the field you have chosen, checking constantly that the glide looks OK.

this system, and the descent through different areas of lift and sink can cause pilots to easily undershoot or overshoot.

The constant aspect approach, is a modified version of the aircraft approach, starting slightly upwind and approaching in a curve It is very effective in allowing flexibility to accurately adjust your altitude if wind and lift conditions are variable.

The constant aspect approach *(Fig 16.2)* relies on conscious noting of the signs that most experience pilots use automatically to judge their glide path and approach to a bottom landing field. Previously you will have used S turns to approach landing fields that your

When it seems right, you simply start your long curving approach to maintain the correct glide angle. If you are climbing above your intending glide-path, widen the turn; if you are sinking, tighten up the turn to get back on track. The idea is to end up some 20-30m above your target and slightly downwind, so that the final approach is straight glide into wind.

If you are high and well clear of a hillside then the approach can be usefully started at about 100m whilst flying downwind, but it can be "joined" at any point on the curve.

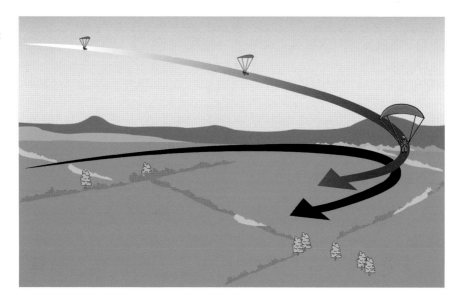

Fig 16.2: The constant aspect approach

If you are in mountains or have flown away from the hill and are unsure of the state of the valley wind or your drift as you approach, you can do a whole circuit, beginning slightly upwind of the target and flying down in a lazy constant aspect circle like a spiral staircase – just the opposite, in fact, to circling upwards in a huge 2m/sec thermal.

It is important with any landing approach to keep checking the sky around you; do not get target fixated!!

This broad curving approach has a big advantage over S turns as it gives you almost infinite flexibility – get a bit high on an S turn approach and you are forced to do a whole new beat, perhaps involving a slight downwind leg close to the ground.

Pilots with sufficient experience may approach from vertically above the landing area by circling or spiralling down, or in some cases by using a rapid descent technique like big-ears to regulate their sink rate or glide. However, these are not recommended techniques (except in very specific circumstances such as powerful lift conditions).

Ensure you have a good Landing area available. This is Iceland. BGD

Consider your landing approach options early.

Not a particularly recommended approach!
(Photo: Red Bull)

Whatever your approach, your aim is to be into wind with your wings level at a minimum of 8 metres (25ft) from the ground, if the field is quite long then you can be much higher, you should be set up for a final glide directly into wind. Let the controls up if you have not done so already, so that you are flying at around 1/4 brake position or, in no wind, at maximum trim speed. Just before the touchdown you need to flare by braking smoothly and as strongly as conditions require. The exact amount of brake is determined by the wind. If there is no wind, a full flare is required. If there is a breeze you will need less. Every flight is different and you will have to practice to discover exactly when, and how hard, you need to flare.

Sometimes you may be faced with the choice of having your wings level or being into wind. (On a beach for example, or approaching a fence or other obstacle). In fact a paraglider has excellent cross-wing landing capability in comparison to other aircraft and a wings level cross-wind landing is perfectly safe provided the flare is well timed and the pilot is prepared to run. Students are drilled by their instructors to land directly into wind, for good reason, but this can sometimes result in a slight obsession with wind direction at the expense of having level

wings and a good flare. Bear in mind that the latter is the most important in a good landing.

Turning a paraglider and landing a paraglider are both easy, but landing whilst turning can be very hazardous.

Many pilots focus on the intended landing spot whereas it is more useful to picture a "window" through which they should be aiming to fly in order to set up the landing approach correctly. – A long narrow field demands a narrow but quite high approach window, whereas a shorter fields requires a lower top limit to their window in order to vector the pilot onto the right spot. *See Fig 16.3*

One cause of problems with landings is that pilots seem to be accelerating towards the ground on approach (due in part to the effect of wind gradient and in part to their reaction to the optical illusion created as the ground fills more and more of their field of vision). Some pilots' very natural reaction to this is to brake more and more as they near the

Fig 16.3: The approach window

ground and in an often sub-conscious attempt to keep their groundspeed low. The result, unfortunately, is that they can inadvertently stall too early and are "dumped" as the canopy stops supporting them.

A different problem is that some pilots lift up their legs as they come in. Your legs are your landing gear and much better equipped to withstand shocks than your backside. You need to make a conscious effort to sit up in the harness and actually reach down for the ground with one foot.

If one foot touches first it is easy to run off any excess speed. If you lift your legs and both feet touch together it gives a very neat landing if you have no forward speed. but, if you are still moving forward, the next move is to fall over.

Touch-down

Once on the ground it is easy to relax, but the flight (and the danger of something going wrong) is not over until the canopy is safely wrapped up. If there is little breeze, the act of "flaring" the canopy to land will induce a stall as your feet touch down and the paraglider will start

to collapse. To ensure that it does not drape over you, it is wise to continue to move forwards and hold the flared position with the controls. This makes the canopy fall behind you and, by keeping the lines stretched, helps to prevent tangles occurring. It's only necessary to flare sufficiently to touch down gently and so, in a breeze, you may only need to brake gently. In this case the canopy may remain inflated above you. There are several options open to you at this point. With some practice you can turn to the reverse launch position, and given an appropriate slope you can use the inflated wing to help pull you back up the hill.

You can continue to walk or run with it still inflated (provided you move more or less into wind). This can be useful if you have touched down in a muddy or rough area or if you need to clear the area for others coming in to land. If you wish to collapse the canopy, the best method is to turn and adopt the reverse launch position and then flare with the brakes or rear risers whilst moving towards the canopy.

If the wind is strong, a very good way of collapsing the canopy is to pull

Flare

Control after touchdown

for a touchdown. This "swing through" technique is very effective when done correctly. But do not be tempted to try it in wind or you may find yourself stalled 3 metres off the ground!

If you should lose your footing or find you have fallen and the canopy is trying to drag you, try to turn so that you are facing the glider, and releasing one control completely, pull the other control hand over hand. This is messy and may make your wing spin once or twice, but it is the best way to kill the wing's power completely if you are being dragged.

More details of landing in strong winds and subsequent canopy control are outlined in Chapter 21, Soaring Flight.

down sharply on the rear risers as you step towards it. This method offers the most effective means of "killing" most canopies.

The act of flaring a canopy has two effects. The first is to generate massive drag and slow or stop the forward motion through the air as the wing stalls. The second is to add lift as the angle of attack is increased. The most effective flares utilise both properties by approaching with some spare airspeed and then strongly but progressively "rounding out" by applying brake, finishing with a hard stab of the brakes to stall the wing as you contact the ground. It is common to see pupils (spurred on by their instructors command to "flare") simply whack the brakes down from their shoulders to their knees in one motion and shock stall the canopy. A slightly more subtle approach as outlined above is actually more effective, as it takes advantage of the lift as well as the drag available.

Experienced pilots landing in very calm conditions, or those flying tandem, will often initiate a slight dive to speed up as they approach the ground, and by converting this energy to lift will actually be climbing when they flare

"...and fly off as if that's what you meant to do all the time..."

After the Elementary/ Parapro 2 stage

17

Once you have completed your initial course you have slightly different options open to you. You may decide that the sport is not really for you, but you'll take your certificate home, and hang it on the wall. For some people this is the best and most sensible decision.

You may continue as before, working your way up to the next level as a club pilot, or the Para Pro 3 level using the school's equipment. This will give you the opportunity to decide for certain that you have found your vocation, whereupon you can consider buying your own equipment.

You can do this with your original school, which does have some advantages of continuity, or you can change schools, possibly to one that has a range of larger sites, or possibly one that teaches abroad. This option is discussed in more detail below.

Another variation is to buy a canopy of your own. If you are to continue learning on your own canopy, you may be able to do so at a reduced cost. (If you buy from the school who will be teaching you then a combined kit/ tuition deal may often save you a proportion of the tuition fees.)

Whether you are using the schools, or your own equipment, you will now need to join the national association as a full member. You should also think about making contact with your local club, as, once qualified, it will be the club members you will be meeting out on the slopes. Most clubs run a variety of social events and have meetings each month or so, in addition to meeting when out flying. They may also publish a guide to your local sites, showing their status and suitability, who to ask for permission and any hazards or rules that apply to them.

Training abroad

You can learn with a foreign school, and many offer excellent tuition. However, do be aware that unless you are fluent in the local language, or the tuition is conducted in your language, the subtleties of some technical discussions may escape you. It will also add a further dimension to passing the exams!

Training in the Alps (Photo: Sup'Air)

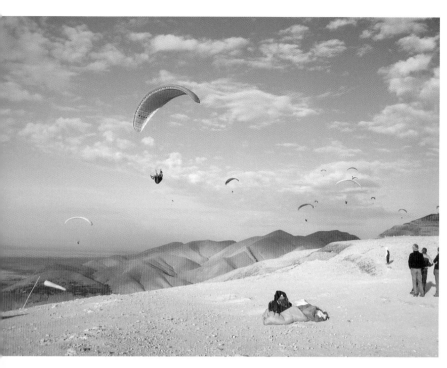

February soaring in Morocco

skills, but much poorer reverse launching and dynamic soaring and top-landing skills than those training on lower and breezier hills.

If you learn abroad on a holiday, do be aware that the fees you pay may be for a course, and if you cannot complete it due to weather etc, and cannot return, you may have to pay again to complete your training somewhere else. Always get a signed log sheet or record of your flights, so that you can show your local club or instructor what you have done.

Most importantly, however, you must be fully confident you can understand any radio commands clearly (even when both you and the instructor may be under stress!)

Returning to your own country, you may find that some aspects of air law or site protocols are different, and that your qualification may not be quite the same as the local one, requiring a few more tasks to be completed and new exams sat.

Typically, learning in a mountainous environment produces pilots with far better Alpine launch and flight planning

Another way is to learn abroad but with a school from your own area. In the UK the Foot and Mouth Crisis in 2001 prompted a relaxation of the BHPA's training abroad regulations, and many BHPA schools teach all courses in various locations with good sites and generally better weather than the UK.

Busy soaring at the Grand Dune de Pyla near Bordeaux in France. (Photo: www.sunsoar-paragliding.com)

More often than not when flying abroad you will have an audience – no pressure! This is Pokhara in Nepal

This seems like a very good idea, provided the school concerned has applied for the correct permission from the BHPA or their own country's governing bodies, and has established good relations with the flyers and schools (if any) in the host country.

In this way you can benefit from the BHPA training system and qualifications, and also the better weather and holiday atmosphere of a foreign trip.

Caution: Some school trips have proved less than suitable because of problems with challenging sites or poor research by the providers. The BHPA ask for the following criteria to be met:

- A history of successful trips to the area.

- Liaison/permission from the local school/club/ site owners.

- Suitable sites.

- Proper preparation for incidents. Knowledge of local emergency services, local guide or person who is fluent in the local language.

Your best bet if considering this option is to check with the BHPA or previous students that the school is conforming to these criteria.

If you are a British reader, the ratio of good days for teaching in the UK is around 20-25%. In several countries with more reliable climates it is three times as high, and you get a sun tan! Wherever you go, it is unrealistic to expect to get perfectly flyable weather every day. (Despite what the brochure might say!)

Whichever route you take you can expect to need around 6- 9 days to complete a course from Elementary to CP level. Or from Para-pro 2 to Para pro 3

By the end of a CP course you can expect to :

- Be able to assess weather conditions and sites.

- Conduct good pre-flight checks.

- Be safe and reasonably competent at forward and reverse launching.

- Be able to soar in dynamic lift and be capable of top landing where appropriate.

- Plan an approach and land reasonably accurately.

- Deal with minor incidents like tucks.

- Understand and be able to use your accelerator system.

- Be able to combat strengthening lift and get down when you need to.

- Land and control your canopy in a variety of conditions.

- Understand your limitations and that of your equipment.

- Have a knowledge of the actions to take in various emergency situations.

- Know how to fly safely with others.

Or to put it another way, you should be capable of flying safely without an instructor. Parapro stage 3 is similar in scope, but requires more high flights and airtime but does not specify top-landings as a requirement.

A 4,200ft take off at Bisanne in the French Alps

Once you have reached this stage you are an independent pilot. But you are of course not an experienced one! Exercise caution, especially when assessing conditions, ask advice. It is much easier and safer if you have joined a club and go flying with more experienced pilots. Many clubs operate a voluntary coaching scheme for the newly-fledged pilots and these are well worth taking advantage of.

After spending lots of money and holiday time training, new pilots often then have a break for several weeks or months (over winter for example) before they fly again. They are rusty and the spring conditions are often powerful, so great care is needed after a break.

The best advice is to try and amass a few hours fairly soon after qualifying, or if you have had a long spell off, go back to school for a day or two.

Soaring in Germany. (Photo: U-Turn GMBH)

18 Other equipment

Harnesses

The right choice of harness can make a huge difference to your flying. A good harness needs to be comfortable to fly in, but must also be easy to get in and out of, provide adequate storage for your glider bag and other items, offer the facility to allow back protection to be fitted, and have a suitable arrangement for mounting a reserve parachute system.

Photo: Skywalk GMBH

Finally, the harness is also part of the foot-operated speed systems that virtually all paragliders are fitted with.

Comfort in flight means that you have no pressure points and that the fit is close enough so that you do not slide around on the seat. Make sure that you can sit back easily on the seat when launching without undue problems, or needing to wriggle about too much as you launch. Even more importantly, you must be able to rotate easily into the upright position as you approach to land. If you are too supine, this can be a struggle, which can have serious consequences.

The harness must be a good fit; most are available in 3 or 4 sizes; too small and it will not be comfortable for long. On the other hand, if it is too large, you will tend to "slide about" when the harness tilts. The seat plate, or articulated support flap, should extend to a point around 03-10cm (one to three finger widths) short of the backs of your knees, any less and it is too large and you may find it a sloppy fit, and it may hard to rotate upright or to run effectively whilst wearing it. If the

Cam-lock adjuster

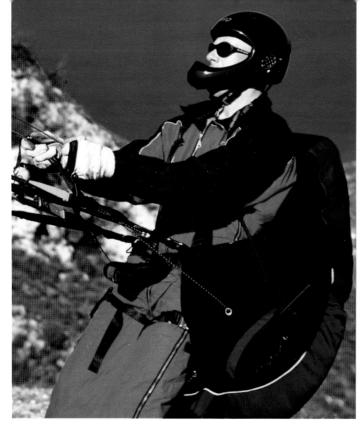

Harness

made of aluminum and have stainless steel pins in the mechanism. This is worth noting as prolonged contact with salt water or a salty atmosphere may result in corrosion where the different materials are in contact. If flying on a coastal site regularly, or if they are immersed in sea-water, a thorough rinse with fresh water is strongly advised. You can also use stainless steel carabiners to a similar design , these are much stronger and withstand knocks and corrosion better than aluminum, but they are heavier. They are usually favoured by tandem or paramotor pilots.

A lightweight option for connecting a harness is a self-locking Kevlar loop. These are stronger than steel and lighter than aluminum, though they are a bit more fiddly to fit.

Virtually all harnesses offer the option to adjust the straps and so alter your angle of recline, and possibly the tilt of the seat. The waist strap is also adjustable, allowing a range of different sized pilots and offering the option to fly "cross-braced" by tightening the waist strap in flight to help reduce the impact of turbulent air. Most harnesses feature a small strap or handle to allow easy adjustment of the waist strap in flight.

The certification class of your paraglider will specify the distance apart of the carabiners when tested. All harnesses will adjust to conform to the tested distance and in many cases it is not very critical.

edge of the seat board is touching the back of your lower leg when relaxed, the pressure point caused by the edge will be noticeable on a long flight – if this gap is more than 3 finger widths the harness is to small and will be hard to get into and uncomfortable.

Apart from a few specialist lightweight models, all harnesses are adjustable – make sure that you are sitting well back on the seat plate, that the straps do not slip off your shoulders, and that you are not too upright or too supine.

The attachments for the risers should be carabiners made especially for the job. These are normally automatically locked on closure, either with a twist-lock or a button lock gate.. These are available from all good dealers. They are usually

However, it is worth noting that a very much larger distance can adversely affect the recovery behaviour in the event of a large collapse. A shorter distance can adversely affect the spin characteristics.

A critical feature is the ability to mount a reserve system neatly into the harness. Check that the reserve handle is going to be visible and easily reached when fitted. A good reserve container should be closed with two "pins" – these can be made of either plastic coated wire or steel. Steel pins must be curved to avoid the possibility of jamming if they are not pulled straight. Any system relying primarily on velcro is no good.

Many models have clear "windows" so that you can check the pins without disturbing the container. Reserves may be mounted on the side, under the seat, over the small of your back, or ventrally (on your stomach). There is no "right" position, and all these options have some advantages and some drawbacks. The important point is that the handle is easily accessible at all times and that the reserve is easy to deploy but not likely to be activated by mistake.

Harnesses generally feature three buckles to secure them onto the pilot. There are two basic varieties of buckles the simple "interlock" type and spring loaded "quick-lock" buckles. Interlock (or pass-through) buckles are a slight nuisance to connect, especially if you have gloves on or cold hands; however, there is no known case of them failing once connected. In an emergency situation such as water landing, the time taken to disengage them may be a problem. For this reason they are not recommended for use where there is a significant risk of a water landing. These are now very uncommon and are generally found only on specialist lightweight harnesses.

Reserve closure pin detail

Quick-lock or automatic buckles are much more convenient; however, as they are more complex, they can malfunction –usually because of sand or snow in the mechanism. It is important that you check that these buckles are fully engaged before flight by testing them with a good tug.

If you habitually fly in sandy or snowy areas it may be worth considering using interlock buckles (pass-through).

The two pictures both show harnesses with an "anti–forget" system. This essentially means that the waist strap cannot be fastened without a strap between the legs also being engaged. This is to prevent the situation of a pilot finding himself starting to slide out of the harness if he launches after forgetting to do up his leg straps… it has happened more than once!

Another important consideration is back protection. A number of harnesses on the market feature some kind of passive protection system that is designed to minimise spinal injury in an emergency situation. These are essentially bags of air that are kept inflated either by being

Kevlar loop

A twist lock carabiner

A twistlock carabiner designed for harnesses with two webbing loops

full of foam padding (the airfoam or Bump'Air), or by being inflated though a valved entry and pressurised by your airspeed (the Cygnus airbag).

The disadvantage to all these protective devices is added bulk and in some cases weight. However, as many paragliding injuries are either minor or involve the spine, they are a major step in making the sport safer. The foam types are rather bulky, but are very effective (except for sharp "point" impacts). They basically hold the shape of the air-bag so that a sudden stop causes the air to escape through the seams and fabric in a controlled way, increasing the stopping distance and so minimising the deceleration force. The "Cygnus" types are even more effective and are less bulky to transport as they function in the same way, but without any foam. The disadvantage is that they take a few seconds of steady airspeed to inflate, so are of limited use in a zero-wind- launch-closely-followed-by-crash scenario. These systems are improving however, with stiffeners added to hold the air-void open before launch. (Ground impacts, by definition, always happen at launch or landing!) Some pilots maintain that an

airbag system is less effective on a second bounce or prolonged drag situation, however as the main cause of injuries ins the initial shock to the spine, this is (in my opinion) more than compensated for by the much more effective impact reduction of an airbag.

Polystyrene or other "solid" materials are also very good at deforming under shock load, and at least one protector is made of this substance. However, unlike air, it is not re-useable, and it only needs to be sat down on once or dropped by an airline baggage handler to lose much of its effectiveness..

An unwelcome side effect to good protection in harnesses is that some pilots behave as if the airfoam padding is an alternative to landing on their feet. It is not.

The DHV testing to determine the effectiveness of these devices tests for a reduction in deceleration from a situation equivalent to falling 1.85m (6ft) squarely onto the padding. The resulting G force transmitted should be sufficiently low to prevent permanent spinal damage. Note that a sideways or angled impact is not presently tested for, and these

Quick lock buckle

Harness interlock buckle

devices will offer far less protection in that (much more likely) situation. Some of the more well-appointed harnesses include lateral impact protection as well, but it is by necessity much thinner and less absorbent. Its principal function is to minimise the likelihood of the pilot sliding off the main protector in an angled impact.

By contrast, falling from 1.85m onto your feet and bending your knees (or better

still, performing a Parachute landing fall) is many times more effective in preventing injury. The message is pretty clear: rotate into an upright position in your harness whenever you are close to the ground and go for a feet-down landing every time…

A few years ago there was a vogue for rigid protectors made of fibreglass, Kevlar and similar materials. Research has shown that in some circumstances these

Airfoam or 'Bump'Air' protector (left) and a Cygnus-type airbag protection system (above).

can actually increase the risk of certain injuries, and if found in older harnesses these protectors should be removed.

The basic choice of harness falls into three main categories.

Recreational: ie With all the features you need for flying, protection, storage, comfort and reserve compartment. Usually pretty tough as well.

Lightweight: These often reverse into themselves to form a bag so reducing the weight and bulk of your pack, but they are slightly less robust and some may also require a separate ventral parachute container.

Performance: These tend to be more supine and usually feature a faired back and a speed bag to enclose the pilots legs, this is great for warmth and comfort on very long flights, but protection and storage are often compromised for low drag. They tend to be a bit more complex and expensive as well.

And of course there are hybrids, fairly lightweight but with full protection and reserve containers, or recreational with the option to add speedbags etc.

Harnesses are available in many shapes and sizes, and there are specialist models for those seeking ultra-low weight or

An enclosed 'pod' harness.
(Photo: U-Turn GMBH)

volume, harnesses for tandem use or those that allow the competitive pilot to adopt a fully supine position to minimise drag. These are not ideal for the first time buyer. It is usually best to ask your instructor for advice.

Helmets

It is impossible to entirely rule out the chance of an accident, and/or hard landing where the pilot falls over or is dragged. For this reason a suitable helmet is a mandatory piece of equipment. There is a CEN standard for airsports helmets to which any paragliding helmet should conform. (Recognised by the CE966 mark on the shell) .

Helmets can be either of the open face variety, which are cooler, lighter and usually cheaper, or the full-face type. These offer greater protection and warmth to the lower face, and can be a

good place to mount a microphone.

Whichever type you choose, it is important that it fits correctly, allows good all round visibility, is in good condition and of course is CE966 certified. Visors or peaks can restrict vision and are not usually a good idea; if glare is a problem good sunglasses are a better bet. Though sunglasses have been implicated in accidents in variable light conditions, *(circling from bright sun into shade close to a rock face is a classic example of this)*. Heads come in a variety of shapes, and some helmets can be "rolled" either forward or backward right off the heads of some people, even with the chin strap fastened. It is worth spending a minute ensuring that this is not the case with yours, as a helmet is clearly useless if it is not on properly.

Helmets designed for other sports such as motorcycling are as good or better in terms of ultimate protection, but are almost always unsuitable, due to restricted upward vision and hearing problems. Those designed for cycling or climbing may not offer adequate protection.

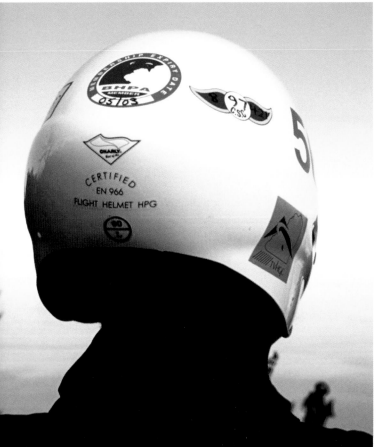

The materials used for flying helmets are generally polycarbonate or carbon fibre (kevlar). Both of these are very intolerant of knocks and care must be taken not to drop them onto a hard surface or much of the protection may be lost. Also take care not to crush the helmet by stacking heavy items on your packed bag or allowing your helmet to go in the hold of an aircaft packed in your glider bag. Never buy a used helmet for this reason.

Primarily because of UV degradation, helmets also have a limited life (around 5 years or so if used regularly) so they need to be replaced periodically. Some stickers or solvents can also damage the integrity of the shell. Never paint or add stickers to your helmet without being certain that the glue or paint type is compatible with the helmet materials.

Reserve parachutes

It may seem strange to carry a reserve system when we are already flying under what appears to be a parachute. However, because our wings require constant air-pressure to remain inflated, excessive control movements or turbulence can collapse them. In these cases, recovery is often quite straightforward. However, there remains a possibility of "wrapping-up" the canopy to the point where it is impossible, or may take too long, to recover. We are not alone in the sky, and there is always the possibility of a mid-air collision, either with another canopy or (perish the thought) with something a lot heavier and faster.

Reserves are rarely used, but they are a second chance: if you fly in a variety of conditions or with groups of other pilots, you may one day need it. They are mandatory equipment for cross-country or alpine flying. A paragliding reserve is usually a small (24-40 sq metre) round parachute.

A quick glance at the marketplace reveals that some reserves of quite different sizes are sold for the same weight pilot. How can this be? Size (whilst very important) is only one of the criteria in how well a reserve decelerates you. There are a number of other design factors that can affect the coefficient of drag of a reserve system.

A pulled-down-apex (PDA) reserve parachute.

Certification label on a reserve parachute

Flying diameter, for example, is usually a much better measurement; to visualise this consider a plate which may have a smaller surface area than a bowl yet have a greater flying diameter (or "projected" area). In fact, some shapes have higher drag coefficients and better sink rates than others, even with the same diameter. Some designs use "drive" to generate lift, and there are variations such as adding a central cap over the vent, or depressing a circular area rather than a single point at the apex.

Another factor is fabric. Some reserve designers use more porous fabric for stability and other reasons, so the reserve needs to be correspondingly larger than one using zero-porosity fabric in order to have the same sink rate.

The criteria used by the CEN testing body demands a 5.4m/sec sink rate at a maximum payload.

The max payload is left to the individual designer or manufacturer to determine, and some calculations are more optimistic than others.

It is very hard to calculate the sink rates of reserves accurately as they may be less stable in some situation than others, but it is fair to say that a CEN certified system should offer any user a maximum sink rate of 5.4m/sec in still air, provided there is no interference from the paraglider itself.

What do these figures actually mean? A 5.4m/sec rate equates to the impact experienced when stepping from a height of 1.5m and 6.8m/sec when stepping from around 2m.

Of course the air is quite likely to be very far from still when you actually use a reserve, (it could be descending very quickly behind a mountain for example) and the paraglider is still connected so that may cause a big variation in the sink rate as well, so a reserve deployment of any kind is a risky business, however of the 50 or so emergency reserve deployments recorded by British pilots in the last few years, using a reserve that is correctly packed, and where the pilot is within the manufacturer's payload limitations, all have been successful and resulted in few injuries. (Hang-gliding is a different story, unfortunately).

Reserves are mounted in or on the harness, with the deployment handle within easy reach. All should have an airworthiness test (CEN or LTF label) and come with instructions for use and repacking.

A reserve should be mounted so that when it is opened the pilot is suspended by both shoulder straps, Ie in a feet down position. Do not be tempted to connect a reserve parachute to your main carabiners.

Reserves must be aired, inspected and repacked at least every year, or more often if they have been exposed to damp or compression. Many pilots attend re-pack sessions run by their local club each spring, or you can send your reserve to a licensed packer who will check and pack your kit for you.

Parachutes are available in a large number of sizes and formats; these can broadly be divided into four three variants.

Reserves with drive

Some designs have slots in the envelope that give the reserve forward motion or "drive", and these have two purposes. The first is to aid stability by controlled bleeding of excess pressure and therefore reduce excess oscillation. The second is to allow the pilot to "steer" by converting the forward momentum into a turn, using brake handles or weight-shift through two or more risers. In order for the drive to work, however, the parachute must be allowed to fly correctly, which is a very difficult situation to achieve when a main canopy is flapping around behind it. Some reserves may be relatively unaffected by this (although you obviously cannot steer them without either dumping completely or at least wrapping up your main wing).

Some reserves with drive are true wings and actually fly just like the paraglider, They can either be of the Ram air (paraglider) configuration or a Rogallo (single surface Delta) shape. Whilst both of these work well in isolation, a possible result of deploying them while connected to a paraglider,is that the reserve will be stalled by the drag of the paraglider, or fly away from the main (downplaning), which can cause a very dangerous situation – perhaps worse than that which caused the deployment.

One pilot who threw a "square" reserve was very lucky to survive a 2,000ft descent of stalls and swooping dives as the main and reserve fought it out, taking turns to stall each other.

You cannot steer a reserve whilst still attached to even a partially inflated paraglider –despite the misleading wording of some advertisements that may seem to imply otherwise. For these reasons true "flying" reserves are well suited to high altitude deployments but not to low level deployment where the pilot has no time to gather in or control their paraglider.

Pulled down apex reserves

These are systems in which a central line holds down the Apex in a shape rather like an inverted saucer. This gives a relatively large flying diameter for relatively little fabric and therefore a good low sink-rate combined with a small light package. Another advantage is that these types operate at high pressure and therefore inflate very quickly – a great bonus as many deployments occur at a surprisingly low altitude (the most common situation is a mid-air collision while ridge soaring).

The pulled apex design does tend to oscillate more than a tri-conical or hemispherical type. Also, in the early days of paragliding the reserves went through a phase of being built very small indeed with correspondingly high sink rates. This was, to a great extent, due to the very optimistic 6.8m per second allowed by the German DHV test – at that time the only recognised standard. Experience has shown that this is a rate that will give the pilot a pretty fair chance of injury, and as a result the newer LTF and CEN test demands a sink rate of no more than 5.4m/sec

LARA, CONAR, and other variations.

In order to decelerate the pilot a reserve needs to generate a significant amount of drag, or lift. Lift is created when the reserve can fly forwards through the air like a paraglider, and this is the type that is used by sport parachutists. However, a true flying reserve is problematical for use with a paraglider as discussed in the earlier paragraph. This leaves drag, which is generated in proportion to sheer size, but can be enhanced by altering the shape, such as pulling the apex, as discussed above.

There are additional design techniques too, that may improve slightly on the classic pulled apex design. One is the apex being depressed in a ring rather than at a single point; this is the basis of the LARA design. This is not as different aerodynamically as it may appear, as, due to the central hole in the apex of the reserve, the inner edge is effectively a ring already. However, it does allow an even flatter profile and a corresponding increase in the flying diameter.

An apex hole of some type is necessary to prevent oscillation, but inevitably reduces the drag efficiency of the reserve; the Conar and similar designs seek to minimise this problem. This can be done with a "cap" immediately above the apex hole which acts to deflect and slow down the escape of the air. Using mesh or making the central part of the reserve with more porous materials has a similar effect.

At the time of writing, the UK is one of the very few countries that still does not insist on an independent test for reserves. To a great extent this is due to the fact that market forces dictate that Certified reserves are almost universally used anyway. However, there are other systems for sale and it is advised in the strongest possible terms that you ONLY purchase a reserve with a CEN or LTF certification.

The factors that determine reserve performance are quite complex. One leading manufacturer discovered their larger model had a worse sink rate than their small one with the same payload! It is therefore not really possible to determine from the adverts or calculations which is best for you. Fortunately, just about every deployment of a correctly sized reserve (i.e within the manufacturer's recommended range) and properly packed reserve has resulted in a successful save; so it is fair to assume that the manufacturers of these systems have got it about right, (or that paraglider pilots are very tough or have been very lucky so far).

Reserves have a life of ten years from the date of manufacture. Emergency deployment can generate considerable stresses and so it is not recommended they are used more than once. So any used reserve must be less than 10 years old and preferably should not have been deployed, (If it has, it must be professionally inspected and certified as airworthy).

Instruments

It is perfectly possible to fly a paraglider well with no more equipment than your wing, harness, helmet and senses. However, to use the available lift to its maximum potential, to thermal efficiently and to navigate cross-country you require some senses nature has not provided. The higher you are above the ground, the less reliable your senses become as the visual clues become less useful.

Variometer

A vario measures how fast you are rising or falling and displays this information as a sound, on a meter, or both. Most dedicated varios work by detecting changes in air-pressure. A human can detect acceleration, such as flying into

a thermal and shooting upwards, but smooth constant gains (or losses) of altitude are undetectable. Your senses can actually work to fool you. Lift of 500ft per minute may suddenly decrease to only 200ft per minute. To the pilot this feels exactly the same as sinking at 300ft per minute and, without a vario, he may make a bad decision and leave the lift. A vario is therefore essential to know what is really happening. They do this through an audible tone and a large LCD display.

There are a number of piloting Apps including a vario function that are available for smartphones and tablets, these are great for air and groundspeed, direction and airspace data, and are useful for powered flight, but are less

A variometer and GPS mounted on a 'cockpit' instrument console

helpful as free-flying varios as the altitude data is gained from GPS readings and it is inevitably not very sensitive and slightly delayed, which makes using it to prompt the immediate and subtle adjustments required to use thermals efficiently is not currently possible.

Altimeter

An altimeter tells you how high you are above a specific pre-set point *(see Chapter 24, Air Law)*. You may think it is obvious how high you are, but until you have had a good deal of practice most people are amazingly bad at judging altitude, especially from greater heights. Why do you need to know your altitude? There are three main reasons:

● Personal interest – "I made my best height of four grand today!" etc.

● To help you navigate your position relative to controlled airspace – are you under the Airway or in it?

● It complements the vario when thermalling. If you are flying in broken lift; that is up, then down, then up again, it is soon impossible to know if you are gradually losing height or gradually gaining. An altimeter gives you this information at a glance. It could occasionally be of use in some competition tasks where you can work out beforehand that you can reach point B if you are at 3000ft or better, at point A.

In practice, most variometers and altimeters are integrated units in one case. Most of these will give you very accurate information and allow you to switch between altimeter settings. For example, you can check your height above takeoff and at the touch of a button check your altitude relative to airspace *(see details of altimeter settings chapter 24, Air Law)* Many units will also remember details of

your peak altitudes and other information from your last few flights. Some more sophisticated units function as a barograph, that is, record a complete trace of your flight that can be downloaded into a computer or printer, and which can form the basis of an official record claim.

All of these functions have a use but only you can decide what is necessary for you.

Compass

Useful for navigating – it is easy to get lost or disorientated after a cross-country flight involving several hundred circles over unfamiliar territory. Again, good navigation is required for avoiding airspace etc. It is a vital tool if you get caught in a cloud, and invaluable simply as an aid if you get caught in the mountains on foot.

Barograph

A barograph is essentially an instrument that records a flight. This information is displayed as a trace that can be read to ascertain your duration of flight and also your altitude at any point during the flight. Modern barographs are electronic and display this information as a print out, or by downloading onto a computer screen. Barograph evidence is a requirement for a flight to be recognised as an official record.

Map

Mandatory for cross-country flights. You must carry an up to date airchart if you are flying XC, as it is the only way you can be sure you are not infringing controlled airspace. Some GPS devices incorporate a digital version that tracks with you as you go, and this is far easier to use than the paper types which are better suited to an enclosed cockpit! The zoom facility of modern tablets and phones make the use of the smaller scale 1:50000 charts much easier than previously.

GPS (Global Positioning Systems)

Originally developed by the US military, the GPS system comprises a constellation of satellites whose relative orbits ensure that several are always above the horizon. Dedicated GPS units are small handsets that can plot a position from these satellites and give a very accurate fix as to your position anywhere on the earth's surface. If enough satellites are above the horizon they can even give you a reasonably accurate altitude. A further facility is that you can program "waypoints". These are positions that you can use as turn points or targets and the GPS can then advise you of the heading to take to navigate accurately to these points. These are very useful indeed for aircraft flying on instruments or for maritime traffic, for which accurate positioning is essential.

UHF (left) and 2m (right) radios

The falling price of these units has meant that some pilots, especially those undertaking long-distance flights over unfamiliar or featureless terrain, have found them irresistible as a safety and navigational aid. The fact that they can tell you exactly where you are, and therefore how far you have left to go, what your groundspeed is, what heading to take to reach your goal, and even whether you've already broken that record before you've even landed are powerful incentives to own one!

Many competitions now accept GPS data a proof of the completion of a task. Only some models have the facility to record tamper-proof data, so if you wish to compete it is important to you ensure you buy the correct one.

One problem with GPS is that they are very battery hungry, so you may need to have a map as backup against battery failure mid-flight.

A lot of pilots now have smart phones or tablets with an integrated GPS and the facility to upload aircharts.

This is a great advantage as tracking your position accurately relative to airspace is of course a perfect solution. As mentioned the vario function is not yet as good as traditional pressure driven devices, so for the moment the best solution is probably to carry a tablet for positioning and navigation and a separate vario and altimeter for using lift and tracking altitude.

Tracking devices

GPS technology has also allowed the development of trackers which a pilot can carry to allow a third party to follow their position. This is now a significant feature of adventure racing, like the X-Alps completion where competitors and followers can see how pilots many kilometers apart are progressing in real time. It is also a great safety feature and pilots flying over hostile or featureless terrain like deserts or jungles can carry one knowing that in the case of problem their back up teams can navigate straight to them.

Radios

It is only legal to transmit from the air on specific airband frequencies in the UK, and you may only use the specified channels if both you and the equipment are licensed. Details of Airband radios are discussed in chapter 24 "airlaw".

There are two other types of radio that deserve a mention. The first are 2-metre VHF radios. They have a good range and are a fraction of the price of airband equipment. They are very common among paraglider pilots, and certain frequencies have been unofficially adopted by groups of pilots. In France and some other countries, the weather information from automated stations at major launch sites is transmitted regularly on a 2m frequency which is very useful in choosing a site.

In the UK (at present) it is not legal to transmit on the 2m frequencies without a radio amateur's licence and not legal at all to transmit from the air. The De facto situation is that for safety and convenience many pilots choose to use this system anyway, and make every effort to stick to the "clear" frequencies which are not allocated, and stay well clear of the frequencies used by the emergency services.

In the last few years the introduction of Ultra high frequency (UHF) radios on the general market. generally known as PMR radios, whilst these have a shorter range than a 2m radio, they offer clear reception, and best of all they are both legal and very cheap.

At the time of writing the CAA are considering the situation with FLARM transponders which can warn of any other FLARM equipped aircraft within 2.5km and display their position and heading on a screen. This option is already available on Flytec's high spec GPS instruments and may become a real help as more and more light aircraft become equipped with this technology. There is a risk that those with this will feel safe and fly "head down" increasing the risks of conflict with aircraft that are not equipped with them.

Buying a paraglider 19

The pace of paraglider development is very rapid and therefore it is impractical to refer to specific models in this section. However, there are a few questions that you should ask both yourself and the seller to make sure that you purchase the correct product.

How much can you afford?

When budgeting to buy a canopy remember that you must allow for a harness, a helmet and probably some extra training too. It will not be long before you will need a reserve and possibly a variometer. However, the newer the wing the longer it will last you, and as changing is an expensive business it is a false economy to buy a worn out or basic wing.

How much do you weigh (fully clothed)?

It is very important that you get the right size. Pilot weight and wing-loading is a vital factor in determining stability; too large and it will be slow and may behave badly in turbulence; too small and it will have poor sink rate performance making soaring difficult. Most manufacturers give an optimum weight range of around 20kg for each size. It is important that your all-up weight (that is, you with all the gear, including the wing) falls within this range. If you are in the middle of the range, that is clearly ideal, but all good paragliders will fly and behave well, even if you are at the top or the bottom of the range. Some pilots who are keen on racing or who habitually fly in windy conditions, will choose to be close to the top; others who float around on smooth coastal sites in sea breezes may prefer to be towards the light end.

As a rough guide, a basic set of gear will add 15kg to your body weight, or 20kg if you have a reserve and a bulky harness and winter clothing. If you have a large glider, a high spec harness with back protection, a reserve, instruments, boots and a flying suit you could be looking at as much as 25kg on top of your clothed body weight.

What airworthiness classification does it have?

If you are a first-time buyer only consider a canopy with the appropriate classification. All suitable canopies will

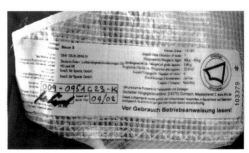

LTF certification label   A DHV certification label

hold one or more of the following ratings: LTF/ CEN A or B. Canopies certified before 2009 may have a DHV rating. The equivalent grades are DHV 1 or 1/ 2 .

However many "B" rated models and a high proportion of DHV1/ 2 's are also unsuitable for the first time buyer, and some A or DHV 1 models may be aimed at school use and be very basic. You will need to take expert advice on what is suitable for you from a trusted professional. More information on these classifications is given below.

Buying a Used Glider

There are a huge range of models available, ranging from very basic older designs which have dreadful performance by current standards, to some excellent models that are either still current or have only recently been superceded. Avoid wings more than about six or seven years old as their useful life will be fairly limited.

Prices of some older or unpopular models can be very low, but this may be a false economy, as the resale value in a year or two is likely to be next to nothing, and in the meantime airtime may be more difficult to achieve. It is vital with a used machine that you get a recent service report. Internal damage, porous material or shrunken lines are often impossible for a visual check to detect.

Buying from a dealer is likely to cost a little more than privately, but you do have some comeback if there is a problem. Most dealers can offer you a choice; a private buyer is going to try and sell you the (only) wing he has.

Buying a New Glider

All the same advice holds good, and of course when buying new you will have no trouble choosing a wing that is not only the right size and certification level for you, but even get one in your favourite colour.

You will get a warranty of some kind, these range from an informal 12-month warranty on faulty workmanship or materials, up to a proper transferable guarantee of the specific properties of the fabric or lines for anything up to 4 years. Some manufactures offer so-called "lifetime warranties" However in reality it is hard to pin the makers down to exactly what that means, in some cases the lifetime of the company has proved to be shorter than that of the glider!

There are a number of purpose-built canopies designed for the new pilot. All certified at LTF A or B

They are ideal for the first time buyer and many recreational pilots. They are usually good value for money. The only problem with this group is that the B certification class is so wide that it is hard to make meaningful comparisons. Some B models are perfect for the ambitious first time buyer and some are not at all suitable.

It used to be the case that different manufacturers produced wings with very distinct flying and handling characteristics, however for the first time

No matter how good a deal it seems at the time, buying a glider the wrong size is never a good investment! (Photo: Julian French)

buyer this is now a very subtle range as all the designers are chasing the same criteria and end up with products that are quite similar in most major respects. The good news is that this means that any first time buyer wing from a major manufacturer is going to be good for the job, there are some variations in style and design and each designer has their own following, but a poor or uncompetitive glider is unlikely to make it to the market.

About airworthiness certification

It is arguable that a canopy should either pass or fail a universal test. However, this would give the customer no information about the wing's behaviour or who it is suitable for. In the real world some pilots with experience are happy to fly wings that other pilots may not be, and of course the relationship between performance and security is always a compromise

The tests are far from perfect; they only report a glider's behaviour at a certain maximum and minimum payload on a certain day. Back in 2001 a tandem wing fully certified at DHV 1 (A) and Tandem level was found to spontaneously enter a deep stall when flown at a certain weight and with the big- ears folded in.. This was only discovered after an accident and subsequent exhaustive "searching" for this problem.

Be aware that the tests are an indicator of the canopy's likely behaviour, not a guarantee. However the present LTF grades are the most thorough tests available and have a proven track record.

Many pilots and instructors rely quite heavily on the certification to show that a wing is "safe". In fact statistics show that whilst the grade of the wing is significant, it is far less critical than the conditions you fly in, in determining your chances of an accident or injury. At the risk of labouring this point, a stable wing in smooth air is the safest, a higher performance wing in smooth air is not quite as secure, a very stable wing flown in rough air is risky and a high performance wing in rough air can be very dangerous in the wrong hands.

Making sense of it all!

Some manufacturers market LTF / CEN "A" models that are a bit basic for more ambitious flyers, whilst several wings with the B placard are actually very high performance machines. This is not a problem in itself as they have proved their safety in unstable situations. But the faster and more energy efficient models do tend to get into trouble a bit faster, if they are "spat out" of a thermal, for example, as the very speed that makes them desirable means that they dive more readily and are therefore more prone to tucking. Whilst it is by no means a rule, if a manufacturer has more than one "B" model it is usual that the "higher" end model is aimed at a second time user.

Read the recommendations of the manufacturer, but always get advice from your instructor on the pros and cons of each machine before deciding. Canopies designed for the more experienced pilot fall into two broad categories. The high-end "B" types are designed for recreational flyers who have reasonable skills and a year or more of experience, some suitable canopies for this group may feature LTF/ CEN "C" certification. These are not suitable for first time buyers.

Top performers

The state-of-the-art canopies as used by competition and experienced cross-country pilots, these wings represent the cutting edge of paragliding technology and deliver excellent performance, particularly in glide and speed range. They are not suitable for first time buyers with even the more docile models needing some expertise to fly well if the air should be turbulent. A few may require a great deal of skill to fly safely. Performance machines are generally "C" or D" rated. If you do have plenty of experience and are seriously competitive, then of course you have got to have one!

Anything without a rating or with "open" or "competition" written on it is strictly for highly skilled or professional pilots who are very comfortable in unstable situations outside the normal flight envelope.

General Pointers

If you can afford to buy new, that is usually the best policy. Although the improvement curve has certainly flattened out compared to the leaps made in the 80's and 90's, the newest canopies are noticeably better than even two or three-year old ones. Not only do you get more flying because of this, but it may well cost you less in the long run as older canopies depreciate very fast. The exceptions are if you can find someone who has quickly got bored, or moved up and has a "nearly new" machine, or an ex demonstrator, etc.

When buying new, always buy from an approved dealer; your instructor may well be the best choice (providing he is offering a good range of products – some schools are tied to one manufacturer and may sell that model even if it is not necessarily the right one for you).

It is often possible to get reduced cost training to soaring standard if you purchase a canopy from the school and fly on your own machine. Buy the right size; you will regret it if you do not. This is especially important advice to remember if buying second hand.

Get a harness you know you are comfortable with: There is a lot more information on the choice of harnesses in this book, a few older harnesses are heavy and not very comfortable, but the basic rule is have a sit in it and preferably a flight or two if you can before buying. Your dealer should advise you.

Ideally see the wing flown or fly it yourself before committing. Always get a second opinion if it is a private sale. If the dealer or seller is not a competent pilot then his advice is not going to be worth much. Do not buy a canopy that has been repaired or modified unless you are 100 per cent satisfied about its history (i.e. who did the repair and whether the manufacturer approves of any modification). NEVER buy a canopy without certification.

Airworthiness Testing

As the previous section makes clear, the certification level of a canopy is a vital indicator of its suitability. Very few canopies are still available new that have not been submitted for an airworthiness test. Those that have not are generally confined to competition prototypes and development gliders. Some countries (usually outside Europe) have small builders who make a few of their own designs or "clones" of other models for sale to their local pilots.

A typical LTF A paraglider – this is a Skywalk Mescal 2 (Photo: Skywalk GMBH)

All reputable manufacturers display a classification by an independent body on their products and advertisements. The major European systems are the CEN /LTF system which is You may also come across the DHV (German) or SHV (Swiss) certification schemes on older equipment but these are rapidly becoming less common as all manufacturers adopt the newer CEN/ LTF programme.

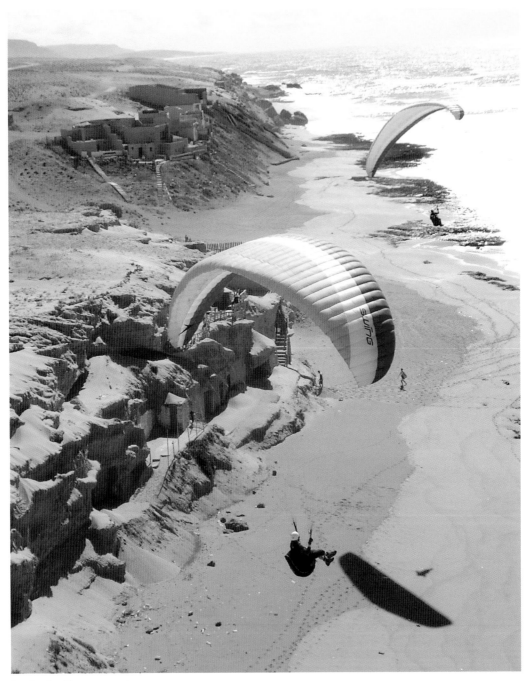

Soaring the Moroccan coast.

One of the most common questions asked by students and first time buyers is, "What does the test actually do and what do the classes mean?" There are a number of routines through which the test canopy is put and its reactions noted by the pilots and by a panel of judges from a high definition video recording.

The LTF certification is designed to be as objective as possible; the glider passes each test or it does not. The results are recorded in the user's manual and on a sticker fixed to the glider so that the pilot is able to be fully aware of the results. The first test is a load test. The wing is steadily loaded to eight times the maximum recommended weight (8g). This is done by pulling it behind a truck. The canopy is also shock loaded with a slack line and a 6g weak link in the system. The truck accelerates away and the canopy is snatched with an instant 6g load. It must pass these tests with no failure. In the second part of the test the glider is put through a range of manoeuvres by a test pilot.

The tests are constantly being evaluated and new exercises are added or existing ones are altered as necessary. See Chapter 38, How a Paraglider is Designed, Built and Tested.

Airworthiness classifications

If you wish to check out the test pilot report on any canopy they can be found on the DHV website at www.dhv.de.

When referring to these tests do remember that they are designed to give a benchmark indication of the relative behaviour of different models. Passing a test at level A for example, where a wing recovers from a 60% asymmetric tuck in less than 4 seconds and with a turn of

less than 90°, does NOT mean the wing is necessarily going to recover in the same way in turbulent air if you make an incorrect input. The canopies are tested in ideal conditions (still air) by highly skilled test pilots.

IF YOU FLY OVER OR UNDERWEIGHT THEN STABILITY IN SOME SITUATIONS CAN BE SEVERELY COMPROMISED.

If this is all a bit much to take in, as is probably the case if you are looking for your first paraglider, here is a shortened guide:

- If you are a new pilot or are not particularly interested in performance, it is recommended you buy a wing with an A rating.

- If you are a first timer but quite ambitious it may also be worth looking at some of the lower end "B" models

- If you have a few hours under your belt, are an ambitious XC pilot and you have had some training in dealing with tucks etc. then the wings that have the LTF B rating are most suitable for you.

- If you are an experienced pilot and have good SIV experience and are interested in top-level competition, then the C or D level wings are likely to give you the edge you need, albeit at a price in reduced security and serious depreciation.

20 Packing & Care of your equipment

How you repack your canopy depends on what sort of terrain and wind conditions you are in and whether you have anyone to help you. You will need to decide which method is most appropriate to your situation.

If it is wet, dirty or dusty, or if there is strong sunlight, the best bet is to "posy up" the canopy completely and drop it onto a clinch or "posy" bag. Simply place it on top of the disc of fabric, and feed it in as you pull the draw-cord, This will protect the wing, and you can either keep it in the bag till the next flight or find a better spot to repack it properly. Using this type of bag regularly is the best way to take care of your wing, as it will help keep it clean and protected against UV damage. *FIG 20.1.*

Packing the wing up into the carry bag: If there is any wind, your first move should be to orientate your canopy so that one tip is pointing into wind. This makes it less likely to blow around while you fold it. Next, make sure that the canopy is laid out flat on its back with no lines underneath it. Place all the lines on top of it (under-surface). The harness is best left attached in most circumstances, as this minimizes the chance of tangles, and can either be passed over the wing so that it is next to the leading edge, or placed close to the trailing edge.

Fold the canopy as neatly as possible. If you are alone, or if the terrain is rough and you do not wish to drag the fabric over the ground, this is best achieved by folding the tips into the middle, then

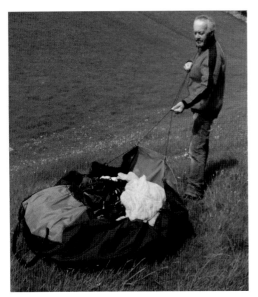

Fig 20.1: Posy up the canopy completely and drop it onto a clinch or "posy" bag

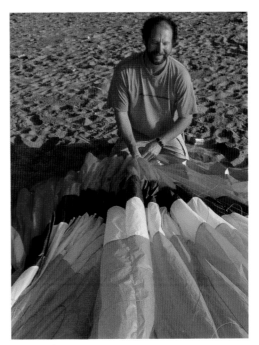

Fig 20.2: Gathering the leading edge rib-to-rib concertina fashion

each end into the middle again, and so on. If you have help, you can either fold the canopy from each tip, one panel at a time, or concertina fashion, one panel at a time, starting at the centre and pulling each panel in as you fold, this process is made much easier if you have an inner concertina bag. *FIG 20.2*

When the canopy is arranged as a double pile of folded panels, press out the air trapped inside. This must be done working from the sealed trailing edge towards the leading edge where the air can escape easily through the cell entries. Fold one side onto the other and press out any remaining air in the same way.

The long "tube" of fabric can be folded to form a square pile of S folds. This should give you a fairly tidy package to which the harness is still attached, but not wrapped up in the fabric. Try to avoid carrying it around like this, as the bundle will inevitably split apart. This is best secured with a strap, or can be slipped into a stuff sac if you have one. The secure bundle can now be placed into your rucksac with

the harness. Some modern harnesses take up a lot of room, so the best way to manage this may be to place the canopy in the seat and secure the waist strap around it.

Concertina bags: the purpose of these bags is to help the pilot fold the cells of the canopy neatly in order to protect the mylar stiffening sheets sewn into the cell walls at the leading edge. Most modern wings now use thin plastic wire stiffeners sewn into the leading edge of the cell walls to do the same job, these are in fact much more resistant to crushing or folding than the old mylar, however if there is time and a clear packing space it can still be helpful to pack these parallel to each other so that they lie flat in the concertina bag. Some pilots, eager to protect their investment, spend a lot of time carefully folding their wings into these bags, however if this means leaving your wing out in the sun for prolonged periods or dragging it cell by cell over rough or dirty surfaces this can have the opposite effect and in hot or dirty environments the quick and simple "posy" or clinch bag is actually more effective way to care for your wing.

Care of the canopy

The fabric used for paragliders is prone to damage by repeated exposure to ultraviolet light, so do not leave it lying out in the sun for long periods. This is particularly important where the sun's rays are very intense, for example at high altitude or at low latitudes. The fabric and lines are of synthetic fibres and are easily damaged by heat. Take care not to smoke near them and never attempt to dry a canopy by applying direct heat. It is advisable to avoid getting the canopy wet, but inevitably it sometimes happens. If so, dry it out fairly soon afterwards, as it is possible to get mould or mildew on fabric that has been left damp for long periods, and this can leave unsightly marks. Paragliders dry in a matter of minutes in a breeze, as long as water is not trapped in the cells.

Never store the canopy near chemicals or fuel as this could affect the material. If you are flying in a hot climate, take care to pack your canopy into its bag and protect it from great heat. Canopies with Dyneema lines risk them shrinking if the temperature exceeds 100° C – this has happened where an unpacked canopy has been left inside a car. Never use chemicals to try and clean the fabric or the lines: some cleaners that will remove oil will also attack the fabric.

Sometimes, of course, paragliders do get damaged. If the damage is to the lines or a riser, or the webbing or metal of the harness, do not fly it until it has been professionally checked and repaired. If the damage is a small tear in the fabric of the harness, it is unlikely to be critical, but it should be attended to as soon as possible. If the tear is to the canopy fabric, then minor tears, that is to say those less than 10 cm long that are not on a seam or line attachment point, can be repaired using self-adhesive rip-stop tape. This is available in a variety of colours from camping shops and sailing equipment shops. If applying this kind of tape, there are a number of pointers to get the best results:

Left: A damaged wing; torn at the line connection point. Right: Blown internal cell after a severe nose-down landing

1. The canopy must be completely dry and clean.

2. The tape should give a generous overlap around the damage.

3. The edges of the tear should be carefully aligned in their original position, otherwise there will be creases and additional strain on the area.

4. Always round off the corners of patches.

5. A patch should always be applied to both sides of the fabric.

6. The internal and external patches should be of different sizes to prevent stress lines.

7. Do not forget to make a special point of checking the repaired area as part of your pre-flight checks.

Lines also need maintenance – tests indicate that they get weaker with use and over time. As the canopy is ground handled the lines do tend to get wet and dirty. This can have the effect of shrinking the outer sheathing of the line and shortening it. As the A and B lines take much more of a load than the other lines, they may be stretched back again each time you fly. As a result canopies with old and dirty lines may fly at a slightly higher angle of attack, as the rearmost lines shrink the most. Stalls and spins become easier to induce and the top speed decreases. A moderate pull of 10 – 15 kg on a line may reveal that they can be re-stretched by anything up to 2 or 3 cm to achieve their proper length. If the lines appear excessively dirty, stretchy, or at all worn – replace them.) Line measurement and load capacity is hard to check without proper equipment, and this is another reason for ensuring your wing receives its annual check.

NEVER ATTEMPT TO REPAIR A LINE BY KNOTTING IT.

IF YOU ARE IN ANY DOUBT, SEEK PROFESSIONAL ADVICE.

Major damage should be referred to your dealer. All good dealers should be able to supply lines and other basic components. Apart from physical damage, canopies can be rendered unsafe through material degradation. The major cause of this, already mentioned in the section on fabric, is ultraviolet light. UV, a constituent of sunlight, gradually weakens the fibres of the cloth, and prolonged exposure will make it increasingly porous and more prone to tearing. This problem is associated with a severe fading of the colours, so, if your canopy appears very faded, ask a professional to check it for you. The tenacity and air-permeability of the fabric at critical points like the leading edge top surface is an integral part of a professional annual service.

Harnesses are usually overbuilt to a significant degree, with a webbing framework able to tolerate loads far in excess of that normally found in normal flying use. However, the fabric of the airbag chambers, zippers and velcro closures all degrade with time and use. Hard landings can damage the underseat fabric and seat plates and dislodge parachute retaining pins. For this reason harnesses also need to be regularly inspected.

Reserve parachutes should be repacked annually and more often if they should get any significant moisture into the container. A reserve parachute has a "placarded" life of 10 years and should be replaced when it reaches that age.

21 | Soaring flight

Soaring can be defined as flight where altitude is maintained or gained purely from natural lift, i.e. without any outside input such as an engine or tow line.

As we already know, a paraglider is just that – a glider. It must be gliding down through the air constantly in order to fly. So how can we soar? The answer is to find some air that is going up faster than we are going down.

Let us assume that your canopy sinks at about 300 feet a minute.(1.3m/sec) If we fly in air rising at 600 feet a minute, (2.6m/sec) after one minute we will have gained 300 feet (80m) of altitude. *(See Fig 21.1).*

Rising air is known as "lift", and there are several sources that a paraglider can use. The most common is ridge lift. This is produced when the wind is forced up over a ridge or cliff and forms a band of rising air we can fly in. *(Fig 21.2)*

From what we know of site assessment and air behaviour we can visualise the "pressure wave" of air forming the lift band in front of the ridge. All we have to do is fly around in this area and we can stay up as long as we wish. This sounds very easy and often it is. However, it can require considerable concentration and effort to visualise and utilise this invisible force effectively. The best advice is to watch and learn from those who are already proficient. This usually other pilots, but birds of prey or gulls generally seem to have the right idea as well.

Unless you have a lot of height and space, when soaring a ridge always make your turns into wind – see Fig 21.3. This is important as it minimises downwind drift, and helps you stay in the lift band. Try to follow a smooth extended figure-eight pattern, remember your site assessment and look for steeper sections of slope or those most directly

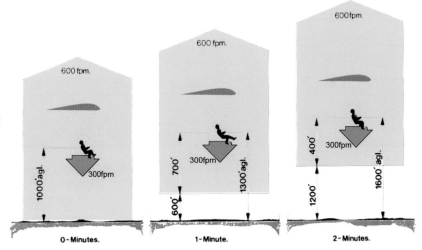

Fig 21.1: Flying down through a block of rising air, i.e a thermal. The glider, with a sink rate of 300fpm is flying through a block of air rising at 600fpm. The net result, after 2 minutes, is a 600ft height gain

into wind for the best lift. If you are ridge soaring it is very likely you are not alone.. Keep a good lookout at all times, avoid any sudden maneuvers or changes of direction or height which might cause a conflict with other soaring pilots, and ensure you are conversant with the anti-collision rules.

Some useful hints:

- Always try to make your turns in an area of good lift.

  Slow down to minimum sink speed in good lift and turn slightly into wind to remain in the lifting patch for longer, speed up to trim speed in sinking air.

- Watch out for gullies or the very end of a ridge where there may be no lift and you can be "hoovered" backwards.

- The higher you get the further out the lift will extend. *See Fig 21.2.*

  Don't overbrake, slowing down helps you lift initially but too much drag makes the wing less efficient

Other sources of rising air

These include thermals, wave and convergence, which are described in other sections of this book. A primary difference between ridge lift and other sources is that whilst it is easy to visualise and explore the position and strength of a static wave of ridge lift, the other sources are often moving, and usually have no visual clues as to their dimensions. It must all be done by feel, making use of these types of lift more challenging than ridge lift alone.

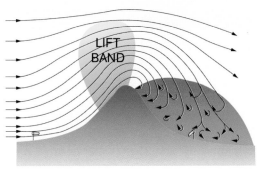

Fig 21.2: Section through ridge showing lift band and dangerous region of turbulence in the lee of the hill.

Fig 21.3: Typical figure-eight soaring patterns – all turns made into wind

Because humans have never evolved the senses to fly (or the sense not to) we can only judge our vertical motion by visual means, and if you are not close to the ground or a ridge this is very difficult.

A variometer gives you the missing information on your vertical movement, so flying thermals or other "random" lift sources means you need a vario to help define the limits and strength of the lift and fly effectively. The base criteria remain the same: to soar you must manage to locate and remain within airmasses that are ascending more quickly than your wing is descending. In the case of thermals, which drift with the wind, this often means circling continuously to stay within the confines of the lift.

Birds have successfully used this technique for millions of years.

In practice, the sources of lift are often mixed or less easy to define. A ridge may have weak dynamic lift, but may also be a source of thermals you can use. Wave lift may be mixed with ridge lift, and converging airmasses can generate standing areas of dynamic lift or be source of thermals.

If you are soaring in thermal lift, it is well worth glancing upwards at regular intervals, this is to check that you are not converging vertically with craft above you, and to see where you are going… many thermals terminate in a cumulus cloud and you can suddenly find everything suddenly goes wet and grey! If you are touching cloudbase, you may want to widen your circle or change your track to ensure you stay near the edge of the cloud and retain visibility.

Top landing

So, you are soaring. The view is wonderful and after a few minutes you can relax and concentrate on exploring the lift and perfecting your control. If your flying site is suitable you are may be in a position to consider landing back on the top (just think, no more long slog up that hill). First, look in the area that you intend to land in. Is it suitable? Are there any potential hazards? Has anyone parked a car there while you have been flying? (Most clubs have defined areas for landing that are kept clear if possible). If it is not a recognised landing area, could it suffer from turbulence and rotors? If in

First top landing.

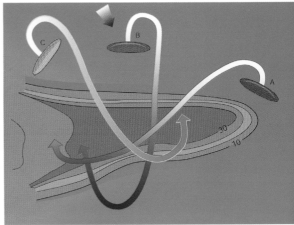

Fig 21.4: Top landing approches.

doubt, don't try it – land at the bottom. Ask other pilots and read your site guide to make sure it is advisable before attempting it.

If everything is OK, you need to plan your approach. Look at *Fig 21.4*; this is perhaps a little exaggerated in terms of good and bad choices, but gives you a good idea of the decision-making process involved. You have three choices: track in from the left (C) or the right (A) or approach directly downwind (B). All three approaches end up, of course, with a turn into wind. For your first top landings, a downwind approach (B) is not usually recommended; this is particularly true when it involves overflying a hazardous area such as the spine back shown in the diagram. So, left or right? If the wind is at 90° to the hill and the ridge is straight, the approach will be similar from either direction. Look at the area again; if you overshoot will it take you into the launch area or off the end of the hill? Choose the direction that gives the greatest margin for error – there are often unexpected patches of lift or sink above the top of a hill. Often the wind is not quite straight onto the face. This makes the choice easier – track to the end of the

downwind leg and start your approach from there. In this example track (A) is the best choice.

1 Decide in good time that you are planning to top land (a good pilot always reads ahead). Do you have enough height? Do not assume that you will be lifted up as you approach the ridge – a painful collision may result if you do. Plan your turn carefully for the approach leg.

2 Commence your turn as you would if you were intending to carry on soaring, then continue the turn until your track will drift you sideways "crabbing" you across the hill top. Be careful not to turn too much with insufficient height, or you may not have room to turn back into wind.

3 Continue to crab until you are over your planned landing area, then turn into wind.

4 As you turn into wind and continue to sink, ease your brakes up, then ease them down if you need to lose any excess speed. Do not forget that you will be landing in a reasonably strong breeze – something you may not have

experienced previously – so feel your way with the controls. Do not flare hard unless it is obviously necessary. If, on your final approach, you find yourself too high, then a few gentle "s" turns will help you lose height. If in any doubt, overshoot and try again. With practice you will learn to judge more accurately and be able to spot land in a pre-determined area

Always keep a good eye on other pilots (Photo: UK Airsports)

Touchdown and canopy control

Once your feet have touched the ground you have a choice to make. You may be able to "walk" the inflated canopy to a suitable area to pack it or to launch again, or you can choose to collapse it where you have landed – if there is only a light breeze you can collapse it simply by flaring as normal – *see chapter 16, Landing*. If, however, there is a reasonable breeze, your first action should be to turn to face the canopy. In this position you have far more control (as per a reverse launch) and you can see and control where the canopy will end up.

To collapse it, pull down hard on both rear risers. This will effectively stall the canopy and it will collapse. It is very important, if you are top-landing in a good breeze, that you should also move towards the canopy to reduce the pressure. Occasionally the glider will dive to one side if the risers are pulled unevenly or you are out of wind. If the canopy rotates and dives into the ground with a good load through the lines to you, it may hit very hard and this could damage the internal cell walls. The more wind there is, the more important it is that you run towards the canopy while collapsing it.

Occasionally you may find that the wind is strong enough to re-inflate the canopy whenever you stop moving towards it. In this case, the only safe position is behind (downwind) of it. If you should find yourself landing moving backwards or in a gusty wind, sprint round to the back of the canopy as soon as it is down. Being dragged by a paraglider is an unnerving and potentially dangerous experience. If you should fall over and find yourself being dragged, try to roll onto your stomach so that you can see where you are going and again, collapse the canopy by pulling one control hand over hand (until you get the fabric if necessary).

Soaring in the Lake District (Photo: UK Airsports)

Accelerator systems 22

Often referred to as "speed systems" these are simply a way of changing the angle of attack of the wing in flight. A few competition gliders, paramotor wings and and tandem wings feature "trimmers"; these are small cam-lock adjusters on the rear riser which can be applied and locked in place to alter the length of the rear riser, and set the trim-speed of the wing.

This is very useful on fast wings, as it allows the angle of attack to be set to the optimum for conditions, and tilting the whole wing is far more efficient at maximising lift than adding lots of drag with the brakes alone. On a tandem wing this system is used because the brake pressures are greater, and because of the harnesses arrangement, tandems cannot use a foot operated speed system.

Virtually all other canopies use a foot –operated stirrup to activate a speed

system which lowers the angle of attack of the whole wing. *(Fig 22.1)*

When the foot stirrup is pressed the front riser is shortened. This would collapse the canopy's leading edge if done alone, but to prevent the airfoil "breaking", the B riser is also pulled down a proportional amount to maintain the even loading of the lines and keep the wing solid. In 4 riser systems (as shown) the C riser may also be shortened very slightly. This basic pattern is how all speed systems work, but there are variations on the theme: some may allow the rear riser to be extended as the A's & B's are shortened, for example.

A lower angle of attack means that induced drag is reduced, and the wing can travel faster and on a steeper glide path. The lower the angle of the canopy, the less resistance it has to diving further if it encounters a lull or any turbulence, and if it gets too low the airfoil can

Normal   **Accelerated**

Fig 22.1: The stirrup is connected to your front risers by cords that run through pulleys mounted on your harness. The cord usually passes through another pair of pulleys on the front riser that gives a 2:1 or 3:1 reduction advantage to make its activation progressive and to reduce the load, ensuring it is easy to operate

Speed bar with a cranked ladder extension for easy 'footing'

can locate them with your feet alone, but if you have problems you can teach down and use one hand to put the bar on your foot.

A small patch of Velcro, or shock cord retainers are a handy way to keep the stirrup itself against the harness when not in use.

Speed system cords should be adjusted so that the system is not activated at all when the risers are tensioned.

Pilots with long legs sometimes worry that they can "over-accelerate". However, this is not the case, as all the speed systems are limited by the distance between the pulleys.

Some pilots prefer to remove their harnesses when packing up. In this case the speed system must also be disengaged. The cords are often secured at the riser end, by either a small maillon, or by a pair of Brummel hooks. These interlocking devices are easy and effective, but you must be very careful that lines cannot get trapped in the slots.

Any connection system with snap hooks or any spring-loaded gate must be discarded as the hooks can trap a line during ground handling. Even the Brummel hooks that are usually provided can be an issue as some modern wings have such thin lines that they have been known to work their way into the 0.5mm slot in the hook, usually when the glider is being packed up. The best advice is to connect up the hooks and leave your harness connected with a sheath or tape over the connected Brummel hooks.

Accelerator systems are there to give a bit of additional speed if you should need it; they are not provided so that you can fly in winds that are too strong to cope with otherwise.

deform and have little resistance to collapse. For this reason, it is wise to use the speed system sparingly in rough air, and to maintain contact pressure on the brakes, so that you can slow and counter any sudden tendency to dive forward.

To actually use your speed system you need to locate the stirrup with your feet, most modern speed stirrups have a secondary wire or plastic loop so that you

Apart from competition use, your speed system (like big ears) should be thought of as a safety device that you keep in reserve for dealing with situations where you have misjudged the conditions, ie if you need to use it routinely on a flight then the conditions are really to strong and you have no remaining margin for error.

To activate your speed system the procedure is:

1 Hook the stirrup extension with one heel and push it out enough so that you can place the other foot on the stirrup itself. You may need to tear away a retaining piece of Velcro during this process.

2 Place the first foot on the stirrup bar as well so that you can push evenly.

3 Smoothly and strongly extend your legs to alter the angle of attack of the wing; -this can require considerable effort.

4 Keep contact pressure on the controls so that if the wing pitches forwards you can react quickly by bending you knees and adding some brake. Note the speed systems are not just on or off, you can push for more speed or relax to back off a little as conditions dictate.

5 Always release the accelerator to trim and remove your feet in good time before landing. If you do not, you run a higher risk of a low level collapse and getting a foot tangled as you touch down.

NOTE: Do not activate big ears when the speed system is extended. If you wish to use both together (which is a good way of reducing height safely and quickly)-, you should always make sure your speed system is off before folding in the ears, once in, you can then reapply speed bar.

Foot stirrup (Photo: Sup Air SARL)

23 Site discipline & Rules of the air

Paragliders are subject to the same rules and laws as any other aircraft *(See Chapter 24, Air Law)*.But, in addition to these there are some other disciplines that must be obeyed for us to fly safely and without causing problems for others.

Sites

In the UK almost all land is owned by somebody, and before you fly from it you should find out whose it is and seek permission. Obviously you must use common sense. If you are flying from a remote peak in the Highlands it is unlikely anyone is going to worry.

However people flying from cultivated land, areas where grouse shooting takes place or where are sheep during lambing time, have already lost sites, just by thoughtlessly flying without permission, or in contravention of local club agreements.

It is vital for the future of the sport that pilots follow sensible guidelines when out flying and are polite to landowners and other land users.

In most of the world the general rule is much the same, any cultivated or land in use by someone (ski pistes etc) require permission to be used as launch areas. Most regular flying sites are adminstered by a local club, many of whom will charge a fee for their use, but occasional launching from unprepared slopes is generally not an issue in most countries.

Site use guidelines

Most major sites are administered by the local club or school

Make sure you know the site rules, & restrictions, you may have to join the local club to obtain this information, or ask a local club member.

- Keep away from livestock
- Do not take dogs onto any hills where there may be sheep
- Do not climb over fences, walls or hedges.
- No lighting fires
- Check that there is no shooting on Moorland, or lambing is not taking place. (February to May in the UK)
- Close all gates
- Park sensibly, specifically, do not obstruct gates or partially block roads or tracks.
- Leave no litter
- Ensure you fly with third party insurance and always pay for any damage.

These guidelines are designed to help others and make us more welcome on someone else's land. We can also help ourselves directly by observing a sensible attitude on the site. For example.

- Do not leave equipment in the landing area
- Make sure everyone knows the site rules.- if a pilot is unfamiliar, check that they are aware of the landing areas, or any hazards.

- Offer to help other pilots. Perhaps by offering advice if they are inexperienced, or by acting as an anchorman if required.

- Do not launch if the sky is too crowded

- Always do a pre-flight check

- Only fly if you are in good health

There re also some mandatory safety rules laid down by the BHPA and most other national organisations, these are not law, but are very important. (Failure to comply could invalidate your insurance for example).

- Wear a suitable helmet (to EN 96 standard).

- Have the relevant qualification for the flying you are undertaking

- Have adequate insurance cover. (BHPA membership presently confers £5,000,000 third party cover).

- Do not fly outside the weight range, or fly a modified paraglider or harness unless the manufacturer has approved the changes.

- NB. This is mentioned in the following chapter: Airlaw, but it is worth reiterating a couple of vital points.

- It is an offence to operate an aircraft whilst under the influence of drugs – this includes alcohol.

- It is an offence to operate any aircraft in a manner that could endanger another person.

The 'aquarium' at the Dune de Pyla, France

Ariel collision avoidance regulations (Anti-collision rules)

For your own safety and that of others it is crucial that you are aware of these rules. There is a certain amount of general Airlaw required to be pilot, and to reduce our risk of conflict with general aviation, but the fact is that the people we are most likely to collide with are each other.

These rules are exactly what they are entitled, rules to help avoid a collision, and they come into force when a collision is imminent.

Although everyone needs to know and follow these rules, the fact is that most pilots rarely need to put them into practice, as the sensible pilot avoids allowing these situations to develop.

The key point is observation. If you have a good mental picture of where other pilots are, you can minimise the risk of having to take avoiding action.

So… Rule one (and the most important of them all) is

I Always keep a good lookout.

In particular always look around before you manoeuvre. "Manoeuvring" means doing anything: Taking off, commencing a turn, letting go of one brake to scratch your nose, etc.

2 When approaching another pilot head-on at a similar altitude; turn to your right.

If this impractical or unsafe because of a ridge or another aircraft, maintain your course and allow the other pilot to turn.

3 When two aircraft are on converging courses, the one on the right has right of way.

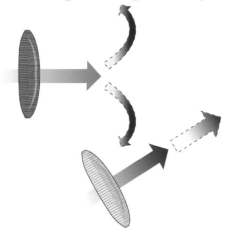

(Often shortened to "on the right in the right") If you are on the left you must alter course to avoid a possible conflict.

4 Give way to pilots who are below you.

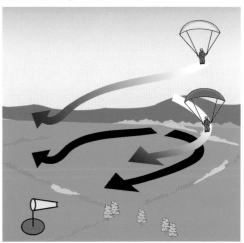

This is especially important, if you are approaching to land, the lower pilot has less room to manoeuvre and a higher workload as he approaches the ground. In any situation where paragliders are flying together, such as in thermal lift, the lower pilot has much reduced upward visibility, so the onus is on the higher pilot to stay clear.

5 Overtaking. Exercise care and a good lookout when overtaking.

There is no right or wrong side to overtake a slower moving pilot, the key is simply to make sure that they are aware of you and there is lots of room. Note that a hill soaring pilot is very much more likely to make their next turn into wind (ie away from the slope) and so avoiding trying to overtake "outside" them reduces the risk of collision.

If in doubt, do not overtake. Rather like a car, a pilot in front of you will have poorer sense of your position, so the overtaking pilot must ensure that there is adequate space.

6 Notwithstanding any of the rules above, it is every pilots' responsibility to take any action necessary to avoid a collision.

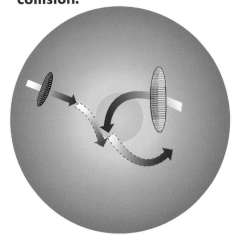

In other words, even if it is your right of way, you are expected to take action if the likely alternative is a collision. This is the overriding rule. In any case where there has been a collision, there is always some share of the responsibility on both pilots.

Thermalling convention: Whilst not enshrined in Airlaw, one of the commonest situations where soaring pilots are in close proximity is when using thermal lift. When circling in thermal lift, always turn in the same direction as other craft.

The direction of turn is set by the first pilot to start using the thermal, and by flying the same way, the closing speeds of the two (or more) aircraft are small and good visual contact can be maintained. This enables several gliders to safely use the same relatively small are of lift.

Putting it into practice:

When you are flying it is a useful exercise to imagine that you are flying in the centre of a sphere or bubble which is your personal space, as long as you keep your bubble away from everyone else's, the anti-collision rules never need to be activated. The size of your "bubble" varies depending on your experience, who you are flying with, how smooth the conditions are and other factors. If you do not think that you have enough space to fly without compromising your space, the wisest move is to stay on the ground.

Sometimes things change during the course of your flight, the lift may weaken, or the conditions become rougher, or more pilots take off.

You may find that you need to move further out from the ridge, or fly away from your thermal or to a less busy area, or simply go and land. It is better to be a disappointed or have to wait to fly again, than to find yourself in a mid-air collision situation.

Note; because of the low relative speeds and the fact that the pilot is exposed (not in a cockpit) it is often practical simply to shout at another pilot if you are not sure that he has seen you.

One final point, some paraglider pilots seem to be under the impression that because their canopies are slow moving, faster aircraft like hang-gliders or sailplanes should give way to them. While there is some truth in the reasoning that those craft have more speed to call upon, it is an EQUAL responsibility to avoid each other, and in situations where we are flying in close proximity, such as some ridges or sharing a thermal, we are all equally dependent upon the other pilots' good airmanship.

Eurocontrol, the "European Organisation for the Safety of Air Navigation", is currently consulting on its proposed Standardised European Rules of the Air (SERA). Once established, the intention is that these harmonised rules will affect all airsports in Europe. However because the scope of rules of the air for all aircraft is so wide, and the variations among countries and types of craft are so diverse, it is proving a difficult task.

The existing systems in place, (like the BHPA anti-collision rules above), have worked very well for 30 years or more and whilst most pilots welcome a regular review of how things can be improved, the SERA proposals have so far been unwieldy and inflexible for the purpose of slope soaring craft like ours flying in close proximity to one another, and some of the language (probably due in part to translation issues) has been far from clear. The consultation continues!

Flying in the Annecy region France, Gliders all over the place.

Air Law 24

Paragliding is an adventure sport, and is often advertised alongside other activities like skiing; mountain biking or climbing. Most flying is not cross country but is done within a few kilometres of the take –off point. Perhaps because of this there can sometimes be a misconception that paragliding is not really "aviation" in the same way as flying a light aircraft from an aerodrome, for example, and is therefore somehow less subject to air law.

This is not the case, and all aircraft, including gliders of all types are expected to know and conform to any relevant airspace regulations and restrictions.

At a school, or when flying on recognised club sites that we know have no airspace restrictions, it is sufficient to know the visual meteorological conditions (VMC) required, and the anti-collision rules to fly safely with others.

When thermalling, and flying cross – country away from a known site, the situation alters, we are sharing the airspace with a wide variety of other users and having laws and regulations helps to keep both them and us safe.

Imagine just for a moment that a paraglider pilot with no airchart or who is working a strong thermal and climbs into an airway, or even just skimming cloudbase;- having a mid-air collision with another aircraft. It could be a microlight, a helicopter, or a military or passenger jet. Whatever the type, the consequences are certain to be extremely serious, and are very likely to included the deaths of everyone involved.

That is the potential problem, so what is the solution? There is no 100% failsafe way to avoid other air users completely but there are a good many ways to hugely reduce the risks.

Firstly the key element is to have good visibility so that we (and other pilots) can see what is around us, including other pilots. UK air law defines the visual meteorological conditions we can fly in and they vary depending on where we are flying. So to make sense of this information you need to know the type of airspace you are in. It is no good having good visibility if you do not look around. A good pilot will scan regularly to check for other air traffic, including above and behind his aircraft. Visibility is a measure of how far you can see. On many days, the visibility from the ground may be much better than from altitude, and of course the presence of clouds has a huge influence. It must also be within the hours of daylight.

- **Above FL100 (see below)**
  VMC is : Visibility 8km. Clear of cloud by 1,000ft vertically & 1500m horizontally.

- **Below 3,000ft Above Mean Sea Level (AMSL) in type E & D Airspace, & above 3,000ft AMSL in type F & G Airspace**
  VMC is : Visibility of 5Km Clear of cloud, in sight of the surface.

- **Below 3,000ft AMSL In type F & G Airspace.**
  VMC is : Visibility of 1,500m, Clear of cloud, in sight of the surface.

That sounds pretty complicated, but in fact FL100 is 10,00ft pressure attitude (see page 144) and so that is highly unlikely to be relevant to us flying paragliders in the UK.

So that leaves two options, above 3,000ft, or in restricted airspace, where we must be clear of cloud and with visibility of 5km, and below 3,000ft or in F or G airspace where we must have visibility of 1,500m, be clear of cloud and be in sight of the surface.

Clearly we also need to know what airspace is what, and to know where we are, and how high we are.

Airspace types.

In the UK the categories are A to G.

- **Class A controlled airspace**
  All traffic within type A airspace is controlled by Air traffic services, and we are unable to comply with commands such as climb to Flight level 1200, it is effectively prohibited to us. Type A airspace is typically found around major airports.

- **Class B Controlled airspace.**
  All airspace in the Uk above FL245 is Class B and is prohibited to us by virtue of lack of oxygen and sub-zero temperatures as well as by law!

- **Class C Controlled airspace.**
  This is also prohibited to us, but we do not care because there is (at the time of writing) no UK airspace designated Class C!

- **Class D Controlled airspace.**
  It is possible for gliders to enter Class D airspace if they are in radio contact with ATC and obtain clearance. Note you will require an RT (Radio telephony) licence and a suitable airband radio to allow this. Some clubs

have negotiated letters of agreement to allow access to some parts of Class D airspace. Your local club will be able to advise you. It is anticipated that in the near future you will also be required to carry a transponder, for which you once again require an RT licence.

- **Class E controlled airspace.**
  Gliders may penetrate Class E airspace without permission subject to VMC (see above)

- **Class F Airspace (Advisory routes).**
  Gliders may penetrate Class F airspace without permission subject to VMC (see above)

Note however that heavy (commercial) traffic may use these advisory airways which are 10 Nautical miles wide.

- **Class G airspace.**
  Class G is uncontrolled airspace, ie everything else, and fortunately for us this makes up most of the sky. Gliders may fly in Type G airspace subject to VMC (see above). Note however that uncontrolled means just that, other general aviation and military craft can also fly here, and the rule is very simply "see and avoid". The need for a good lookout cannot be overemphasised.

There are lots of other types of airspace within these broad categories and these all have to be taken into account. But knowing about them is not much use if you do not know where they are and more to the point where you are in relation to them. For this reason every pilot flying cross country in the UK should carry an up to date airchart, and altimeter and know how to read the relevant features.

At the time of writing the European Organisation for the Safety of Air Navigation is nearing the end of a long (10 years and counting) period of consultation into the creation of a "Single European Sky". Essentially this is about simplifying the large number of national air traffic regions, each with their own protocols and (the present proposal) having just nine air traffic "blocks" covering all of Europe. This all sounds very splendid and logical but unfortunately as the emphasis is so heavily on commercial traffic that soaring pilots like paragliders are sometimes caught up in the regulations, even though it is not designed with any thought to their needs. So far this has had no serious impact on recreational pilots in Europe but initiatives such as making all airspace above 10,000ft into controlled airspace, or a requirements for gliders to carry transponders, could, if passed as legislation, have a significant impact in the future. The BHPA and other national bodies representing soaring pilots are working hard making the case on behalf of their member pilots, but at the time of writing it appears likely that some of the proposals will be adopted and the airspace landscape described in this book will change significantly in Europe.

One part of this initiative that is almost upon us the requirement for all aircraft entering class D airspace to carry transponders (short for Transmitter responders) these devices can be interrogated by secondary surveillance radar from air traffic control or other aircraft and give the precise height, heading and identification of the aircraft they are fitted to. Whilst this does not affect us directly, because most pilots now use GPS systems, it is likely that the areas immediately outside the controlled area

Instrument console with moving digital airchart on a PDA.

will become very busy as general aviation pilots who are not using transponders, all skirt these areas closely, and especially where there are narrow corridors of uncontrolled airspace, this means that the resulting funnelling of traffic around the edges of controlled airspace could make some parts of the sky very busy places.

Aircharts

These come in two varieties, the half-million charts which have a scale of 8 miles to one inch or 500,000 to 1. These show all airspace. However for low and slow flying like ours, they are difficult to read in the air (especially if you need reading glasses!) and much of the higher level information is not likely to be of much use to us. They do however cover a very large area and if you are an experienced pilot expecting to do a long flight or expect to fly at 5,000ft or more then they are the most comprehensive choice. The availability of GPS devices that can accept digital aircharts, has made the half-million series more popular as the screens can often be zoomed, neatly getting round the scale issues.

The 1: 250,000 charts (quarter million) are scaled at 4 miles to the inch and have

An excerpt from a 1: 250 000 airchart and a 1: 500 000 attendant key

a lot more topographical information making them easier to use, however the airspace is only marked up to 5,000ft or FL550, meaning that at greater altitude you may not be aware of some airspace, and on a long flight there is a danger that you may fly off the edge of the map.

Digital charts can allow you to swap charts in mid air on some devices, which is a very helpful feature.

Aircharts are updated regularly and it is the pilots' responsibility to ensure they are flying with the latest edition as airspace is subject to changes. Updates are available from all good retailers.

Perhaps the best and most practical way to familiarise ourselves with the various types of airspace is to identify them on an airchart

Interesting things you might come across on an airchart!

Airways

These are the Motorways of the air, they are usually 10nautical miles wide and have a lower and upper limit. These heights vary, and for each one you need to consult an up to date airchart. The levels are printed along each one like a road number, and may say (for example) FL75 This means that the base of the airway is at a flight level of 7,500ft. Virtually all UK airways are prohibited to us, though there can be letters of variation issued that can allow penetration in some cases. (Your local club will advise you). If you do enter one your situation is not unlike a hedgehog crossing a road, and the rules are the same! Cross quickly at 90° and in a straight line, for obvious reason you must keep a good lookout and be flying in full VMC.

Fig 24.3: Aerodrome showing the air traffic zone and an airway "stepping down" to meet it. The illustration shows only one airway stopping at the boundary. In fact there may be more than one and they may well continue above, through and beyond the controlled area.

Control Traffic Area (CTA)

Control areas are found above aerodromes, they are the roundabouts of the sky where the airways meet, the bottom of the airway will generally descend in steps to the control area.

Some control areas are known as **Control zones**. As a general rule in airspace terms a zone is something that extends from the ground to a specific altitude, whereas an area is something that goes from one altitude to another. (As always there are exceptions to this, Danger areas for example (over military ranges) start at ground level.

Penetration of control areas is prohibited to paragliders (except where prior permission has been obtained, or when the area is stated as being inactive at specific times).

Terminal Control Area (TMA)

Similar to a Control area but on a larger scale a TMA is found over major international airports. They are category A airspace where a high density of commercial traffic is flying under Instrument flying rules.

Within them the traffic is under the direct control of the airport control tower, who tracks them with radar. Whilst it is perfectly possible to talk to ATC if you have the right equipment and a suitable licence to use it, it is clearly impractical for a paraglider to conform to ATC instructions so of course they are prohibited to us.

Air Traffic Zone (ATZ)

These comprise the restricted airspace belonging to smaller aerodromes, many of which will have no air traffic control. They form a cylinder of controlled

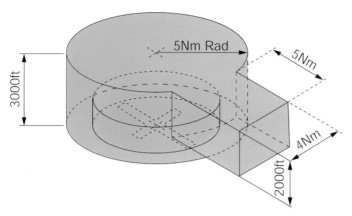

Fig 24.3: The dimensions of a typical military aerodrome traffic zone
(MATZ). (The ATZ is shown in orange).
Note the "stub" is in line with the
longest runway. More than one MATZ
is visible on the airchart extract in Fig
24.1.

airspace from the surface up to 2,000ft.
The cylinder is located over the centre
point of the runway or runways and
normally has a radius of 2 nautical miles.
If the longest runway is longer than 1,850
metres, the boundary is considered too
close to the end of the runway so the
radius is increased to 2.5Nm.. There are
a variety of grades of ATZ ranging from
fully prohibited to those that require prior
permission or radio contact to penetrate.
Your club can advise you on the situation
locally. But if you are not certain you have
clearance, do not enter an ATZ.

Military air traffic Zone (MATZ)

Because of the speed and weight of some
military traffic the ATZ of a military
airbase has a further shell of controlled
airspace outside the normal ATZ. Gliders
are permitted to penetrate this outer area,
however like all high traffic areas, it is
very unwise to spend any more time than
strictly necessary in a piece of sky where
pilots with a very high workload, and
who are often under training are likely to
be encountered.

A MATZ typically has a radius for 5Nm
from the centre of the longest runway and
extends to 3,000ft above ground level. In
addition there is usually a "stub" (see fig
24.3) five nautical miles long and four
wide extending from 1,000ft to 3,000ft in
line with the main runway.

If more than one MATZ are overlapping
they are designated a Combined Military
Air traffic Zone (CMATZ).

Areas of Intense Ariel Activity (AIAA)

This is a catch all for any other areas
where there is a high risk of encountering
other aircraft, such as an area used
for aerobatics. Whilst not specifically
prohibited to gliders the same provisos
apply as for a MATZ

Danger Areas, Prohibited Areas, and Restricted Areas

Dotted all over your airchart you will
also find areas of prohibited or restricted
airspace. These reflect ground based
activities such as sensitive military bases,
nuclear power stations etc.

Danger areas are often military firing
ranges or a similar hazard. They can
be active permanently or only at
certain times. If you have certain prior
knowledge that they are inactive then
they can be crossed. (This may require a
confirmation through radio contact with
ATC) Otherwise they are prohibited.

Each danger area has a code number. For example D503/12. This means that this are is number 503 (in fact Number 3 above 50degress latitude) and extends to an altitude of 12,000ft.

High Intensity Radio Transmissions (HIRTA)

Airspace of defined dimensions within which there is radio energy of an intensity that may cause interference or even damage to radio and navigation instruments. Certain areas emit signals (microwaves etc) that can be harmful to pilots.

Bird Sanctuaries

Usually these are breeding colonies of protected birds. Unfortunately for us, some like Gannets like to nest in areas of good ridge lift! Some are out of bounds in the breeding season and a few are prohibited at all times.

Temporary restricted airspace

This can sometimes be created – primarily for flying displays, and also for Royal flights

By its very nature these restrictions are not shown on the aircharts, they are often listed on various airspace websites such as NOTAMPLOT or NOTAM INFO or there is a dedicated AIS information line 0500 354802

Sharing uncontrolled airspace

As we all fly the same terrain and use lift in a similar way, the major risk of a collision in uncontrolled airspace is with other gliders (whether rigid sailplanes, hang-gliders or paragliders). The anti collision rules for flying with other

gliders are reproduced in the previous chapter. The second group of air users that concern us comprises military aircraft with crews under training. Their operations are very often carried out at low level, high speed and often with their pilot doing their best to remain hidden by the terrain. Training is concentrated in the more remote and hilly areas of the UK.- the parts most used by paragliders.

Fortunately the Royal Air Force usually operates on weekdays except for major exercises which are generally publicised well in advance. As sport paragliding is predominantly a weekend activity, the risk is reduced. However there is still a very real risk of conflict on weekdays, and in order to minimise the risk of collision, there is a system in place for sport flyers to notify the military of their intended areas of activity. For major exercises the military also issue a NOTAM giving warning to other air users.

Paraglider pilots are strongly advised to use the Civil Advance Notification Procedure (CANP) to inform the military authorities of their intended activity. This is especially important if you expect to be flying during the week and in a known military training area such as Wales, the Highlands of Scotland or the Yorkshire Dales or Lake District.

Using CANP

The system is very easy to use. Simply call the free phone number **0800 515544** and you will be asked about your activity. Typically the information you need to supply is:

- Your name and contact number

- Where you will be flying The site may have a reference number which is noted in the clubs site guide, or you can give a 6 figure grid reference. – The nearest town name is also helpful.

- The time of activity, (12 noon till dusk for example)

- The expected height of activity (surface to 3,000ft for example).

- How many pilots will be flying. – *Recently the controllers have informed some callers that if there are less then 5 pilots they are not obliged to inform the low flying booking cell. However it is always good practice to do so, and it is quite usual for several individuals or small groups to converge on one site, so the risk is that no individual will use the system, leaving the site without cover.*

The agent will then call you back a few minutes later when your data has been entered and give you a confirmation reference number.

Military crews are being briefed and launching all the time, and so to work effectively you need to give as much notice as possible. Ideally this should be 5 hours or more, but even if it is less, it is still worth doing as the percentage of notified crews will increase as the day goes on.

Note that the resulting CANP is simply to alert military pilots of your presence and likely position so that they can keep and eye out for you. It does not guarantee you an avoidance zone that they must stay away from. Though if you call with 12 hours notice or more , crews are advised to make their flight plans with this information incorporated- which effectively means they will avoid your site. You can of course notify more than one site if you are not sure where you are going, though it is courteous to call back and cancel one of you change your mind

Do use the CANP system. It is very easy, and your club site guide will have the reference code and grid references of the sites. It is far better for two or three pilot to notify the same site on the same day, than for everyone to assume someone else will do it, with potentially fatal results. The system is not used as much as it should be in the UK and it will be very sad day if two or more pilots' families learn their husband/son/mother or fathers were killed because they did not bother to make a free 'phone call. Sadly the CANP system is very underused by paraglider pilots in the UK and at the time of writing it is under review and may changed (perhaps by being converted to smart phone app) or may be discontinued entirely.

If flying away from the notified site on a cross-country, then the NOTAM is no longer applicable, and the rule is simply keep a good lookout. Most military low flying exercises are conducted at heights of 250ft to 900ft AGL and particular care is required at these altitudes, and a careful all-round scan of the sky is recommended when you are getting low or thinking of landing.

General flying rules

The Air Navigation Order is a large piece of legislation covering all aspect of flying, but the rules below are of particular relevance to paraglider pilots.

1 An aircraft should not be operated in a negligent or careless manner* so as to endanger life or property, nor be flown in such proximity to other aircraft as to create a danger of collision nor in formation without the prior consent of the pilots.

2 No person may be carried except in that part of the aircraft designed

for the purpose, or be drunk in the aircraft

3 Nothing may be dropped from the aircraft other than a person by parachute in an emergency, articles for life saving, or ballast in the form of fine dry sand or water. (Or tow ropes at an airfield)

4 An aircraft shall not be flown within 1km of an outdoor gathering of more than 1,000 people or below such height as will enable it to land clear. (ie you cannot fly into your local football stadium!)

5 Gliders may not fly over a built-up area below either such height that will enable it to land clear or 1,000ft above the highest fixed object, whichever is the higher.

6 An aircraft must not be flown nearer than 500ft to any person, vehicle, vessel or structure except when taking off, landing or hill soaring. **

* There is no specification of what is a negligent or careless manner, though there is, at the time of writing a prosecution in which an untrained pilot has collided with a hill walker and injured them. It is the opinion of some lawyers that flying without training or qualification is a reasonable definition of "negligent and careless".

** A paraglider can always be said to be hill soaring, taking off or landing, but this rule is important because if you should add a motor it becomes applicable, and places an important restriction on paramotoring activity.

Altitude. As airspace is three-dimensional in nature, pilots need to know their altitude as well as their position. For example a pilot flying at 900ft might be uncontrolled airspace under the stub of a military air traffic zone (MATZ) and his VMC requirements are different to a pilot 500ft above him (at 1,400ft) who is within the zone. Another pilot flying a further 1,500ft above him (at 3,100ft) is clear of the airspace again, though by virtue of his altitude is still obliged to fly in full VMC.

The words height, altitude and flight level are all important and all have slightly different definitions; that pilots need to be clear about.

Height is how high you are above the ground.

Altitude is how high you are above mean sea level (Amsl)

Flight level (or FL) is how high you are above mean sea level assuming the standard atmospheric pressure and temperature. On air charts and in aviation jargon, Flight levels are quoted without the final two zeros, so FL 75 is 7500ft. Airspace above 3,000ft is normally given as a flight level as this is where you are likely to meet aircraft who may have set their altimeters in a different pressure region. (Often in a different country!)

Changing Pressure

The standardisation of flight levels is important as changes in pressure in different weather conditions can make a big difference. If two planes who had both zeroed their altimeters to AMSL, one in a high pressure area and one in a low pressure area – were to converge, one may have a an indicated altitude of say 10,000ft and one an altitude of 10,500ft, but they could still actually be the same height above the ground and collide.

Pressure is measured in millibars and can vary by as much as 40 or more millibars. One millibar is "worth" 30ft or so at sea level. This is why you usually have to reset your altimeter to zero on different flying days. If the pressure is lower then the altimeter will over-read, so the pilot may be lower than his instruments tell him. Let us say you set your altimeter to zero using the Standard pressure setting of 1013.2mb to give flight levels, and then you are flying in a low pressure area of 996mb, at sea level the altimeter will be over-reading by 510ft.

Altimeters

To go ridge soaring on your local site you do not need an altimeter, but for the reasons given above it is a mandatory requirement to carry one (together with your aircraft) when flying cross-country. Most paraglider pilots will choose an integrated vario/ altimeter, a few more basic models will have only one setting but many will feature two or three altimeters that you can switch between in flight. One setting should be zeroed at take –off (or above your expected landing field if different). This setting is known as QFE. – (*So called because incoming pilots can radio to their destination airfield and ask "Query Field Elevation" so that they could set their altimeters to the right value for entering a circuit pattern.*) QFE

is therefore your **Height** above a certain point on the ground.

If you wish to set your altimeter to mean sea level, this setting is known as QNH (*"Nautical height" is a handy way to remember this*). At QNH you will know your **Altitude**: ie how high you are above sea level, and therefore the mapped terrain in the area.

Because aircharts have the altitude of active airfields marked on them, you can very easily work out that if your QNH is 3,500ft and the airfield you are approaching has a ATZ up to 2,000ft that you cannot enter, but the airfield itself is at 1,000ft AMSL... then clearly you are only 500ft clear, which may not be enough to overfly the ATZ safely..

Pressure altitude. This means the altimeter is set to the sea level assuming a standard pressure and temperature of 1013.2mb and 15Degrees C (the ICAO standard atmosphere). The value given is expressed as a **Flight level**. Flight levels are generally used for everything above 3,000ft in the Uk. This switch point from AMSL to FL is known as the transition level. If you are crossing immediately below an airway for example with the base at FL55, your FL must be less than

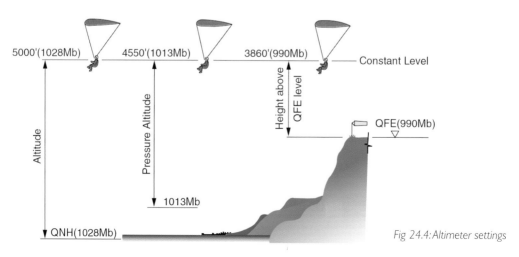

Fig 24.4: Altimeter settings

5,500ft to remain clear, if you are flying on a QNH setting then you could be hundreds of feet into the airway without knowing it.

Radios

It is illegal to transmit from the air with other than a licensed airband radio. To use the vast majority of airband frequencies requires a radio telephony licence. This is necessary if you wish to talk to an air traffic controller in order to get permission to enter his ATZ for example.

There are however a few frequencies that are set aside for sport pilots, and the main one allocated for Hang-gliding and Paragliding is 118.675Mhz.

You do not need to take an exam or obtain a licence to use these frequencies, but you must maintain radio discipline and not use them to chat. The other

frequencies currently available in the UK are : 129.900 129.950 130.100 130.125 130.400

Note that these may be used by other aircraft types, especially gliders, balloons and parachutists.

The emergency distress channel of 121.500 is constantly monitored.

For the purposes of clarity there is an ICAO phonetic alphabet that is used to ensure accurate transmission and reception, particularly where reception is poor, or vital information such as call signs are being transmitted. This is given in table 24.5.

Many paraglider pilots do not use airband transceivers. Though they are essential if you are flying in or around controlled airspace. There are other types of radio available and details of these are given in Chapter 19. Additional equipment.

Fig 24.5 ICAO phonetics

ICAO Phonetic Alphabet & Useful terms

A	Alpha	J	Juliet	S	Sierra		.	Decimal
B	Bravo	K	Kilo	T	Tango		5	Fife
C	Charlie	L	Lima	U	Uniform		9	Niner
D	Delta	M	Mike	V	Victor		0	Zero
E	Echo	N	November	W	Whiskey		Emergency	Mayday
F	Foxtrot	O	Oscar	X	X-Ray		No	Negative
G	Golf	P	Papa	Y	Yankee		Yes	Affirmative
H	Hotel	Q	Quebec	Z	Zulu		Will Comply	Wilco
I	India	R	Romeo				Wait	Stand by

The present UK airlaw framework is about 40 years old, and although it has been under constant review, and has worked very well so far, it is likely that the advent of new technology such as transponders that make any aircraft far more conspicuous, and a general growth in the number of airusers will prompt a

good deal more change in the next few years.

It is important that the information in this chapter is seen as time sensitive, and that pilots should take steps to make use that they are informed of the most up to date requirements of air law.

25 **Meteorology**

The weather is a colossal subject. In this section the intention is to consider the basic weather patterns that affect us, and look at the local "micrometeorology" systems that a paraglider pilot is likely to encounter or that are of particular interest to us.

Forecasts

Weather forecasts are available from a variety of sources. The most obvious are TV and the internet. The UK BBC or Met Office forecasts are excellent for establishing a visual picture of what is happening and, if you are familiar with the synoptic (pressure) charts (*see Fig 25.1*), you can glean a good deal of information that the presenter does not have time to spell out. Satellite photos are useful for assessing cloud cover. The downfall of these forecasts from our point of view is that they are very general and give no indication of the change of wind speed with height, and they rarely mention convection, though code phrases such as " cloud will build up" or "sunshine and showers" can give a clue.

Radio forecasts fall into three main categories. General "it will be a nice day in the south" are of little use to us. Specific forecasts, particularly the shipping ones, are good for approaching weather and surface winds, especially for coastal flying. You will need to know where the coastal stations and sea areas like "Dogger" or "Fastnet" actually are.

Internet Forecasts

There are a huge number of weather information providers on the net. A list is given in the useful addresses section. But a good place to start is.

www.bbc.co.uk/ weather
or
www.met-office.gov.uk

A good pilot is constantly aware of conditions mid-flight and any impending changes.

These forecasts are often available for a small region like "the Malvern hills" or the "Southern coast of Cornwall" This does make them more useful as local conditions, such as a hill or coastal fog, tide states etc, may be mentioned. Many rely on you entering a postcode or nearest town, such forecasts are likely to under-read wind strengths at launch points or above as they are aimed at ground level users.

There is also an internet weather service in the UK known as Airmet. Designed for pilots, Airmet offers two services. One gives the weather for the following 24 hours, and one for the following 12 (i.e. that day). These are excellent as they give the most valuable information from our point of view – wind speeds at different heights. They also warn of turbulence, freezing levels and cloud types and coverage. A gliding supplement and a ballooning supplement is available both of which gives information about wave or thermal activity, cloud types etc. Airmet is a prime source of weather information for many pilots.

RASP (Regional Atmospheric Soaring Prediction) This is a more specialised forecasting site which provides information on expected convection (thermal) strengths. This is most useful to pilots who are in a hurry… ie planning

Fig 25.1: Synoptic pressure chart

long cross-country flights or competing, as it can help them in their decisions on how high to leave a source of lift, with a good estimate of how strong the next thermal will be.

Actual live weather data

A useful development in forecasting involve paragliding clubs actually building their own weather stations, which they site in a suitable spot and which use a mobile phone or are wired to a nearby line. Current technology allows the forecast data to be converted into a simulated voice that can be rung to give us our own "actual" data.

In the UK the "wendy windblows" stations are the prime source of actual weather data. This is invaluable to many pilots as you can call up the flying site before setting off and this can save a lot of time and effort in travelling to the wrong hill or turning up when it is too strong or the hill top is in cloud. Actual weather data is also available from other sources such as airports and some coastal stations.

Using the forecasts

As a general rule, pilots look out of the window first then watch the TV. If the forecast is good – "a bright sunny day with light westerly winds" – then they set out. If it is poor – "gales and sleet" – they obviously do not bother. If the forecast implies that it may be OK, then logging on to Airmet may be advisable. If you are planning a cross-country flight it is worthwhile obtaining the gliding supplement or perhaps a RASP forecast.

If you have a local actual weather source like wendy windblows, that is usually also worth a call to confirm the forecast is correct.

In much of Europe weather data from popular take-off points is transmitted regularly on 2m radio frequencies. A few sites, usually at skiing venues, now feature webcams so that you can log on and actually see who is flying and how they are doing! The ultimate forecast (or torture if you are stuck in the office).

Text Forecasts

You can get a 6 hour local weather forecast texted direct to your mobile phone if you message your postcode to the met office. Check the met office website for details of this service.

Doing your own forecasting on site

Once on site you have the advantage of being able to measure the wind speed and direction and being able to look upwind to see what weather is heading your way. Here are a few clues you should be looking for.

Cloud types

Clouds are categorised according to their altitude and shape. There are three main categories:

- **Cirrus**
  These are the highest clouds, at 16,000ft (5,000m) or more, and they are composed of ice crystals.

- **Stratus**
  These are featureless layers of cloud.

- **Cumulus**
  Heaped piles of cloud caused by convection.

The latter two categories can be sub-divided again by height. The prefix "Alto" is added to identify clouds above 6,500ft (2,000m) and the prefix "Cirro" to identify those at cirrus levels. The term Nimbus (or Nimbo as a prefix) indicates rain bearing clouds. The prefix "Fracta or Fracto" means the cloud is broken in nature.

As a general rule, the high level clouds do not affect us directly, though they do of course affect the amount of sunlight reaching the surface and are a valuable indicator of what the weather is likely to do in the next few hours.

The cloud types that directly concern us are, firstly, low stratus clouds. Are they going to cover the hills or cause visibility problems when airborne? A specific type of low stratus is orographic cloud. This is a blanket of cloud that clings to the surface, usually on the windward face of a hill. It is worth pointing out that these clouds can form quite quickly, and if you are already airborne, and notice wisps forming over the surface of the hill, you should land immediately. Orographic cloud forms when the dewpoint is below the level of the hilltop, this is typically the case in early morning on bigger mountains, but as the temperature falls in the evening orographic cloud can form quite quickly, sometimes while you are flying, -creating a potential hazard.

The second type of cloud we are concerned with is cumulus cloud. Cumulus clouds are formed by the condensation of water vapour in rising air (convection) and therefore indicate areas of lift. Where there is lift there is also turbulence, so they also signal caution for the inexperienced pilot.

Cumulus clouds vary from the tiny "balls of cotton wool" that have little or no effect on us, through weak, medium and strong thermal clouds right up to the

Orographic cloud forming on a ridge behind the pilot.. (Photo: U-Turn GMBH)

Valley fog seen from above in the French Alps

Cumulus cloud over the Kyrenia ridge, North Cyprus

Radiant fog over the Yorkshire Dales (Photo: RAD Aviation)

149

dark-bottomed cumulo-nimbus clouds which mark violent updraughts and severe turbulence. *Cumulus clouds are mentioned again under "thermals" and in chapter 26, Cross Country.*

Another cloud type that directly concerns us is a type of alto-cumulus known as a lenticular. Lenticular clouds are easily identified as they are smooth and lens-shaped and they do not move across the sky with the wind. They are usually arranged in "stacks" or as a series of "Bars" at 90° to the wind direction. These clouds mark the presence of atmospheric wave, which is an important source of lift and turbulence. Wave is discussed in detail later in this chapter.

Depressions, fronts and high-pressure systems

The dynamics of weather systems make up an interesting but complex subject that is well explained in several books. Very briefly, the sun heats the earth more in some places than others, for example at the equator and in the middle of the day (where its radiation passes through the atmosphere at almost 90° to the earth's surface) and a much lower angle at the poles, or later in the day. This sets up a circulation as the heated air rises, moves horizontally, cools and then sinks and flows into regions of lower pressure again.

Large continental land masses and large areas of ocean also generate large and predictable airmasses. In some parts of the world this gives rise to regular and settled weather patterns.

In those areas sandwiched between "competing" polar and equatorial systems, or between oceanic and continental regions, the weather is changeable and much more difficult to predict. The UK (as we are only too aware) falls into both

these categories. We can, however, read the weather as it approaches if we have some understanding of the main features.

Depressions and fronts

Depressions or 'Cyclonic' regions are areas of relatively low atmospheric pressure. Air can rise easily in these regions and, as a result, depressions are frequently associated with cloud and rain. Depressions often form where air masses of different temperatures meet. The division between these air masses is known as a front. Because of the different characteristics of the air masses on each side, these fronts may develop "waves" along their length. The actual process is triggered by the Jetstream and is beyond the scope of this book. A wave on a front is the first sign of a depression being created *(Fig 25.2)*. As the depression develops and the airmasses rotate, the pressure drops and the winds increase. The air masses are now arranged in sectors and are divided by a warm front followed by a cold front. As the depression gradually fills and weakens, the cold front overtakes the warm front and the result is an occluded front.

An occlusion can be active, with the warm and cold fronts passing 'back to back', or it can be quite weak especially as the depression is in its later stages and can be marked by no more than a band of high cloud.

To clarify the different characteristics, *Fig 25.3* shows a cross section through a simple example of a cold and a warm front.

As a warm front approaches, cirrus cloud appears, and this cloud gradually lowers and thickens into nimbo-stratus or strato-cumulus; the wind "backs" – that is, swings anti-clockwise, and strengthens.

Fig 25.2:
The formation
of a depression

A katacold front for example is a term describing a situation where the cold airmass is descending and there is therefore less convection and cloud. If you are interested in finding out more about the weather patterns that affect our flying, a list of books is given in the appendix.

As the front passes the rain slackens. Cloudbase rises and the wind "veers" (swings clockwise from south-west to west, for example).

A cold front is marked by active cloud and (often heavy) rain, perhaps even thunder with cumulo-nimbus clouds if the front is an active one. There may be a "gust front" extending well ahead of cu-nim clouds, making flying in their vicinity very dangerous. As the front arrives, the wind increases and veers. After the passage of a cold front the cloudbase rises again and the cold air may give a sharp temperature gradient. This leads to active convection and the formation of cumulus clouds in the cold sector behind the front.

There are differing varieties of front depending on the character of the aimasses involved, their temperatures and relative humidity.

Paraglider pilots do not need to understand how the weather develops in order to fly, but the more we understand, the easier it is to make accurate predictions of what is coming next. This obviously offers benefits both in safety and in saving wasted journeys. Take the potential cross-country pilot: by studying a synoptic chart (one showing depressions with isobars, and fronts represented by broad lines) the pilot can see that there is (say) a north westerly breeze and cold front expected to pass quickly overhead on Friday. This means that by Saturday afternoon he can expect a good temperature gradient (temperature falling rapidly with altitude gain) in the cold sector and, therefore, there are likely to be strong convection currents (thermals). This means good weather for altitude and distance flying.

Another common example is that a pilot noticing cirrus clouds building in the west, sometimes noticeable as a "halo" around the sun, can deduce that a warm front is approaching and that the weather will soon deteriorate. Or you may note

Cold front   **Warm front**

Fig 25.3: Cross-section through typical cold and warm fronts

that although there is little wind now, the day is warm and the coast is nearby so it is likely that a sea breeze will develop.

Fronts are shown as lines on a weather map. These lines indicate the position of the front on the ground. In reality, the gradient of a warm front is around 1° or 2° , so a frontal zone can easily be 150 miles wide. The illustrations have an exaggerated vertical scale so that they will fit on the page!

Remember Buy's Ballots Law – this is a simple rule to help you remember your position relative to a depression. In the northern hemisphere, if you stand with your back to the wind, the centre of the low will be on your left.

High-pressure systems

These are the opposite of depressions. Because the pressure is high there is little rising air. The sky is often cloudless and in the central region there is little wind. If the pressure remains high for some time, dust and dirt in the atmosphere may not be circulated and so the air at low level (often trapped beneath a temperature "inversion", see below) becomes hazy and visibility diminishes. In the winter it may mean mist and fog in low lying areas. If there is sufficient wind to fly, the

conditions are often very smooth, but the lack of any convection means that cross country flying is virtually impossible as all the air is gradually sinking. The airflow around a high-pressure system is in a clockwise direction in the northern hemisphere.

Thermals

The radiation given out by the sun covers a wide spectrum of wavelengths. The heat radiation, however, has very little effect on the atmosphere (unless it happens to be very wet or dirty) and most of it is reflected or reaches the ground. Some surfaces, such as water or green grass, reflect much of the heat and are slow to warm up. Other surfaces, such as dry sand, Tarmac or rocks, absorb heat and may warm quite quickly. This difference in warming is also compounded by uneven ground or aspect (a south facing slope is warmer than a north face, a west face is warmer in the evening and so on), and by other factors.

A result of this differential warming is that the hotter surfaces then radiate their heat warming the air above and around them. Like most other substances, when air is heated its molecules become excited and bounce around more vigorously.

The warm air expands and, in doing so, it becomes less dense. If the sun is still shining and the warming process continues, the "bubble " of warm air will grow larger and larger and become lighter and lighter as its pressure drops.

Eventually, it will break away from the surface and float up through the denser and cooler air around it, gradually cooling as it goes. Ultimately, it reaches a level where the surrounding air is at a similar temperature and pressure, and there it stops.

The warm air very often contains more moisture than the surrounding cooler air, and as the thermal rises it may reach the condensation level (dew point), and a cloud is formed. The condensation level occurs when the parcel of air is cooled to the point of saturation and the moisture it contains condenses as a cloud – air holds less moisture at lower temperatures. The process of condensation is a heat producing reaction, so the thermal receives a final boost, which is one reason why cumulus clouds are heaped up and not just flat.

A thermal may be stopped at a low altitude if there is a layer of warmer air. These layers are known as inversions (because they are inverse to the usual gradient of temperature reducing with height). Very often the temperature does not reduce uniformly as you climb, so the thermal may be rising strongly then slow down, or vice-versa, as it passes through these layers. It is possible to plot the progress of a thermal if you know the temperature gradient. *Fig 25.6* shows a temperature trace for a particular day. As you can see, it generally becomes cooler as you gain altitude. This cooling is known as the lapse rate, and various factors affect this rate.

Dry air has a specific rate of cooling with altitude. This is known as the Dry Adiabatic Lapse Rate (DALR). The DALR is approximately a cooling of 1°C with every 100 metres of altitude (3°C with every 1,000 ft).

There is also a Saturated Adiabatic Lapse Rate (SALR), which is approximately half the dry rate, at 0.5°C per 100 metres (or 1.5°C per 1,000 feet). The saturated lapse rate is the cooling rate of air saturated with water vapour .

In practice the lapse rates vary enormously, due to all kinds of outside factors, and the environmental or ambient air lapse rate more often varies

Cumulus Cloud

Cloud base

Eventual decay

Warm air supply exhausted

Warm air

Fig 25.5: The birth and growth of a thermal to form a cumulus cloud

around the 0.7°C per 100m or 1.5-2°C per 1,000ft mark.

Armed with this knowledge, a temperature trace (or a thermometer and an altimeter) you can predict the climb rate of thermals and the height of the cloudbase.

Pressure also decreases with height. On most weather forecasts the pressure is shown in millibars (mb) or hectopascals (hPa). Both units have identical values and are interchangeable. For our purposes we can assume, pressure drops by one millibar every 30ft or 9.8 metres. In fact it is slightly less than that at sea level and slightly more at 5,000ft.

The solid line on the temperature graph or tephigram (Fig 25.6) shows a temperature trace that is realistic for an "unstable" day with some useful thermals. The broken line is included to illustrate two other features that may occur.

The first is an isothermal layer. This is simply a layer of air that does not change temperature. The second is an inversion – a layer of air that actually increases in

temperature with height. This generally occurs in a region of high pressure – the air has been descending and this process compresses and warms the airmass. Thermals will, of course, be slowed or stopped by such features (depending on the strength and temperature of the thermal relative to the warm layer). This explains why a thermal can suddenly stop or can climb in bursts, or why only one or two thermals from particularly hot sources can penetrate to form clouds. The inversion may be quite high, so thermals can still be felt, even though they never reach high enough to form clouds. Note that the temperature increases again slightly at dewpoint. This is because inside a cloud the process of condensation releases heat and drives the further vertical development of the cloud.

Because the dry and saturated lapse rates are linked, you can determine the strength of a thermal from its vertical development. Towering cumulus clouds mean powerful lift, wispy ones (unless just forming) mean weaker lift.

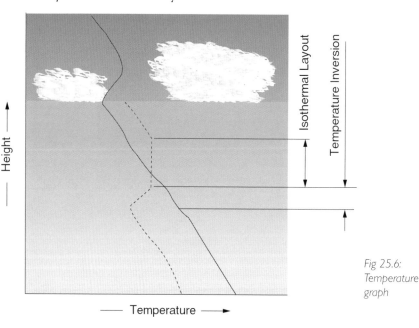

Fig 25.6:
Temperature graph

Wave

Wave, also know as 'mountain' or 'lee' wave is a phenomenon usually caused when the wind is blowing over a series of hills. As we have seen in the section on ridge soaring, the air is accelerated as it is squeezed over the brow of a hill. This process adds energy to the flow. If the hill is solitary, the energy is usually dissipated as airflow downwind of the hill gradually flattens out again into a horizontal flow. Rather like ripples downstream of an obstacle in water. However If there is another into wind slope at the right distance downwind, the energy has no time to dissipate before it is being reinforced by another injection of faster air with a vertical component.

The result of this happening several times is that each fresh input pushes the wave of lifting air higher than the last. *(Fig 25.7)* If there is a layer of stable air above the hills, the process is strengthened as it sinks back quickly after being pushed up by the rising air. The oscillation can then build up a powerful system. It is not unusual for a series of ridges perhaps only a few hundred feet high to set up wave lift extending to 10,000 or 20,000 feet. When the moist low-level air is pushed up to these heights, the moisture condenses and clouds are formed. These

Lenticular cloud over the Yorkshire Dales, UK.

lenticular clouds are arranged along the crest of the wave of air, so are at 90° to the wind direction. Because they are being formed at the front by rising air but then dissipating as the air descends again, they remain stationary. These clouds can cause characteristic lines or 'bars' in the sky.

The crest of the wave may occur some way downwind of the hill that is causing it, hence the term "lee wave". At the bottom of the wave the wind – which may have considerable velocity – may have

Fig 25.7: Formation of a lee wave system and lenticular clouds

Turbulence   Strong wind   Light wind   20,000 ft

to make a sudden change in direction. The result is the same as when there is an obstruction on the ground – the air "tumbles" and forms a rotor. This can result in very severe turbulence. As the windspeed changes the wave position can move very quickly and may suddenly disappear altogether as the hills become "out of phase" for that strength. A spot that was enjoying good lift can be transformed fairly quickly into one that has descending air or even rotor.

Wave may be identified by the changes of windspeed on the ground. It is not unusual to pass trees blowing in a good wind and a few miles further on to see smoke drifting slowly. If you are on a hill and the wind is light but it seems to be strong at altitude or nearby, exercise caution as it is likely that you are in a localised "out of phase" sector.

Once you are actually flying within the rising wave, the lift tends to be very smooth indeed and the greatest heights achieved by hang gliders and paragliders in the UK have been in this form of lift. *Fig 25.7* shows the ideal conditions for wave production: increasing wind strength with height and a suitable set of hills or mountains in phase with the wave length.

Certain conditions seem to favour wave production, in west-south-westerly winds in the north of England for example the wave systems can be seen by satellite photos to sometimes extend as far as the Czech republic! On other days wave has been reported when there are no upwind hills, the "bounce effect" having being set up by frontal systems alone. A good example of this on the western coast of Scotland where the nearest upwind

Wave day at Wether fell in the Yorkshire Dales : Pic Chris Fountain

hills are in North America, yet wave has sometimes been encountered.

Sea-breeze fronts

One other phenomenon that can give excellent flying conditions is a sea-breeze front. On hot, light wind days, the land is much warmer than the sea. As the warmer air over the land gradually reduces in density and pressure, the cooler air from the sea pushes in below it to form an on-shore breeze *(Fig 25.8)*. These breezes may be soarable on coastal sites but the interesting thing is when this onshore breeze contacts a basically offshore wind.

The conflict between these airmasses is resolved exactly like a "normal" weather front, with the lighter warm air flowing up over the wedge of cool dense air. If the coastline is steep or the gradient of the incoming maritime air is sufficient, an invisible ridge is formed which can create sufficient lift to be soarable. When there is no significant obstacle on the ground, the sea breeze can penetrate many miles inland.

Fig 25.8: Sea breeze formation

26 Cross Country

To soar over the open countryside, having to navigate and find lift as you go is one of the greatest challenges and the most memorable experiences of paragliding.

It is scarcely believable that pilots have crossed mountain ranges, jungles and deserts and gained and maintained altitudes of thousands on metres using an aircraft that they can carry in a rucksack.

Having once experienced it, pilots fly in the hope of being able to fly even further next time. Cross-country flights can be achieved using any of the list sources detailed in this book, but typically rely on thermal s. The potential XC pilot must first be able to recognise and be prepared for, the right day.

Preparation

Good preparation is essential. First check the forecast, if it is possible that you might fly a long way, you may need to arrange a plan to get back home afterwards, Plan your likely route. At the present level of performance pilots flying in the UK on a day with any significant wind will be obliged to travel in a predominantly downwind direction. You will need a suitable up to date airchart or a map on which airspace and other hazards should be accurately marked.

Check your instruments. There is nothing worse that the batteries dying in your vario just as you leave the hill behind. Make sure that you are properly clothed; it is far colder at altitude than on the ground. Assuming a fairly typical lapse rate the temperature will drop about

2°C with every thousand feet of altitude. Many early cross-country attempts have been cut short because of freezing fingertips.

Timing

On your first couple of cross-countries it is best to go for it as soon as you get a good climb, especially if there are others in the thermal with you. This is because it is a mental wrench to abandon the hill and the longer pilots wait the more they hesitate, waiting for the perfect thermal.

Once familiar with making the break, the best way to maximise your distance is to choose the best time of day to leave the hill. This varies from site to site, but a rough rule of thumb is with an active sky and thermals growing quickly, try and get away early as the growing clouds may overdevelop into cumulo-nimbus clouds with dangerously strong lift and turbulence, or may thicken or spread into extensive cloud cover putting the ground into shadow and so preventing any new thermal development.

Many of the longest cross-country flights in the Uk are done is spring and early autumn as the cooler air can result in a much longer thermal cycle than in mid-summer. On the other hand, if the thermals are too far apart or the sky downwind is too blue your chance of a reasonable distance may be reduced and

A stunning view over Buttermere in the Lake District on a perfect cross country day (Photo: UK Airsports)

leave lift unless you can see another source within gliding range that will give some advantage.

To fly cross country in any but no wind conditions or in certain timed competitions, the trick is to stay off the ground for as long as possible. Allow the drift of the wind to provide your distance for you, (One top pilot asked about his "secrets" to fly a long distance said "just don't land".)

it may be wiser to wait for conditions to improve. Cloudbase typically lifts during the day, and a higher base means a bigger search radius for the next thermal.

When actually circling in a thermal. Try to fly actively and adjust your flight path to "core" the centre of the strongest lift. The lift may only be temporary and the thermal will be going up faster than you are, so it is easy to get left behind. Every climb is a race to cloudbase before you fall out of the bottom of the thermal. Do not change the direction of your circle, but open out your pattern as the lift weakens and tighten it as it strengthens, try to build a mental picture of the of the lifting area and work hard to maximise your climb rate. Your may be able to fly a little more slowly than usual in strong lift, but be prepared to compensate quickly if you are tightening your turn as you could find yourself close to an incipient spin. This can happen especially if you fly out of the lift into sinking air.

Once at cloudbase there is definite temptation to go speeding off and explore downwind. At a good altitude your groundspeed may seem negligible and many pilots compensate by speeding up. The golden rule with an aircraft as slow and inefficient as a paraglider is never

Another reason not to leave rising air is that it is often surrounded by sinking air and leaving too soon may lose your altitude as fast as you have gained it.

After circling for a few kilometres your cloud finally ceases to lift. Look around for an active cloud to fly towards. With luck any sink will be very slight by this stage and your glider performance will be enough to get you to the next lift source without losing too much height. If there are no obvious clouds waiting for you, study the ground. Is there an area that has been in sunshine for a while? Is there a likely thermal trigger point (a quarry, a small town or a perhaps a windward ridge)?

Always try and be aware of the position of the sun; in the same way as a sunbather trying to get a tan, you need to know where the suns' energy is most intense. This is your fuel source and the sheltered side of a slope that is angled into the sun for instance will be a much better bet than an area where the suns' rays are striking the surface at a shallow angle. Needless to say, if you see a real giveaway such as circling birds or other gliders, that is where to go.

It is worth mentioning at this point that especially on your early XC flights it is far easier if you do not go alone. Another paraglider, or even a hang-glider or sailplane will give you a wealth of information about the position and strength of lifting or sinking air. Almost all long XC flights are achieved when several pilots leave together..

If you elect to go crosswind to a marked thermal or a likely spot, your groundspeed will reduce and if the lift is not as good as you had hoped you may have reduced your distance. For this reason the more cross-wind the target, the surer you need to be that it is worth the cost.

Heading back upwind is rarely a good idea unless the marked thermal is very close or unless you are very low and going for a solid area of lift such as ridge.

If you have no preference, then head directly downwind; this way your chances are as good as any other and you will be covering ground at a better pace.

If the lift is strong, look up. If the cloud is large, or dark and solid looking, or the clouds around you have good vertical development it may be worth flying in a straight line for a while to determine the extent of the lift; you may wish to fly nearer to the edge of the cloud so that you can escape if the lift becomes too severe.

Do not allow yourself to be sucked into cloud. Apart from the possibility of turbulence in powerful clouds, they are also wet, so prolonged exposure will not do your wings performance much good. You will become disorientated in a matter of seconds and the chance of a mid-air collision increases dramatically. If you are very lucky you may find one of those cumulus clouds where it is possible to circle up the side without going

right into it. Climbing above cloudbase on a paraglider is a rare and amazing experience.

Do not forget that you are in uncontrolled airspace (or you certainly should be) and there may be other traffic around. The visual flight rules are see and avoid. Throughout your flight you should scan all around you periodically to make sure no other aircraft are too close. Do not let your eyes become glued to your instruments.

Flying with others

You already know about circling in the same direction as other pilots in a thermal. It is equally important to give those below you plenty of room as they cannot see you very well. If you wish to take any action such as flying away from the core and coming back, make sure you do it is such a way that other pilots can see you and do not have to disrupt their patterns. Never tuck in directly behind another pilot, he cannot see you very well and you may be flying in his wake vortices, which may reduce your control. Always try to stay on the opposite side of a thermal core to another glider at the same altitude. If you have a good pattern established you may get the illusion that you are remaining stationary, rotating on the spot while the other pilot whizzes around you in a huge circle. Don't worry, it looks just the same to them.

The situation is just the same whether you are flying close to a paraglider, hang-glider or sailplane, though be especially careful if you are below the latter and climbing , as they have very poor downward visibility. If you reach cloudbase with other pilots, be very careful not to enter the cloud.

If you are in radio contact with your fellow pilots, it is well worth choosing a side of a cloud and letting them know where you are. Even without contact you can help each other by flying your downwind glide at a reasonable separation distance to increase your chances of contacting lift.

Flying like this in a group is known as "gaggle" flying and is hugely beneficial in maximising the conditions, if one pilot contacts good lift and starts to circle the others can join them to climb out again, and on the next glide the gaggle can separate again and repeat the process.

Thermal and cross-country flying with others is a great shared experience and a good way to improve your skills. In strong or turbulent lift and the poor visibility at cloudbase the risk of mid-air collision is magnified considerably and demands a high level of concentration,

Landing

Never fly cross-country over terrain where you are not within range of somewhere to land safely.

Paragliders can land in a very tight field, compared to any other aircraft, but large bodies of water, or forests, or some other terrain like narrow valleys in windy conditions can find the pilot in a very dangerous situation if they are forced down, especially if no one knows where you are. Deep valleys in particular are a problem as radio transmissions including mobile phones may be affected. Flying too low to glide clear of towns or restricted airspace regions if the lift is lost is not only dangerous but illegal.

In the absence of further lift (or sinking air) If you have a height of 500m and are flying with a 10mph tailwind, that will

give you an effective downwind search "fan" of about 6km and about 7 minutes to reach a suitable landing spot. You require a field that is big enough, and free of crops, livestock and turbulent airflow, and which has an approach which is clear of powerlines or similar obstacles. Lines are hard to see from the air, check for the poles or pylons. Landing late in the day with poor visibility is a big risk as lines become virtually invisible.

Check the wind direction at ground level; this can be surprisingly hard to judge and may have changed since you launched. Cloud shadows and your own drift are good indicators, if possible do a constant aspect approach or if you have enough height a 360° turn above the landing area, and your relative drift will allow you to fine tune your direction as you approach.

After landing from an XC flight always try and make a point of thanking the landowner or farmer if you can find them. This will often result in the offer of a cup of tea in Britain. If it is a sparsely populated area it is may be worth sacrificing a bit of distance to land close to a road. If you have one you may be able to give your retrieve driver your GPS co-ordinates; – or directions from your map if you don't have a GPS. Now all you need to do is get back to your car.

Out and Return flights

In the sailplane world, defined flights or closed cross-country flights have been the norm for many years. They generally take the form of an out and return flight or a defined triangle. The benefits of a long flight where you end up back at your launch point are obvious and as distances steadily increase hang-gliders too are using this option more and more often. As yet paragliders are unable to make any significant progress into a moderate wind, and so in the Uk defined XC flights are most usually cross-wind out and returns, sometimes utilising a mountain ridge system to help position the pilot for the next leg.

In the last couple of years a few top pilots flying the latest competition wings, have started to emulate the very light wind alpine cross-country pattern, and make significant increases in the triangle flights being achieved in the UK , using the more mountainous regions of Britain, particularly the Scottish highlands.

Turn points are recorded either by photographic evidence or for record claims by a suitable GPS track plot.

The progress of our sport has always mirrored Hang-gliding and the defined XC has become one of the major competition tasks and area of significant improvement in performance. Defined XC flights require meticulous planning and careful decision making to be successful.

More information on turn points and camera sectors is given in the section on competition flying.

Navigation

When you fly away from the relative security of a known flying site, it is vital to know precisely where you are, and to negotiate airspace requires and airchart (in fact flying with one is a legal requirement). On longer flights or those aimed a specific goal you may also need to navigate using compass bearings.

Pic: Ozone Gliders

Navigating falls into two categories. Planning and map reading; planning is done before take-off and will consist of following your intended track on an up to date airchart, ensuring you know and have planned for any hazards, and worked out any compass bearings you may need. A very useful exercise especially on defined XC flights is to mark a point perhaps 20% along your intended track to the goal, and time yourself to this point. In this way you can easily calculate your groundspeed and likely remaining time and distance to your goal or turn-point.

Compass bearings are complicated slightly by the fact that the compass with point to magnetic north whereas the grid lines on your map will refer to true north. The difference between these is known as variation. If you look at the map you are using it will tell you the amount of variation in that areas when the map was printed. (This does alter depending on your position and to a lesser extent changes with time as well).

Pic: Neil Cruickshank

Map reading in the air is vital to paraglider pilots. Unlike a powered aircraft we cannot simply stick to our intended track, we tend to go where the lift takes us. If you have done the groundspeed exercise, then knowing the time since launch and your compass heading you should be able to plot your expected position, which you can then confirm with ground features like road junctions.

These functions can of course all be done for you by GPS and more details of using a GPS can be found in the section on instruments.

Until you have done it, it is hard to believe how easy it is to get lost while you are flying, especially if you are over unfamiliar or similar looking terrain, or visibility is not very good. Quite a few top pilots have been known to land in the wrong place simply by navigating inaccurately.

Measuring and recording your flight

After you get home from your epic Cross-country flight you will want to log your distance. Many flight instruments with GPS will have the facility to upload this data to your computer and print out a track log. These can be very interesting and informative to you and some other pilots, though it is just a squiggly line to anyone else!

Many instruments can also give a reading of flight time, height gain and actual distance flown. (As opposed to the straight line distance). In the UK you can log onto the national XC league website and by entering your take-off and landing co-ordinates the site will calculate your distance for you. (You can do this yourself using the Pythagoras theorem to triangulate co-ordinates and calculate the distance between any two points).

Note that for record claims or official competitions you will need a suitable certified flight record.

Flying Cross-country and using an airchart.

As a pilot flying cross-country you will be concerned with searching for lift, flying as efficiently as you can, staying out of cloud, keeping a good lookout for other air traffic and navigating. The following section is a rough guide to what is involved, and using the key information on your airchart to navigate and make decisions as you go. Reading this through in conjunction with the airchart excerpt below should give you some idea of the challenges.

The situation

It is a weekday, but you are due a day off and it is looking like a good cross-country day with light to moderate westerly winds, so after rechecking fthe forecast you set off at 10.00am towards Tailbridge hill on the border of North Yorkshire and Cumbria. A couple of miles from this site is the Northern Paragliding shop, so you drop into see if anyone else is going out and to pick up some new batteries for your vario . You also know that there is a new edition of the Northern England 1:500,000 airchart due and sure enough the nice people there take your card details and fold a new map for you. They also tell you that the school is out training that day and have already NOTAM'd the flying site using the CANP system. (Must remember to that yourself next time).

It is now 12.15 and you can see a few gliders up as you approach the hill. Ten minutes later you are at take- off and the sky is looking good. But before you launch you put the new chart in your map

case, put new batteries in your vario, set your altimeter to zero at take- off, and check your radio. You might note that the take- off is 2,100ft above sea level.

Pre-flight checks done, a quick sandwich and a pee and you are off. It is now 13.00.

13.30 you catch a good solid thermal and care it to cloudbase, you glance at your altimeter which reads 2,500ft. It feels pretty good and you circle at base, drifting with the developing cumulus. If take off was at 2,100ft and you have now climbed a further 2,500ft you are at about 4,600ft above sea level so the VMC requirements are 5km visibility etc. It is a clear day with small to medium puffy cumulus clouds so far, so no problem there, although you know that if you get close to cloud there will be very little reaction time if a jet should be letting down through the clouds.

You are now committed and at about 12kilometers downwind you check your map. The first piece of airspace is coming up soon I it is an airway and a quick look at the map informs you it is at FL 100-190 That is 10,000 to 19,000ft. Your altimeter reads 3,100ft so add that to your take off altitude of 2,600ft and you are now at 5,200ft AMSL. Wow, this is the first time you have climbed to over 5,000ft. It feels good although a bit chilly, and it also means your altimeter is now not very accurate, as above 3,000ft the airspace is defined by flight level.

If you can switch your altimeter to a standard pressure setting, now is the time it would be useful. If not you should have checked the pressure before take-off to allow you to manually set an approximate value. Fortunately on this particular day you are thousands of feet below the base level of the airway, so it is safe to press on. This area is often used for low flying practice by military aircraft and you may see jets passing below you. Almost all low flying training is conducted between 1,000ft and 250ft above the surface. Something to remember when you are on your final glide!

Now you are coming up on a hatched box on your chart. This is a danger area, number 408 to exact, it is up to 2,500ft so lots of room at the moment, but it also says 5.5 OCNL. This means occiasional use to 5,500ft altitude. You are now down to below FL50 according to your altimeter. You do not know if the danger area is active today so you have no choice but to track south a few degrees to avoid it. You get fairly low and switch your altimeter back to QFE, but fortunately there are planty of thermals and pretty soon you are climbing well again, though now your altimeter is only reading 1,500ft QFE. You are crossing a clear visual reference point, the AI / A66 motorway junction at scotch corner and are now approaching the stub of a military air traffic zone. In fact you can just see the huge runway of RAF Leeming to your south. How high is this airspace? A MATZ goes from 1,000ft to 3,000ft AGL. Does that mean I am in it? The altimeter still says 1,500ft QFE but you are obviously much higher above the ground. It was set at 2,100ft at take-off, so what is your height now? You need to know how high the ground is here.

The Lemming ATZ has a number next to it: 132, is that the airfield altitude or the radio frequency?

Radio frequencies have decimal points, so it must be the altitude. 1500ft on your altimeter plus 2,100ft at take-off means that you are at 3,600ft above sea level, the airfield is only at 132ft, so you are still a few hundred feet above the stub of the

MATZ and still in lift so worth going for it.

Of course if the lift dies part way across it is not the end of the world as the MATZ is still OK to penetrate in full VMC, although as it is a weekday the airfield is likely to be active. It is a NW/SE runway so as the wind is westerly today the traffic will be approaching to land from the SE so it is crucial to keep a particularly good lookout in that direction. This is good news for your position, however if any aircraft are visible on the runway it is a good bet they are going to take off in a NW direction, straight towards you.

Just over half way across the MATZ it overlaps Teesside airport CTA. This is category D airspace and so is prohibited to paragliders. It is from 1,500ft height to 6,000ft, so no real chance of climbing over it. But there is still plenty of lift around so rather than abort the flight you can try and track further south to avoid the CTA. It starts about 5km NW of the town of Northallerton which is another clear visual reference point, so a compass heading of 120° should keep you clear. After another 5 km or so you are out of the MATZ and the CTA, but another MATZ (Topcliffe) is looming ahead. You are now losing a bit of height as well so climbing over the stub is looking hard. You can slip under it at below 1,000ft but that only gives you a couple of minutes before you are looking for somewhere to land. A late thermal saves you and hoists you high enough to fly over the stub as before. You are now flying over the North Yorkshire moors and your height above ground is now much less as the terrain is much higher here. To the north you can see sailplanes being launched and the chart shows that this is an active gliding site.

Dead ahead is a very high mast. This is Bilsdale TV transmitter and although it is very high and braced with almost invisible cables it is safe to fly close to it as it not classed as an area of high intensity radiation. You track just to south of this as you can see sailplanes circling in that direction. You circle in weak lift in the company of a sailplane for a few kilometres over a succession of westerly ridges, the chart shows you are heading towards a large cross-hatched circular area. The map says "Fylingdales: See note 3" But you cannot refold your map in mid-air so you do not know if it safe to enter this area. There is no sign of a runway but there is a large and oddly shaped building ahead. Your sailplane friend has headed back upwind at 100kts, so there are no clues there. In fact Fylingdales is an RAF listening station and the hatched area denotes a region of high intensity radio transmission area. This is prohibited airspace. Ideally you should have looked ahead before take off to anticipate all the airspace you may encounter but if you do not know what something is on a chart then your only option is to divert and avoid it or to land.

You glide south cross-wind to get as close as possible to the main road for an easier retrieve, and just possibly pick up another late thermal, but soon it is all over and as you touch down you notice your QFE altimeter now reads minus 1,100ft.

This example is based on a real flight and gives a good idea of how important it can be to have an up to date chart, a properly set altimeter and a compass in order to be able to make well informed and safe decisions about your cross country flight. It also shows how a few minutes spent planning a possible flight and with the luxury of looking up notes, or anticipating airspace and other hazards can dramatically reduce your workload in the air, making it much easier to concentrate on staying up.

If you have local flying sites that you expect to go cross-country from, it is worth planning a broadly downwind track and identifying hazards in this way for each site.

27 The Polar Curve

Pilots and instructors spend quite a bit of time discussing the performance of their paragliders, but it is sometimes difficult to visualise how to obtain the best from it in various situations.

Fortunately it is possible to gather various bits of information from tests that let us know for example that this model sinks at a rate of 1.4 metres per second at 17mph and so on. When we have sufficient data we can plot them on a graph and the result is a performance "map" of the craft. This graph is known as a polar diagram *(Fig 27.1)*.

The polar curve of a craft is time-consuming and painstaking to produce, but once drawn, it allows us to predict the glider's performance and so helps both designers and pilots.

If we wish to know our sink rate at 20kph we can simply read off the figure where the sink rate axis corresponds to 20kph. Our best (i.e lowest) sink rate is at the highest point on the graph, and our best glide ratio in nil wind is at the

point where a straight line drawn from 0mph on the axis just intersects the curve *(Fig 27.1)*.

We can also discover the performance in different situations. For example, if the canopy sinks at 1.2m/sec at 19kph, but we have a headwind of 13kph, how fast should we fly to achieve our best gliding (ie distance over the ground) performance? We can plot this by drawing another straight line that just touches the curve but is drawn from the 13kph point on the horizontal speed axis *(Fig 27.1)*. You can now apply the same technique to assess the performance of the craft in any combination of lifting or sinking air, headwind or tailwind.

The fact is that the useful speed range on a paraglider is very small and a slight variation in your airspeed is not very significant compared to the options available to a hang-glider or a sailplane, but even a small advantage can pay big dividends in cross country flight or competition.

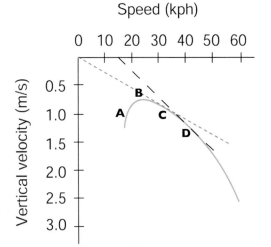

Fig 27.1: The polar curve

A = *Point of stall at 18km/h*

B = *Minimum sink 0.75m/s at 23km/h*

C = *Maximum glide at 32km/h with 0.8m/s sink rate*

D = *Best speed to fly with a 13km/h headwind (=40km/h)*

What does this actually mean to us in practice? Scrutinising a typical paraglider polar diagram, it soon becomes apparent that in sinking air or a headwind, adding speed is a good idea if you wish to make progress over the ground, but in lifting air or a tailwind it is usually better to fly at trim speed or minimum sink.

In practical terms, the polar tells us that, in sinking air (of say 300ft/min), you should be using your speed bar for best glide results, however glide is not everything, if you are still airborne because you are flying more slowly you still have a chance to connect with a fresh area of lift, – a good fast glide may take you further but it will inevitably put you on the ground sooner.

Because of this pilots actually use the knowledge of their gliders polar curve in conjunction with their reading of the

likely strength and frequency of thermals, and of course their requirements… a pilot racing to a goal line has a different priority to one who is trying to gain height in a specific area before crossing a hazard like controlled airspace.

Perhaps the most useful tip to glean from looking at our gliders polar curve is that in sinking air or headwinds, a lot of pilots still tend to fly too slowly for best performance.

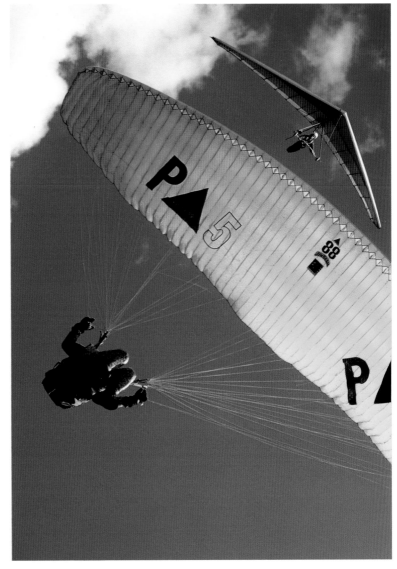

The minimum sink rate performance of hang-gliders and paragliders is very similar. However a paraglider benefits from a lower minimum airspeed whereas a hang-glider has much better high speed performance.
(Photo: DW Photography)

28 Instability and recovery

A paraglider canopy is virtually unique among aircraft in that it relies upon the weight of the pilot to maintain its shape and, therefore, the structural integrity of the wing. If the weight is reduced, removed or distributed wrongly, the wing may collapse.

The aerofoil shape is maintained by internal air pressure, which in turn relies on a certain amount of airspeed, and maintaining a limited range in the angle of attack between the wing and the airflow. If this pressure is reduced or lost, the wing is prone to distortion and collapse.

These factors are in addition to the usual characteristics of any aerofoil when stalled. It is therefore vital that the pilot understands his craft's behaviour and is able to help prevent, or anticipate, any problems. The pilot must also be capable of taking the correct action to help the wing recover promptly should he find himself in an unstable situation.

Dealing with turbulence

Prevention is better than cure. Before discussing how to recover from unstable situations, it is worth trying to understand how they can occur and how to prevent them. Gusts, thermals and turbulent air are invisible: the only way you have of detecting them (apart from basic site and weather assessment, of course) is by feel. Flying in rough air is all about feeling the canopy and reacting very quickly to the feedback it is giving you.

The first rule is to maintain some pressure on the controls all the time in rough air. This gives you the option to speed up or slow down and also serves to "pressurise" the canopy to some extent, helping to minimise wing tip tucks, etc.

The second rule is to try to keep the canopy directly above your head! This requires active input from you and is known as active flying.

GUST

Fig 28.1: Active flying dealing with gusty conditions.
1. Flying around mid-brake position
2. Encounters gust – canopy pitches back – brakes high to provide speed.
3. Flying into lull behind gust – canopy pitches forward – brakes applied to slow canopy down.
4. Return to normal level flight.

The most common situation is that the wing suddenly surges forward. The reason could be a shear (the interface between two airmasses moving in different directions), a vertical component from behind or a lull (sinking air) in front of you, on exit from a thermal for example. Your reaction must be to very quickly apply the correct amount of brake to arrest the surge, and prevent it turning into a dive.

If the wing manages to dive forwards and get ahead of you, the angle of attack will get too low, and the next thing to happen is that it will lose pressure as the lines go slack and it will start to collapse along the leading edge. For this reason damping the dive may take a quick and deep application of brake.

Sometimes a head-on gust or thermal will try to push the canopy back increasing the angle of attack, you can react to this by adding speed, but be careful – where there is a gust there is usually a lull behind it and you do not want to hit that at full speed just as gravity is swinging you back under the canopy. So be ready to brake again the moment the canopy starts coming back. Inexperienced pilots often make this situation worse by speeding up at the wrong moment, so a safe course of action is to maintain 30% brake pressure and simply let the glider re-establish normal attitude.

Thirdly, maintain your course. Do not allow turbulence (or a tuck) to turn you without countering it with both weight-shift and the opposite brake. It is not always easy to identify what is causing you

to turn, but your reaction should be the same, – try to maintain your direction with a combination of weight-shift and a normal turn brake input.

If it has collapsed, then use weight-shift and some opposite control to hold course, most A & B rated glider require no more than this, but if the tuck is not clearing itself, depress the brake deeply and

Large assymetric collapse during glider testing (Photo: Swing Gliders)

smoothly on the collapsed side until you feel contact with the wing again and then let it back up again. It may take more than one of these "pumps" to clear the tuck.

If you begin to lose pressure on both controls when braking deeply, let up smoothly as you may be approaching the stall.

If the canopy surges upwards and forwards then you have encountered a thermal. If it surges upwards and backwards it is probably a gust. If you do not feel in control of the situation do not hesitate to land and fly again another day – don't forget you are doing this for fun!

CAUTION – while it is desirable to be practiced and competent at recovery from stalls, spins and tucks, it is recommended that before undertaking any of these manoeuvres you receive on-site briefing from an experienced pilot or instructor. Practice them over water, carry a reserve parachute system and allow a one hundred per cent margin for error when estimating the height and space required for recovery.

Asymmetric tuck

This is perhaps the most common situation. Some of the outermost cells at one end of the canopy depressurise and collapse while the other side is still flying. Tucks can be small, involving just a few cells like a single big ear, and these will self- recover almost immediately, a mid range tuck of up to 50% of the wing, will require pilot input to hold course, or they can be quite severe, tucks of 60% and

more will cause the wing to turn steeply toward the collapsed side and start to dive.

Recovery

If the canopy is turning towards the collapsed side and especially if there is a danger of collision with the hill or with another pilot, immediately apply some opposite weight shift, and opposite brake control to arrest or slow the turn. Be careful not to overbrake; it is possible to stall the remaining wing in this way and make the situation worse. If you can maintain direction then that is best, but even if you are still turning slightly, the wing will start to reinflate.

If the wing is slow to re-inflate, you can help. Give a long, firm pull on the control on the collapsed side. This forces air forwards and opens the cell entries to the airflow. When part of the wing is deflated, the controls on the collapsed side may have little air to move, and this deep pumping action helps force air through the internal cross-port vents in the cell walls, from the inflated to the deflated side.

If the collapsed area is 75% or more of the wing, it will surge forward and down, and damping the dive becomes your priority, so brake on both sides.

Full front tuck

This occurs when the even load on the canopy is disturbed, either if the pilot goes weightless for a moment in turbulent air, or if the canopy dives forward to the point where the load on the front lines is substantially reduced, this can happen in strong turbulence, such as exiting a powerful thermal or rotor, or if the canopy has lost energy in a manouevre such as a wingover or diving forward in a stall recovery.

Give a firm deep pull on both the controls; This stops the canopy surging forwards whilst your weight swings back under the wing and also helps prevent the leading edge curling under. As the weight is reapplied, the canopy will re-inflate almost instantly.

Full (dynamic) stall

This occurs when the canopy loses virtually all forward airspeed and, consequently, internal pressure. It can only be induced by "flaring", that is by applying full brake on both sides, very rarely it could be caused by very extreme turbulence or because of a build up snow or rain in the canopy.

In the stalled state the canopy produces no lift but a large amount of drag and it falls behind the pilot, if caused by heavy braking it will usually drop back tips first in a "horseshoe" shape.

Recovery

Firstly wait – you are much heavier than the canopy and you will swing back to a relatively normal position below it. If you have induced the stall, keep the controls depressed. If you let up too soon, the sudden reduction of drag just as the canopy is swinging forwards anyway may cause he canopy to dive down in front of you and tuck. Once the wing is stabilised in a position above you (though still collapsed) smoothly, let up the controls to about 30 per cent. The wing will try and

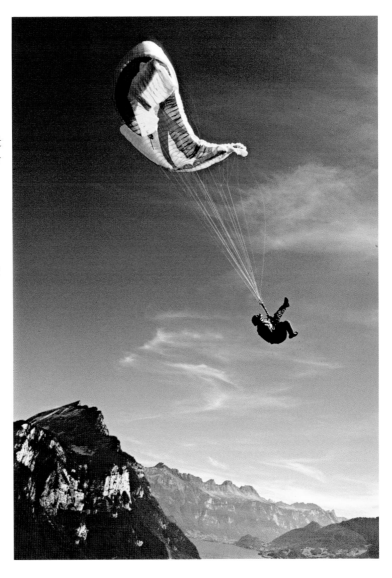

*A dynamic full stall
(Photo: Swing Gliders)*

surge forward and re-inflate. Be prepared to brake again to damp the dive if the canopy tries to overfly you. The worst thing is to overreact to a stall and let the brakes up suddenly or all the way.

Caution: Some canopies "dislike" being in the horseshoe mode and thrash about above you, so care must be taken as they may recover unevenly and enter a spin.

Deep (parachutal) stall

A small number of canopies can be stabilised in a deep stall. This is the state in which the canopy has little forward motion and the airflow over it is predominantly turbulent, creating no lift. However, the wing retains its shape and does not collapse. Its sink rate is very fast and normal control inputs are ineffective as there is little airflow over the controls. Some canopies can be deep stalled through gradually increasing braking. Others can only reach this state through stalling on the rear risers or poor recovery from B lining or big ears. Old gliders on which the fabric has become too porous are prone to deep stall. It can also occur if snow or sand find their way into the trailing edge of a wing.

If you experience a deep stall, it is worth having your glider checked for line shrinkage or porosity.

Recovery

Some models can be recovered by vigorously depressing one brake. The canopy enters a turn, gains airspeed and resumes normal flight. The other recovery technique is to brake with both controls and cause the glider to rock back into an incipient full stall then release, allowing the glider to surge forward into normal flight.

Spins

A spin is an unstable state where half the wing is stalled and half is flying. This causes the canopy to rotate violently, often on its own axis. There is a risk of the canopy collapsing (half of it may be flying backwards) and it is possible for the lines to become twisted between the canopy and the pilot. A spin is induced when the paraglider is flown at a high angle of attack (ie with deep brake) and then the controls are simultaneously raised on one side and depressed on the other. This can happen through poor thermalling technique or "scratching" the commonest situation is an inexperienced pilot inadvertently spinning when flying a downwind leg too close to a ridge, (confusing groundspeed with airspeed and so flying with marginal airspeed and then trying to turn tightly).

Changing to a higher performance wing with shorter brake travel, 360° turns that are suddenly tightened to avoid the terrain or another pilot, or pilots' reacting poorly to a tuck and overbraking on one side can also sometimes cause a spin.

Recovery

Let up both controls to gain speed. As the wing regains flying speed, steer out of the turn.

Caution: It is possible to gain considerable airspeed in a spin and on recovery you must be prepared to damp out any tendency for the canopy to surge forwards as this can result in a tuck.

In a severe spin, or one with a tuck, your lines may become twisted. While this may be recoverable given time and altitude, if in doubt the best course of action is to deploy your reserve.

Other manoeuvres

360° turns

This is simply flying around in a circle. 360's are worth noting because they involve flying on a downwind leg (if there is any wind). Therefore, some planning is required – how far downwind will the drift be, etc. A 360 is particularly useful for approaching some landing areas, and for thermalling, where you can drift at the same speed as the thermal and so stay with it as it moves.

Inexperienced pilots are sometimes caught out when attempting 360 turns in ridge lift, and end up too close to the hillside or too far behind the edge. Always allow a lot more height and space than you think you will need when doing 360's in wind and close to hillsides.

Spiral dives

A spiral dive is simply a series of tight 360° turns. It is very inefficient and so the canopy can lose height very rapidly – very useful for getting down quickly or combating strong lift. A spiral dive is induced by strongly depressing one control and raising the other, gradually steepening the turn until the pilot is swung out from the canopy which can eventually be at almost 90° to the ground.

Recovery

To recover normal flight from a spiral dive, simply ease up on your input and gradually reduce the turn radius and angle of bank, this should be done over at least one and preferably two further 360° turns.

Caution: when recovering from a spiral dive you may have excessive airspeed. A canopy that may have a top speed of

Spiral dive from below

say 45kph without accelerator in normal flight may reach 65kph-plus in a 2g spiral) The canopy must be " damped" as you exit gradually. If you exit quickly by opposite braking, the wing converts this energy into a climb, or you may either stall at the top of the climb-out or the canopy may tuck as the load on the front risers is momentarily reduced. Finally the increased G force can affect your depth perception and you may be closer to the ground than you think. For these reasons a spiral dive should always be aborted with plenty of altitude remaining.

In short it is a great way of getting from 3,000ft to 1,000ft but a bad way of getting from 500ft to the ground.

"Big ears"

This is the common name given to the practice of deliberately collapsing the calls at the tips. This has the effect of reducing the flying surface and so increasing the sink rate. It can be very useful indeed for combating strong lift (unlike a spiral dive it can be done at lower altitudes and without involving drifting downwind). Modern canopies are "big eared" by pulling down on the outermost one or two A lines on each side to induce the outermost cells to tuck.

Big ears (Photo: U-Turn GMBH)

Almost all modern designs feature a separate "mini" riser or split A risers that give a convenient handhold for performing big ears.

Always pull strongly but smoothly and, always close one side, wait a moment for the wing to stabilise, and then close the other. To re-inflate the tip cells simply release the risers or lines. If the ears do not clear themselves, you can "pump" the controls as you would for a minor tuck. Again it is wise to do this on one side at a time.

Note: When in "big ears" mode the wing loading, and the drag of the canopy is increased and therefore the the wing is closer to the stall point. To add additional drag by pumping the controls in this situation can quickly induce a stall. For this reason it is recommended that ears are not cleared by pumping both controls.

For the same reason, do not use big ears when flying though turbulence or wind shears or in close proximity to the ground. See the notes below on using your Ears and speed bar together.

"B" line stall

Some canopies can also be made to sink very quickly in a stable state by pulling down the centre (B) risers and "breaking the back" of the canopy. This disrupts the airflow and destroys the aerofoil

"B" lining is a useful manoeuvre to lose height quickly. However, there are some potential problems. Some canopies will remain deep stalled, particularly if the pilot lets up very slowly. During a B line stall, all the weight is through as little as six lines: that can put terrific strain on the lines and the attachment points. Know your canopy: always release smoothly but quickly and in the case of being stuck in a deep stall use a dab of deep brake and then let up to allow the wing to surge forward. This will re-establish a correct airflow and the canopy will recover. If you pull very hard on the B lines the tips may come forward, forming a forward horseshoe shape, and descent will be very rapid. Before attempting this, check the canopy's suitability with your instructor, dealer or manufacturer. If the canopy starts to turn during this manoeuvre the pilot may be tempted to try and turn by letting up one riser more than the other. Do not do it. The canopy may enter a spin in this way. If the wing is turning, you must recover to normal flight before attempting to steer.

Front centre line stall

Like the B line stall, this breaks the back of the canopy, but fore and aft rather than across the span. This places a great strain on the centre lines. This manoeuvre is rarely performed, as it has no useful purpose. The same provisos apply as for B lining.

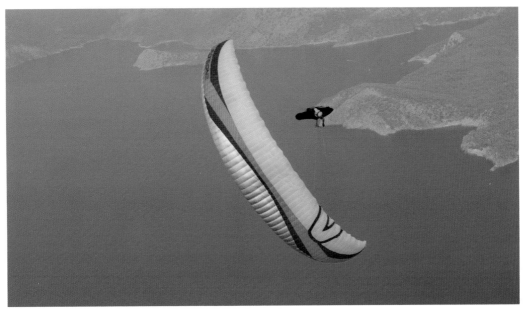

Wing overs. (Photo: Skywalk GMBH)

Wing-overs

By reversing the controls and using radical weight shift a paraglider can be speeded up to the point where there is sufficient energy to make a past vertical turn (ie with more than 90° of bank) and still remain fully inflated and flying normally. This is a wing-over.

Pilots who are skilled at performing wing-overs can achieve angles of bank of 130° or more.

Caution: wing-overs should never be attempted close to the ground, it is a very dynamic manoeuvre and a small loss of energy, or miscalculation can result in a violent impact.

Mixing it up.

It can be very dangerous to combine manoeuvres as this can place the wing in a situation outside its tested envelope – spirals with ears in, for example, can seriously overload a wing and has led to in-flight failures.

However in the hands of a skilled pilot the energy from a big wingover can lead straight into a tumble (loop) or a spin can be controlled in a "helicopter" descent. This discipline is Acrobatic flying or "Acro" and requires a lot of skill, altitude, and good equipment. There is more on Acro flying in Chapter 39 *Pushing the limits.*

Big ears and Speed bar together.

The exception for most pilots is combining big-ears with using the speed system, which is a useful and effective way to deal with strong lift or wind. However if you apply ears with your speed bar already extended you run a greatly increased risk of a tuck, so it is important that you apply the ears first and then speedbar. If you tried speed bar first, this means you need to bend your knees and let it off for a few moments while you close the ears before reapplying pressure to the speed bar.

29 Emergency Procedures

These fall into two distinct categories – equipment failure and "sticky situations". Both can almost invariably be prevented by pre-flight checks and good flight planning. The piece of equipment most likely to let a pilot down is between his ears!

Equipment failure

Broken or lost control line

A limited form of steering is available by adding pressure to the rear riser. All canopies can be well controlled by weight shift. As it is difficult to flare with the rear risers alone you should be prepared for a fast landing which may mean running or a PLF.

Other damaged lines

Generally, a paraglider will fly quite well with only a couple of lines missing (though it may have a tendency to turn). However the increased strain the next line connection point may cause it to fail, and broken lines have resulted in a cascade failure where the whole wing has "unzipped". Fly gently, land as soon as possible and have them replaced. If a lot are broken, after a mid air collision, for example, throw your reserve.

Major damage to the canopy, harness or connections

If you have any control, it is best to fly down as best you can. The only other option is to throw your reserve, which, of course, can neither be steered nor flared.

Canopy inextricably twisted or tangled due to spin, severe turbulence or mid air collision

Deploy your reserve, subject to the provisos above.

Deploying a reserve

Once you have decided you are in trouble do not hesitate. Grab your reserve handle and pull hard; the reserve in its deployment bag should be hanging from the strap in your hand. Fling it away from your body; this will certainly be a weak throw as your body swings away in reaction, so the reserve will drop away until the lines reach full stretch and the deployment bag opens. If it does not open for some reason grab the bridle and tug it hard, this should shake the bag off the canopy itself. As the air channel fills the reserve will snap open with tremendous force and you will feel yourself pulled hard by the shoulders. The main canopy will tend to dive forward and may well go below you. If you can grab a bit of leading edge or trailing edge, do so, as it will minimise the paraglider re-inflating or thrashing around.

If you do have to deploy the reserve during a spin, always try to throw it in the direction of the spin, as it is less

Reserve deployment (Photo: Sup'Air)

likely to get twisted up. Avoid throwing it between your legs. If you have time, you may be able to collapse the main canopy even if you missed the fabric, by pulling in the lines until the canopy itself can be grabbed. When approaching the ground, assume the position for a Parachute landing fall.

Sticky situations

Poor penetration: Being blown back over a hill

If you feel you are losing forward penetration it is important you act quickly as the further back you go the fewer your options.

First check that any trim devices are fully off and that the controls are at maximum speed (against the keepers). Apply your speed-bar. If your speed-bar does not provide sufficient penetration alone, let it off, apply your ears, then apply the speed-bar again, with your ears in. Your forward speed will increase slightly and your descent rate markedly. If these ploys do not work, you are committed to top land.

Look back over your shoulder. Can you land safely in the area where you will end up? If so, wait until the touch-down and the turn and run after the canopy, collapsing it as you go. (a rear riser collapse is best). If the area looks unsuitable, try to track to the most suitable spot within range.

Flying right off the end of a ridge might be an option. If the area behind you is really diabolical, such as a cliff top or a spine backed ridge, and you have any significant height, continue to soar the ridge at minimum sink speed, trying to gain as much height as possible. You may find that the lift extends a good way behind the crest. When you are as high and as far back as possible,

turn downwind and make a run for it, retaining a little brake and being prepared for turbulence as you fly through any rotor.

Note: if you have any control as you approach the ground, try to establish the wind direction. If you are in rotor, it may be from any direction. Be prepared to PLF.

Remember that the above situation need never occur if you assess conditions properly, treat ridges with poor top landings with respect and leave a greater margin for error. Be aware of changing weather. If penetration does seem to be reducing, land quickly or at least stay well forward of the ridge or track to one end of the ridge where flying out of the lift is possible if required.

Water landings

Once again, the emphasis here is on prevention through good flight planning, rather than cure. However, if you should find yourself in a situation where a water landing is inevitable, try to prepare before you touch down.

I   Take off your gloves if you are wearing them.

2   Undo your chest strap – the harness will feel strange as the risers are now further apart but you will not fall out unless you lean right forwards.

Water landing!

3 If you have time you can also slacken or even undo your leg straps.

4 Land as normal, but ensure that the canopy does not end up on top of you. This is best achieved in light winds by flaring very little. If there is any wind, land cross or downwind and allow the canopy to fall in front of you. It will then stay full of air.

5 Wriggle out of, or unbuckle the leg straps. Try to avoid the lines.

6 If you are well away from land, you can use the canopy as a float by trapping air in the cells. It also acts as an efficient marker for any rescue attempt.

If you habitually fly near water, carry a hook knife. These can slice through your lines or risers in seconds and free you if necessary. Avoid surf; it is probably better to land hard and PLF downwind on a beach than get caught in moderate surf as you could be tangled up and pulled around quite easily.

Note: It has been advised to jump out of your harness completely if you are committed to landing in water, whilst this sounds good in theory, the fact is it is very hard to judge your height over a large body of smooth water, and at least one pilot has been seriously injured by bailing out too early and suffering a severe impact with the water.

Water is about 600 times denser than air, so a wing full of water will weigh tons… paraglider lines will float and tangle around you very easily. If you do end up in the water (especially if there are waves) the best advice is to get away from your wing. A canopy can only be safely recovered by gradually pulling it into a boat or onto a beach, emptying the water as you go.

A pilot has been drowned whilst attempting to gather up and swim in to shore with his paraglider in the Canary islands. Even though he had shouted to onlookers he was Ok after landing.

Tree landings

If you hit a tree, hit it hard and hang on. Pilots will instinctively aim for a path or clearing even it is too small to land in. In fact the main danger is not in hitting a tree, but in falling out of the tree or getting pulled out of it by a gust of wind. So the safest course is to land firmly and hang on to a solid branch.

Keep your legs together. Try to protect your eyes; turn your head or use one forearm. Gather in the canopy quickly if you are able to, or release yourself from it. Again a hook knife is a potential life saver if you habitually fly over trees.

Nesting season comes early at the Dune de Pyla!

Power lines

Do not hit power lines. It is worth taking virtually any avoiding action including stalling at low level or crashing downwind to ensure that you do not contact power lines. Two broken legs are preferable to 40% burns or death, both of which have been the results of pilots tangling with power lines in recent years. If "hung-up" or assisting another pilot, it is essential to wait for the power to be properly cut off by the authorities before attempting to get down or start helping. Many power lines have an automated system that switches the power back on to attempt to "blow" branches off the lines. Even a broken cable on the ground can kill you if you approach too closely by transmitting the voltage through the earth.

Power lines are a major hazard if you are flying in poor visibility, at dusk they virtually disappear against the ground when approached from above. Sunset flights and power or 'phone lines are a toxic mixture.

Even Low Tension power lines (the type mounted on poles rather than pylons) carry a current sufficient to kill you 100 time over. Frightened? You should be!

Snow and heavy rain

Should it begin to snow or rain heavily while you are flying, lose height and land as quickly as possible. A weight of snow or water building up inside the trailing edge of the canopy can affect its flying characteristics and possibly cause an unrecoverable stall.

Flying in cloud

If you should find that a powerful cloud is sucking you upwards, the preferred method of losing height is a B line stall or a spiral dive. If these are ineffective, the cloud must be a cu-nim or strong wave. The up-currents and turbulence within

Clouds such as this giant cumulo-nimbus are capable of sucking a paragliders to unsurvivable altitudes

clouds of this type can be severe. Induce a full stall and hold it until you have lost sufficient altitude. Do not throw your reserve in very strong lift. A spiral or stall will get you down much more effectively and safely.

Accidents

The best thing to do about accidents is avoid them! Most accidents are recorded and the statistics are published. Here is a summary of how to hugely reduce the chances of having an accident.

- Do not fly in strong winds or rough conditions.

- Get proper instruction.

- Buy equipment the right size and skill level for you.

- Only buy equipment with a Certificate of Airworthiness. Have it serviced annually.

- Don't show off "hot dogging" near others in the air or on the ground.

- Wear decent boots, a helmet, a harness with back protection and carry a reserve parachute.

- Do not attempt instability manoeuvres over land.

- Do not take delivery of your new wing just before a trip to a new area or a competition. Get used to it on familiar territory.

- Never take off from lower down on a hill because it is too strong on top.

- Be very cautious of flying slowly close to a hill when the wind is "off".

- Take local advice.

- Never fly to impress others.

- Always pre-flight check and take good care of your equipment.

- Do not fly in strong winds or rough conditions.

Accidents do sometimes occur (often for one of the reasons above). If you suffer, or witness an accident (or an "incident"), it is essential that you report it. The reasons are self evident: if the national safety committee discovers that a large number of a certain type of canopy are involved in similar accidents or close shaves, then it can take some action to prevent a repetition. If each incident is considered unimportant and ignored, then obviously the problem will persist for much longer before coming to light.

The same applies to tightening up some aspect of training, etc. An accident that is not reported promptly may also jeopardise any subsequent insurance claim. Your club safety officer or instructor will have report forms for this purpose, or they can be accessed on the BHPA Website.

Incidents that should be reported

- Those involving any injury, either to pilot or third party.

- Those involving any damage.

- Those in which an insurance or legal claim may arise.

- Those in which any equipment failed to function.

- Those involving use of non standard procedures or training.

- Anything that may highlight safety points or was unusual.

Actions after an injury or fatality

- Administer first aid.

- Call an ambulance / rescue services (mountain rescue can be reached through the usual emergency services number).

- Call police (essential if fatal).

- Do not disturb equipment.

- Photograph any equipment in the area.

- Take names and addresses of witnesses or bystanders. Inform the next of kin, or (in the case of fatalities) ensure that the police do so

- Inform the national association without delay

The numbers of the BHPA Safety and Development Officer and the Chairman of the Safety and Training Committee are published in the monthly magazine, Skywings, or your instructor or club committee will have them.

Administering first aid

It is beyond the scope of this manual to cover all but the most basic first aid, but there are some practical points that are worth noting. Injuries generally fall into three categories:

Slight injuries
That is to say that the injured person is not in any great danger. If there is any doubt at all, these people should still be referred to hospital. Very often, the shock of an injury and the wish to be OK makes the person belittle or not appreciate the damage. Many "sprained" ankles and "badly bruised" arms turn out to be fractured. Someone should always stay with the patient until they are passed into someone else's care.

Major injuries
Major fractures or a combination of injuries are dangerous, not only in themselves, but because shock can kill (particularly out on a cold hillside for long periods). Administer first aid as soon as possible. DO NOT attempt to move the casualty and make sure that the emergency services are told about

the location and injuries. If you need a helicopter, or mountain rescue service ask for it. Do not wait for the emergency services to arrive before informing them that you are up on a mountain miles from the road.

If you are in a remote location, station people at the road/track junction to help direct the ambulance to you. A canopy offers insulation and excellent protection from the elements. If a helicopter is called for, make sure that the area is cleared of unpacked canopies etc. A canopy left out, well weighted down with stones is a useful marker.

Extremely serious/fatal injuries
In addition to the steps above, you must contact the police and BHPA straight away. Do try to take photos of the site and the equipment. Do not disturb any of the equipment if possible. The police will want to see it "in situ". Make sure that the names and addresses of witnesses are taken (this includes bystanders as well as other pilots).

Important basics

A.B.C. This stands for Airway, Breathing and Circulation which are your priorities.

Airway
Make sure an unconscious casualty's airway is clear (head back, neck extended and chin lifted), and obstructions – teeth etc – are removed

Check for breathing
If the unconscious casualty is breathing, you must be poised to move them into a position where their airway is open, and able to drain fluid (The "recovery" position). If on a slope the head must be lower than the body). If you suspect a spinal injury which is likely in the case of a paraglider impacting a hillside you must take great care to rotate the whole body and neck at the same rate, this requires

at least three people and preferable more. If they vomit or have blood in the mouth then they must be moved before they choke.

If they are not breathing : You should call for help immediately. Once help is on its way commence CPR (chest compressions) .These should be at the rate of about 80 per minute. If you have been trained then you can also add rescue breaths at a rate of 2 breaths every 30 compressions, but these are far less important than the chest compressions.

Circulation

If a casualty is bleeding badly, then apply direct pressure by gripping the wound firmly. Elevate the wound as high above the heart as you can and get plenty of padding to try and stop the bleeding.

Fluid loss is the prime cause of shock. If the casualty is lying on a hill or mountainside, or is obviously badly injured, do not attempt to move him unless it is necessary to keep him breathing, as he may have spinal injuries. Do not remove helmets (unless required to do mouth to mouth). If the casualty is breathing, but unconscious, and you do not suspect spinal injuries, place him in the recovery position.

Keep him warm and if he is conscious, try to keep him that way. Keep a note of his condition (level of consciousness, pulse etc) – it may help the medical services.

Many clubs run first aid courses. It is always useful to try and make an effort to attend one: there are few feelings worse than helplessness in a situation such as this.

*Once a casualty's heart has stopped completely it cannot be re-started except by a defibrillator. Statistics complied by the paramedic services in Scotland show that CPR can move enough blood to keep the brain functioning longer than if CPR is not given, by several minutes.

However, without a defibrillation shock being applied within about 15 minutes of the heart stopping, the fatality rate is virtually 100%. (The rare exceptions are people who have been "frozen" by drowning in freezing water.)

This means that if a casualty is (say) 20 minutes or more from a paramedic unit and their heart has stopped completely then there is little point in continuing CPR for prolonged periods.

A pilot with a broken pelvis is prepared for airlift to hospital

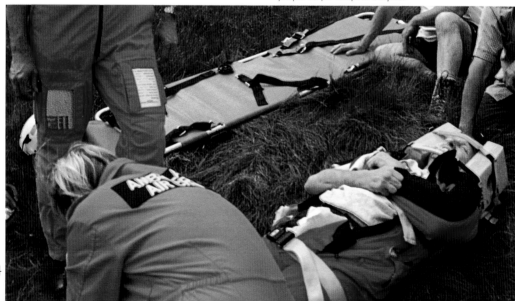

Human Factors **30**

Safety is a primary concern of schools, instructors and of most pilots. Ensuring your safety is essentially a question of controlling the variable factors as far as you can. It is possible to ensure your equipment is suitable and in good condition; you cannot control the weather, but you can decide when and where to fly. However, even with perfect weather, a great flying site and good equipment accidents do sometimes happen. In many accidents and incidents the prime cause is simply "Pilot Error" -arguably the most difficult factor to assess are the human factors: to put it simply, your own decision making and capability.

A crucial element of being a safe pilot is effectively assessing yourself.

This process starts when you first consider taking up the sport, pilots choose to fly for many reasons, one of these is simply ego, we all take pleasure in mastering a new skill and the approbation of others. Another is risk, humans are natural gamblers, and taking a risk and winning is a very satisfying activity. The sensation of flying like a bird, looking down at the terrain flowing past below you is almost irresistible to many of us, and for all these reasons paragliding is very satisfying and almost addictive to some people.

Because flying, especially in the early stages is an alien activity to us we require a high degree of concentration and focus to absorb the new skills, it is important

Pic: Skywalk Gliders

that we are not overloaded and changing a lot of things at one like a new site, glider and exercise together is a classic recipe for things to go wrong.

To fly safely it is important that we understand ourselves and manage the human factors that affect our decisions and performance.

Preparedness is vital, having a routine for pre-flight checking, and including a "self check" – am I ready for this?

A safe pilot must be able to honestly evaluate their own preparedness to fly, and decision making ability. If you follow a pre-flight check routine, one item on your check list is "am I OK?" Do take a moment to think seriously about this. It is just as crucial as doing up the buckles on your harness. If you are ill, tired, emotional or frightened, it will impact on your ability to fly safely. One paramotor pilot is now short of two fingers, purely because they allowed their normal pre-flight check to be interrupted by a bystander asking questions, and missed out his check of the throttle cable which turned out to be jammed open.

Pre-flight check routines help you focus on the coming flight, and act as a system to catch problems early. One day you will find that something is not quite right, and if your attention has wandered and you have made an error, or if a piece of equipment is not quite right, the routine should help you discover any problems.

Being fit and healthy, (ie not tired, under the influence of drugs or hung-over) is very important in all aviation and especially so in paragliding where we operate so close to the terrain and each other. Poor vigilance and lookout is a key factor in many accidents and incidents.

Paragliding training is (in comparison to many skills) very quick and has a steep learning curve, by their very nature many pilots are both competent and competitive people with an adventurous streak and they are often prepared to take risks that others would consider excessive. Being mature enough to consider that conditions or certain tasks may be beyond your capability is a huge benefit to pilot safety and a wise pilot is one who is not swayed too much by peer pressure, an audiences' expectations or their own ego.

Experience and an ability to make sound judgements about the weather conditions are vital but inevitably take some time to accrue. For this reason it is helpful to fly in a club environment and be prepared to ask coaches and more experienced pilots for advice.

Shortly after getting qualified there is a period of a few months, or hours airtime where the risks are quite high, as pilots lack much experience. Once a pilot has achieved a certain level of experience (often about 25 hours or so), statistics tell us that flying becomes much safer, but interestingly after about 200 hours and few years' experience there is a another small spike on the risk scale. Possibly this is when pilots' grow overconfident, and start to push the boundaries, knowing they have the skills to cope, or they become a bit less cautious, or start flying more demanding kit or in more difficult conditions, or just start to get a bit bored or complacent.

Knowing this is the case is the first step towards ensuring it does not happen to you.

In recent years the rise of discount voucher companies and the search for a quick and thrilling experience has seen an increase in the number of people taking one day taster sessions or tandem flights. A small but significant minority of these people have been given this as a present or would not normally have chosen to try something like paragliding, and are not well informed about the risks or requirements of free flight.

There are also people who take the sport up and perhaps do not really appreciate the potential for disaster if they make an error or if they don't know what they are doing. 95% of paragliding is easy and fun, but very occasionally you may find yourself in a situation which requires instant and decisive action in order to avoid serious injury to yourself or others. Paragliding makes it easy to get into the air, but the sad fact is that there are a significant proportion of the population who are not well suited either physically or psychologically to being in this environment when things go wrong.

To be a pilot it is important that you can be honest with yourself about your own capabilities, and have the strength of

A nice wingover sequence. Pic: Bruce Goldsmith Design

character to be able to walk away if the site or conditions or volume of traffic seem too much for you.

Eventually most pilots will find themselves very high above a ground, with no-one in contact and having to deal with unexpected situations. This self-reliance is one of the greatest appeals of the sport in a world full of rules and controls, but it does not suit everyone.

Fear

All pilots who are reasonably mentally balanced will experience fear when flying at some point. One of the elements of paragliding that appeals to many people is the fact that it feels exciting because there is a risk involved.

If someone is very competent and doing a task that is well within their capabilities they will not feel any anxiety. What they are doing is simply play. If they are pushing their comfort envelope a little, trying a new wing or site or just getting higher than ever before it is normal to feel both anxious and excited and these are the situations that give the pilot the greatest rewards, and consequently are what most pilots seek.

But if the situation escalates to be outside the pilots' ability to control, say a large collapse of the wing, very turbulent air or a near miss with another aircraft, – the pilot may react with an adrenaline spike and the excitement transforms into a rush of fear.

Some people are able to almost immediately overcome their fear, and start to take action to deal with the situation, others are "frozen" by fear –particularly when they have no experience of the problem and so have no resources to draw on. Being able to overcome the fear, and still function well enough take action or (in the case of students) still listen to and follow instructions, is critical for paraglider pilots.

A key factor is knowledge and training, if a pilot knows what action he should be taking, he has a resource to draw on in a time of stress. For this reason, proper initial training is vital. Further training courses in dealing with instability situations, and dealing with scenarios like deploying a reserve parachute are well worth doing as a pilot progresses in their flying career.

However, no matter how good a pilot you are, no matter how well prepared or careful, and no matter how good your equipment may be, paragliding carries a risk of serious injury or death that cannot be entirely eliminated. To be a pilot you need to decide that this risk is acceptable to you.

One of the world's leading competition pilots, claimed, (hopefully ironically) that his greatest assets in dealing with fear were a lack of imagination and a short memory! Another claimed that after each landing he felt ecstatic that he had cheated death once again, though possibly this says more about competition pilots than the sport as a whole.

Maximising performance

In cross-country, and especially competition flying, the mental game becomes critical for performance as well as safety. Firstly you require self-belief. If you don't expect to win your chances of actually winning are close to zero. You also need a degree of commitment bordering on selfishness to do well. – If you are flying cross country but using all your brainpower thinking about which field below you to land in for a quick lift back to your car, or how much trouble you will be in when you get home late, you are not likely to get very far. Sports psychologists have developed various techniques for sportsmen and women to get themselves into a winning frame of mind, one cross-country pilot was "caught out" by leaving his radio transmitting to his mates as he talked to himself, his conversation with himself varying between wanting his mum (in turbulence) to assuring himself he was a master of the universe when he was in good lift;- whatever works for you! – probably worth checking your microphone is not switched to voice activated though.

In conclusion

Good self-knowledge of your abilities and experience, self-belief backed by the practised and perfected technical skills to cope with what you are doing, are crucial.

To be a successful and safe pilot you need the strength of character to walk away if it is too much for you, patience, a methodical approach to preparation, a willingness to accept to seek advice, and a healthy and realistic appreciation of the risks.

As the old chestnut has it, *"There are old pilots and bold pilots, but not many old bold pilots"*.

Tow launching & Launching from Skis

31

Tow launching is generally done using a boat, vehicle or winch to provide the motive power, and launches to over more than 1,000ft are commonplace. In the UK, the tow-launching of both round and ram air canopies has been well established for several years, usually using a Land Rover or similar vehicle and a fixed line over land, or a boat with a fixed line over water.

With the advent of soaring flight and lighter, better performing but less forgiving canopies, procedures have been altered somewhat to reflect the changes. Weak links are now commonly used to prevent overstressing (125kg is about correct for a tow pressure of around 100kg). Payout systems are often used to maximise height, and powered winches that work by exerting a constant pull towards them enabling the pilot to climb as they approach the winch. These latter can be easily used without the need for a long smooth runway.

By adding another element to the flying (in this case a pull of about one "g"), you do alter the dynamics and stresses on the wing. Towing places twice as much stress on the canopy and because there are more variables there are more things that can go wrong. For example, if the canopy drifts to one side, it could reach a situation where the towing force is actually pulling it sideways into the ground, rather like a kite that is poorly controlled. This is known as "lockout".

Towing over the Utah salt flats, USA (Photo: Loren Cox/Ozone)

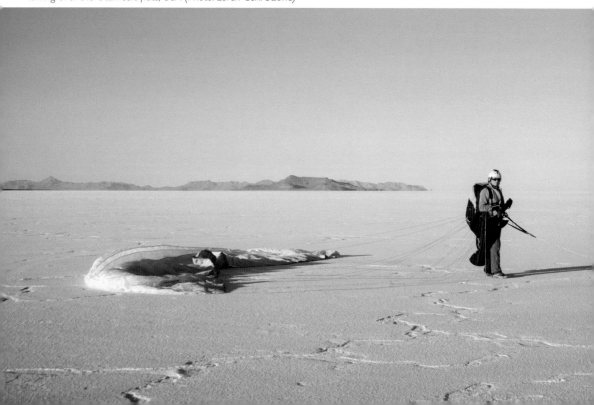

The consequences of a partial collapse or a stall while under tow may also be more serious than in free flight. Finally, there are also more people and more items of equipment that could malfunction. For all these reasons, tow launching must only take place with tested and approved equipment and, most of all, with an experienced and qualified instructor/operator.

There are a range of checks that must be learned, including the release mechanism, signals to the driver or operator and so on. Typically, there is a release mechanism at the pilot's end and an emergency release at the operator's end. The tension of the towline is kept constant, either through a tensiometer or by an automatic process like a clutch.

A typical tow launch in the UK usually follows a set pattern:

- The canopy and the winch are pre-flight checked.
- The line is attached to the pilots' quick release.
- The pilot tries a test release to check everything is OK.
- Reattach.
- The signaller tells the operator to "take up slack" (either by radio or by under-arm swings of a bat).

A payout winch mounted on the back of a boat

- When the line is straight and some tension is established, the pilot launches the canopy. When inflated, stabilised overhead and checked, the pilot gives the command to go (usually "all out" or "push"). This is passed on by the signaller (overhead swings of the bat). If the pilot (or anyone else) wishes to abort the launch, he shouts "Stop" and the signal is a stationary vertical bat.

- The tension comes on and after a couple of steps the pilot is lifted into the sky. When he is well clear of the ground, the operator may increase the power slightly to give a better climb rate.

- During the climb, the pilot uses small control inputs to keep in line with the tow line. He can signal for more or less power to be released should he wish. At any point, the operator can cut the power and, when the line goes slack, the pilot releases, checks that the line has fallen away, and flies down (or up if he can find lift!).

- As the line falls (supported by a small drogue 'chute), it is rewound by the operator ready to be laid out for the next launch.

People have, in the past, attempted to launch by tying a rope to a fixed object and allowing the wind to "kite" them up. This can work, but the pressures are impossible to predict or control making it extremely dangerous, several people have been killed or seriously injured attempting this. Unsurprisingly static kiting is banned by the BHPA (*The last person who tried it was not a member and the accident was only discovered by the BHPA when the safety officer was asked to attend their inquest*).

If you are a foot launch pilot thinking of towing for the first time, it is vital you get expert help. There are also a few points that are worth highlighting.

Ensure the canopy is fully inflated and flying straight before requesting the tow to commence at normal power.

Glance up to check the canopy is evenly inflated before signalling for the power to be applied for launch.

Be very careful not to use lots of brake at launch as you could stall or deep stall the canopy as it takes off, which is a very difficult situation for both the pilot and winch operator to deal with.

Remember that the control pressure will be increased while you are under tow.

Do not forget to check that the line has gone when you have operated the release.

Air law also extends to tow launching – it could be a disaster if pilots started towing up to a couple of thousand feet from their local fields all over the country. It would only be a matter of time before low-flying aircraft flew into invisible and unmarked lines. The Civil Aviation Authority has granted permission for towing activities at various locations throughout the UK (almost always airfields) to qualified groups. These groups or clubs may tow to the height stated on the permit, (usually a maximum of 2,000ft).

Any towing from a site without CAA permission must still be by qualified personnel and is limited to 200ft AGL (60m). Towing activities are marked on air charts.

Because it is easy to gain substantial altitude while having no hill behind you, towing is an excellent way to practice instability exercises. Over water is recommended until you have established some expertise.

Launching from skis

Paragliding was really born in the Alpine ski resorts and, naturally, some of the first pilots were skiers. On snowy mountainsides with little wind, it is often not possible to run anyway, so skis allow a fast and effective way to become airborne. The technique is the same as for an Alpine launch, but great care must be taken not to ski over the lines. It is very easy to damage them with the edge of a ski, particularly if there are rocks beneath the snow or if it is icy. It is difficult to get any traction, so in order to pull the canopy up you require a reasonably steep slope – your body weight should then provide the forward force.

The combination of a steep slope with snow and skis may make stopping difficult once you are committed, so be meticulous in laying out your canopy and in your checks. Be careful when moving the canopy about to keep the snow out as far as possible. If much snow gets inside, it can make the launch more difficult and, at worst, can affect the flying characteristics of the paraglider.

If launching in wind, you may require help to forward launch, as it is hard to sidestep quickly with skis on your feet, if the wind is very light you require a steep slope and a sufficiently large take off area to generate the airspeed to launch, so beware of take off's too close to the tree line, lift cables or other hazards.

Note: Although there may be plenty at take –off, the landing area may well be without snow; think about it before you take off!

Speed riding

The prime advantage of ski launching is that you can achieve a good high groundspeed compared to running, and as a result it is perfectly possible to fly a very small fast wing. As there is often little lift on still winter days in the mountains, the most fun to be had is to fly fast and close to slope, and since about 2003 more and more pilots are choosing smaller and faster wings that are ideally suited to steep launches, and fast ground hugging flight patterns.

Known collectively as speedwings these vary from 19sq metre gliders that are

fully certified but smaller than usual paragliders, to 15 or 16 metre models that operate at close to the double the wing loading of a soaring wing, and can be foot launched in higher winds, or ski launched in snow. These are both very small and light enough to carry or climb with, and give the pilot a fast and furious flight, usually from the top to the bottom of a mountain.

Or right at the sharp end of speed riding are the tiny 8-12sqm "miniwings" that owe as much to free-fall parachutes or kites as to paragliders and are simply the fastest way down.

Because of the small size, high speed and steep glide of these wings they lend themselves to ski launching and very steep terrain, and make previously un-skiable slopes with big rock-faces accessible. In the right hands the steep carving turns and touch and go capability of these wings make for some spectacular rides. However they can require considerable skill to fly well, as something as simple as steeply banked 360° turn can result in a height loss of hundreds of feet. As speed riders may well spend half the descent in contact with the slope, a high standard of skiing is also required for this type of flying.

Speed gliders generally offer mountaineers a new element to their sport with quick descents from high peaks, and fliers have already made some spectacular descents, from very inaccessible peaks in the Alps, and Himalayas. Sometimes cutting the descent times from summit to base camp from days to minutes!

Photo: Ozone

Tandem Flying 32

Tandem flying is great fun and an excellent way to teach certain disciplines such as soaring and thermalling. For the experienced pilot it is a good way to share the sport and it really adds to your own enjoyment to share the air, especially on smooth "boring soaring" days. Many pilots and instructors who have seen tandem operating have shown great interest in doing it themselves. Most manufacturers have a tandem wing in their range, and canopies carrying two people are a routine sight.

How do you become a tandem pilot?

You must be a very experienced and careful pilot and you will need to pass a tandem assessment.

The assessment criteria include practical demonstration of skills discussed below, correct briefings and a good understanding of the ramifications (practical, legal and political!) of flying two people on one wing.

There are some preconditions to applying for a UK tandem assessment:

- You must be a full annual member of the BHPA.

- You must be a very experienced and capable pilot with a minimum 100 hours logged. (or 100 tows for tow pilots).

- You must hold the "pilot" rating.

- You must have flown a minimum of 12 tandem flights with an existing tandem rated pilot (or under the supervision of a tandem instructor). Two of these flights must be in the student position. (*The BHPA, or any centre offering a tandem course, can provide details of precisely what is required*).

Note: In the case of instructors, the exam shall include assessment of the candidate's understanding of the use of tandem as an instructional tool.

Each candidate is assessed by a tandem instructor who will demand a very high degree of competence to award the rating.

This qualification is VITAL, otherwise your insurance (BHPA or otherwise) will not be valid, and if you have an accident flying tandem, consequences both for yourself and for the whole sport could be catastrophic.

The law in the UK states that there must be no commercial gain or payment of any kind unless the P2 (passenger) is on a proper course of instruction (i.e. on a course and flying with a qualified instructor).

The pilot in command is often referred to as the P1 and the passenger as P2.

The Equipment

To fly tandem you need specialised equipment.

- A purpose-made tandem wing. Only paragliders certified by LTF/CEN for tandem operations may be used. They must be used with proper regard to the manufacturers stated weight range and other recommendations.

- Both P1 and P2 require a properly fitting harness and CEN certified helmet (see below). The pilots harness should ideally be a purpose built tandem harness and have wide or flared seat plate so that they can stretch their legs comfortably around the passenger. Many tandem pilot prefer "split leg" harnesses which allow a fast run and which are more comfortable if the P2 is wider than the pilot!

- A spreader bar system that places the P2 slightly lower and in front of the pilot to prevent them being squashed together is strongly recommended. (A good tandem canopy should come with these fitted.)

- A full-face helmet is highly recommended for the P1 – your chin will be perhaps 25cm above and behind the P2's helmet and even a good landing could easily result in contact. Passengers may look up sharply on take off and a crack on the chin is easy to come by.

- A tandem reserve sufficiently large to give a safe sink rate at the maximum payload is a mandatory requirement.

- A spine protector of some description is a good idea for the pilot, as even a gentle stumble backwards will mean the other person's weight can fall on you as well.

- A log book of tandem flights must be raised and maintained.

Points to consider before launch

Personnel

Obviously you must be a qualified tandem pilot (or be under training with a tandem instructor) to fly as the P1. But there are also some considerations when considering your passengers.

If you wish to fly children, make sure you are still within the canopy's specified weight range. Ensure that you also get written parental consent for under 18's, and exercise extreme caution.

If the flight is part of a course, the pilot must be an instructor and the P2 must be a member of the BHPA and enrolled on the rating system. *(This is the ONLY way a tandem flight can take place if any money or other "valuable consideration" is involved. Flying for hire or reward is not allowed in the UK).*

A word of caution

It is not unknown for people to claim to wish to fly with you when actually they are very nervous about the idea.(This includes your own wife/ husband/girlfriend/ children and mother!)

Flying tandem at the Dune de Pyla, France

Before launching, do take a minute to look them in the eyes and ask them (alone) whether they are happy about it. This is especially true with groups, as peer pressure can be a hazard. If you have some doubts, make an excuse and don't do it. (It's no fun when the passenger stops dead when you get close to cliff edge, or is sick on you in flight!!)

Whilst you do not want to frighten your passenger, it is important that the briefing includes explaining the possible risks. Passengers should not be under the influence of drugs, including alcohol.

It is very helpful for safe operation that another experienced pilot is present to act as anchor-man, helper and to pre-flight check the P2's equipment. For both practical and insurance reasons, this should be a BHPA member.

P2's should usually be fit enough to be able to cope with flight themselves. If you wish to fly a disabled person, you should first contact the BHPA office for advice.

There are some technical considerations too. A very light P2 will tend to move up and may obscure the pilot's vision. This change in relative positions may also mean that you cannot reach the "ears ". On some set-ups, flying with a very light P2 such as a child can even put the brake handles out of reach if they are released.

Very tall P2's may make launching difficult: if in doubt, try a small hop first.

Because of the P2's lower position, a tandem wing set up for the P1 to fly will mean that the P2 (if a pupil under instruction) must fly with the brakes up near their ears; a "normal" brake position may induce a stall. (This is particularly true when landing). If your tandem flying is usually as an instructor, it may be worth setting up the canopy for normal brake position when flown by the P2 and using "wraps" when flying yourself and landing, some schools use brake extensions for training. (i.e. two sets of handles at different heights).

The site and conditions

Flying tandem does impose a few restrictions on your choice of take-off and landing site. Co-ordinating two pairs of legs over flat or uphill ground makes it very difficult to move forwards. A sharp edge in light winds is also a problem, as the P2's weight leaving the ground first will pull you and the wing forwards. If you haven't sufficient pressure in the wing at this stage the launch could be dangerous.

Ideally, you need a shallow slope falling away to a steeper one. This also helps with the actual inflation technique and if you are flying multiple P2's, helps to speed up your turnaround time.

The conditions you can fly tandem in are much the same as usual. With a good technique it is easy to launch and land in nil wind even with a 190kg payload. If you are top landing, you need to be certain you are not drifting backwards at all, as with four legs to co-ordinate, a quick pivot and run is not practical. Turbulence is, of course, worrying to a non-flying P2, but certainly with almost all tandem wings, the extra wing loading makes the wing feel more solid than a solo canopy.

Launch technique

The P2 must be properly briefed about what to expect. His equipment must be pre-flight checked by an experienced helper. He must know how long the flight is expected to last, where you are expecting to land and that he must not fully depress the brakes or make violent inputs if he has control.

Above all, he must know not to sit down or stop running during launch until he is told to do so by the pilot.

It is quite possible for the P2 to face forwards while the pilot does a cross-brake reverse launch. This is perhaps the most useful method in the UK, where you are likely to be launching in gentle soarable winds. But if the canopy does not come up straight, this can be problematic, as you cannot easily sidestep to make a correction. In stronger soarable winds, where you may come off the ground as you reverse launch, an assisted alpine launch can be used, but you do need a competent helper for this.

The cross-brake reverse launch technique is identical to a solo launch except that, because of the position of the passenger, one riser is much further away from you than the other. You must compensate for this as you pull the wing up. It is easy to do provided you are already fluent with this launch technique solo. Takeoff and landing are the fun parts. In a breeze you may need an anchorman to hold you or your passenger's waist strap while you get the canopy up.

Launching in a soarable breeze in Morocco with extra skilled assistance

Your cross-brake and Alpine launch techniques must be to a very high standard, as "blowing it" on a tandem may mean an ignominious tumble over your passenger.

In very light winds the Alpine is the preferred system, though if there is sufficient wind to support the wing a cross-brake reverse is appropriate. In a good wind the safest system is to revert back to high wind Alpine launches with a skilled helper. Zero-wind launches can be interesting. The preferred technique is to run side by side with your passenger using a flexible spreader system. If you are running behind them and they slow down or stop you are in trouble!

A very useful launch technique for tandem pilots, especially in a good wind is to "de-power" the wing as it climbs. The easiest way to do this is to launch from well off-centre of the canopy and pull it up with the A riser from just one side, whilst controlling it with the brake from the same side. This avoids pulling the wing through the "power band" in the dead-downwind position. Again a high degree of ground handling skill is required. (This is sometimes referred to as the "cobra" technique and is a useful skill for the tandem pilot).

Nice tandem launch in the French Alps

Flying Technique

Flying tandem is pretty much like flying alone, with the pleasure of some company, but there are some differences. You may have to deal with a nervous or enthusiastic passenger and this can affect concentration. The actual canopy is larger and will be travelling slightly faster than a solo wing; this means you need more room for manoeuvres as the turn radius is bigger, and you may well be constantly catching up with solo pilots on a ridge.

The tandem wing, being more heavily laden, leaves a more powerful wake vortex as it travels, and this can disrupt other pilots who fly near you. It is the tandem pilot's responsibility therefore to avoid other traffic by a good margin. The controls are also heavier and it can be quite tiring on a long flight.

On the plus side you will have a good glide at speed and can cover a lot of sky, and the resistance to slightly turbulent air is slightly better than a solo wing.

During flight, all movements should be progressive, and the pilot should tell the P2 everything that he is doing and why. If all is well when they have plenty of

room, an instructor may hand over control to the P2, keeping his own hands just above the risers so that he can guide or restrain any inputs if necessary. Within five minutes, most people can fly around with no trouble. (The term "instructor" is used here because to hand over control introduces an element of instruction). If the pilot is not an instructor, any incident or problem while the P2 has control would probably put them on very shaky legal ground.

If you are not an instructor, do not let a passenger take the controls.

Training Tandem

If training tandem it is useful to use the aviation terminology "I have control" or "You have control" to prevent any confusion. Do not let the pilot under instruction try spiral dives or any similar manoeuvre, and BE CAREFUL – because of the P2's lower position, a tandem set up for the pilot to fly will mean that the P2 may need to fly with the brakes near their ears. Talk with your P2 all the time. It is very reassuring and you can tell by the way that they talk back (or not) if they are happy or tense. Warn them in plenty of time of impending glider wash or any manoeuvre you are doing and always make sure they are sitting forwards in their seat in time for landing.

If you are top landing in a good breeze it is good practice to have your helper ready to grab you and help dump the canopy, as it is easier to fall over with, and much harder to stop a 40m+ canopy dragging you. When teaching, it is usually advisable to keep the flights to not more than 20 minutes.

If the site and conditions allow, it is helpful to aim to land on a slight slope so that you can launch again without moving. For best results with teaching, the brakes should be long enough for the student to use normally, which means you will often have to launch and fly with a wrap. You will find that the control pressures are greater than usual (particularly with flaring), so be prepared to take a couple of wraps to land and give yourself a rest every three flights or so.

A key skill when flying any passengers and making them comfortable is to keep talking to them.

This relaxes them and lets them know what is happening; to suddenly turn without warning is frightening, but to say "we will be turning left in a moment at the end of this ridge" is helpful.

Landing is straightforward until you touch down. Once on the deck it requires good technique to dump the wing safely without falling over your passenger whose legs may well have "gone" after 15 minutes airborne!

If top landing in fresh winds you should be confident of landing right on your chosen spot so that you can hand-off your controls to your (qualified) helper, who can "shock stall" the wing for you by stepping sharply backwards with them.

Clearly all these techniques require practice and a good level of expertise to master, and it is no coincidence that most tandem pilots are professional instructors.

Renewing your rating

In the UK a CFI's support is required for both registration and annual renewal of a tandem rating. An annual fee is payable to maintain your rating and your insurance cover.

Tandem pilots and candidates are reminded that they must remain in current practice and on-going training is necessary should they fly in differing conditions, fly a different model of tandem wing, or use a different harness arrangement.

In the current litigious climate an accident involving a member of the public on a tandem wing is almost certain to result in a claim against the pilot. For this reason it is foolhardy to attempt to fly tandem without suitable qualifications or insurance. It is even more foolhardy to fly as a passenger with an unqualified pilot!

33 Flying in new environments

Before setting out to fly in completely unfamiliar territory, it is always worthwhile seeking information from your fellow club members or from the local pilots when you arrive. The more you know about the site and the region, the safer and more enjoyable the flying will be.

Do not be in a hurry to be the first to launch – always wait and see what the local flyers are doing. Always ask before flying – they may be a local school, or the club may have specific rules about who can fly. A little courtesy costs nothing and could pay dividends in advice and help later on.

All these points apply equally to flying nearer home, of course. Before flying abroad, always take out medical and repatriation insurance – the cost of a helicopter rescue and treatment in many parts of the world are chargeable and expensive!

Mountains: If you are going up in a cable-car or similar, always take your flying licence or membership card as some operators will not let you up the mountain without them. Do not take anything you cannot easily fly down with. A mountain is nothing but a large hill – some are ridge-soarable but others are simply used as launch points to contact thermals rising from the valley floor or sides. Because of their scale, mountains create their own "micro-meteorology" – that is to say that the wind and thermal development may be influenced as much by the mountain itself as by the prevailing conditions.

Terrain doesn't come more extreme than this! Eddie Colfox on Bubeli Peak in the Pakistan Karakorum (Photo: John Silvester)

An important example of this is the airflow patterns throughout the day *(Fig 33.1)*.

In the morning there may well be a gentle katabatic flow (downhill) as the cool air sinks from the mountain-top into the valley bottom. There is no point in rushing over to the other side of the mountain, as the flow will be the same there.

It is not unusual to find cloud in the valley bottoms in the morning. As the sun climbs and the valley sides warm up (rocky areas facing the sun first), the air will start to rise up the mountain-sides (anabatic flow) out of the valley and may become soarable *(see Fig 33.1)*. As the rocks and slopes warm up, the thermals grow more and more powerful and turbulent. In summer it is not advisable to fly at all in some regions when activity is strongest. As the sun sinks, the convection gradually decreases and large weak thermals are found. This is a good time for the inexperienced pilot to get used to the site. As the day ends, the air becomes calm and the lift dies. This scenario is fairly typical of mountain flying conditions throughout the world.

Large mountains have several effects on the airflow and it is not unusual to find an apparent wind blowing up both sides of a large ridge. This can give a convergence effect that can be usefully employed to fly many kilometres along the ridge crest. The same effect means that mountains facing in different directions can often be soarable simultaneously.

Valley winds

If there is a wind blowing it may only be felt at the tops of the mountains as a light breeze, but in deep Alpine valleys,

Dawn / Dusk   Noon

Fig 33.1: The effect of daytime heating and night time cooling on airflow in valleys

the wind patterns can be quite different as the mountains can have the effect of constricting and accelerating the flow (the venturi effect), giving stronger winds in the valley bottom. It is common for the valley wind to gradually increase during the day, sometimes to the point where the valley bottom may well be a very windy and turbulent area. The best bet is to seek local knowledge by asking the local pilots,

An approaching weather front will also tend to push up the valleys before it is noticeable at launch. The basic rule as that the longer and deeper the valley the stronger the wind will become, factors such as a gradient of the valley floor can also have an effect. The way to deal with this is always approach the landing area high, check the wind below you if you can, and lose height above your chosen spot, a long shallow glide into wind is not advisable.

If you have a choice always choose to land in wide valleys, failing that the second choice is narrow valleys and the worst choice is at the junction of two or more valleys, where the conditions can be very unpredictable. There is more information on valley winds in the "Weather" chapter.

Be very cautious of wind in the high mountains. In this photo you can see spindrift blowing from the crest of the ridge in the background (Photo: John Silvester)

large margin for error and approach your field with spare altitude. Approach by circling over the field to establish the strength and direction (by noting your drift).

Foehn

Foehn is a term used to describe a wind condition that is found in the Alps, The Foehn is, typically, a wind blowing across, or out from, the mountain range. The airmass may lose moisture as cloud often forms on the upwind side of the peaks where the altitude causes the vapour to reach dew point and where it may sometimes fall as snow. This moving air-mass can cause rotor effects in the valleys and wave formations above the peaks. It is generally considered dangerous to fly in these conditions – something similar occurs in mountainous areas throughout the world. Telltale signs are dry wind blowing in the morning and poor visibility at low level. Local pilots will be adept at identifying the Foehn conditions, so it is always worth asking advice.

Flight planning from mountains & different terrain.

If there is a large altitude difference between launch and landing area, there is a chance that the wind in the landing area will be different in speed and direction from that at launch. Always allow a

In very high mountains the air density is markedly lower, and this means that you may need a fast or long run for launch, so a shallow slope or one covered in deep snow may not be practical. High altitude launches also mean that the dewpoint and therefore the cloudbase level may be below you. This can mean that you will have smooth air to launch, but as you lose height you may be faced with a developing cloud layer below you. This can have implications for visibility and for turbulent air.

If you are going for a long fly-down it may be wise to launch early to avoid the cloud cover closing before you get there.

Different conditions and different terrain can have other implications for the unwary pilot. Flying in very hot regions even at low level you may find that wind creates less lift than expected due to the low density of the warm airmass. Conversely in very cold conditions what might be acceptable wind strength at home may cause you penetration problems.

Launching in sand, and particularly snow can be challenging if you are not experienced in dealing with it, take care not to get too much in your canopy as it will affect the handling and speed. Launches from steep snow slopes can be quite technical and some pilots find that using 3 or 4 small pegs pushed into the snow at the leading edge can help keep your wing from sliding downhill before you are ready to launch.

More than one pilot has discovered that being trapped out on a snowfield by failing light or poor weather has quickly turned a day out into a life-threatening situation, especially if they are injured. Paragliders do make excellent insulators and if flying in remote snowy areas a collapsible snow shovel can be a lifesaver in helping dig a suitable shelter or snowhole.

European pilots are used to generally friendly launching and landing areas. In many parts of the world the hazards posed by thorny trees and bushes and even by rocky terrain can be serious. If flying away from recognised landing fields always give yourself plenty of space to manoeuvre by setting up an approach with spare height.

If flying cross-country it is important that your communications and plan for a pick up are well organised. More than one pilot has found himself down in an unknown area with a 'phone that will not work and without speaking the local language.

Until you have plenty of experience it is well worth flying in a new environment with an experienced guide or on an organised tour. A good guide with local knowledge can make all the difference between an enjoyable trip and a disaster, not to mention the knowledge that if something does go wrong someone is there to help you. In remote or difficult to access areas like jungle, carry a tracker device can a major advantage in arranging safe retrieves.

The real big stuff – Nepal

34 Competitions

Many pilots enjoy flying competitively and there is a range of events, from club level up to world championships, that are hotly contested.

A typical task might be to fly cross-country as far as possible or around a number of turn points and landing at a "goal".

Tasks like these test the pilots' skill and judgement in the most comprehensive way. Competition flying does carry an increased risk, as the pilots often push themselves further than they might otherwise, and many pilots may be competing for a small area of lift.

Competitions may take the form of one versus all or, in large events, several groups. In the latter case there is a "cut" after the first few tasks so that only, say, 30 per cent of the pilots go through to the final contest. There may be tasks that are timed from take-off to landing, but these are hard to marshal, so the usual method is a launch "window". This means that any competitor is free to launch at any time during the preset time window and the fastest, or the furthest, wins.

Judging exactly when to launch becomes a major part of the competition. However the technique for winning tasks where you are flying with a group, is straight forward : select the thermal that has the biggest (or best) group of pilots and stick with it. All you have to do is employ your superior skills to fly better than anyone else in your "gaggle" and you are assured of a reasonable placing. Of course, someone unexpected may score better than you but if you keep winning the "A" team gaggle, eventually you will come out on top or very near it. Simple!

Hints

Good equipment is vital, not only a canopy but a reliable camera & GPS (used to prove that you have reached the turn points), other instruments and a reserve. Know the rules! Competitions have been won (and lost) because only a few pilots realised that the rules biased points in favour of speed over distance or a target landing over speed, etc. Do not rush – inexperienced competition pilots often fly too early. You must know the weather forecast to decide whether it will improve or not. You must also keep tabs on how you are doing in the competition – if you are not aware of everyone else's position as the competition progresses, you will not know who you should "target" in the tasks. Should you play safe? Or should you go for it if you have nothing to lose?

But don't forget, you are doing it for fun!

Increasingly, competition tasks are judged on photo evidence of turn points rounded or by GPS flight logs. For photo evidence it is important that you understand the rules, particularly the FAI photo sector regulation *(see Fig 34.1)*. For GPS logs only certain models are acceptable. Check with the organisers for details.

Another fiercly contested area of competition is accuracy landing. This has grown from paracending and tow field operations and the skilled accuracy pilot can measure their deviation from the dead centre of the target in centimetres. The wings used for this type of competition are usually of lower performance and so have a steeper glide path than most free-flight wings but the skill involved is undeniable, and it is a great spectator event!

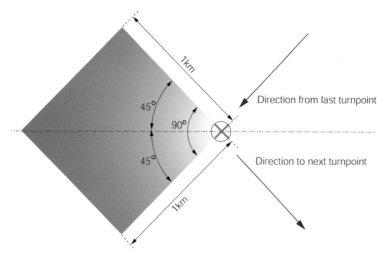

Fig 34.1: An FAI sector. To be judged to have passed the turnpoint correctly, the pilot must have flown through the green sector and taken a photo or logged this on his GPS

Many pilots do not enjoy fighting for thermals, but they do enjoy cross-country flying and measuring their achievements against themselves and others. For this reason the BHPA have a Cross-country league, and pilots can log and enter their best flights, which are published on the web and in Skywings magazine.

When you look at the distances covered by pilots in a single good day in the UK, it is astounding how much skilled flying is being done.

XC flight is often done alone and so it is not quite competition in the true sense, but it is an excellent way to measure your skills, and the tables also allow club rivalry to be given an outlet and consistently high scoring pilots in the XC leagues (which are open to any qualified pilot) are invited to join the national competition circuit.

Like many countries the UK has a busy competition calendar. This is a great benefit to the competing pilots in driving improvements in skills, and to other pilots in that the manufacturers can measure, compare and improve their products in this way.

The top few pilots in each country are invited to join a national team for international meets; these are generally run on a team basis with an aggregate score for each country's team. With several teams in each major comp it can get a bit frenetic but the safety record is surprisingly good!

There are slightly differing competition circuits. As well as club and National level competitions, there is also a European championship.

There are of course other international competitions as well, from friendly "fly-ins" to Acro competitons.

One of the most famous flying events is the X-Alps challenge. Pilots aim to get themselves along almost the entire length of the Alps through a combination of flying and walking. This annual contest has seen some of the most impressive feats of flying, with pilots choosing different routes and tactics to complete the challenge. The competitors are tracked as they fly (or walk) and it is possible to track their progress live on the internet as the days progress… This is perhaps toughest competitive test of flying skill and endurance.

The PWC (Paragliding World Cup) is a series of comps that is based on individual merit rather than national selection. These are held at venues thoughout the world.

Finally there is a world championship, which again is a national team event although as it is a totting up of individual scores there is of course a world champion at the end!

Everyone loves a winner! (Photo: Sup'Air)

Becoming an instructor or coach 35

An instructor is a person who is qualified to train his or her pupils new skills or tasks. In Britain, most of the responsibility for selecting, training and using instructors lies with the Chief Flying Instructor (CFI) of a training centre. If you are interested in teaching, you first need to approach a CFI and convince him that you have the right stuff to make an instructor. If he agrees you will be signed on as a Trainee Instructor (TI) and begin to help at the school. At this stage, you cannot take charge of students and must be under the supervision of a senior instructor, though after some time and if he thinks you are capable enough, he may decide to take a larger group than usual. At this point (usually after a couple of weeks or so) it is usual for the school to pay a nominal rate. To Register as a Trainee instructor you must hold at least the Pilot rating.

Whilst doing your practical training you will also need to attend a trainee instructor course. These are intensive two-day courses and cover all aspects of administration and instructional theory. After a period of working in the school and gaining some experience, you will need to attend a further coaching course to polish your skills.

If your flying, instructing and first-aid qualifications are suitable, you have successfully completed the required courses, and you have amassed sufficient experience, your CFI may put you forward for an examination. An exam takes all day and is conducted by an experienced instructor.

You will be asked to do some hands on training, demonstrate your flying skills, deliver a theory lecture and have an interview. You will be informed as to whether you have passed or failed on the same day. If you have failed, you and your CFI will be told why. You may be advised to reapply when any weak points are resolved. When you are a qualified instructor, a senior instructor may give you charge of a group or class of your own, although the final decisions will be made by the senior instructor on site.

When you have amassed considerable experience as an instructor, including helping supervise new instructors, you may apply for the senior instructor rating. You will need to attend and pass another two-day course, which sets a high standard not only in instructing skills but also in the administration of a training centre. After a further examination day or two you may achieve senior rating, which is a requirement for appointment as a CFI.

That is the bare bones of the BHPA system. However, the most important element is the on-the-job experience and practice. The courses and exams are really only a confirmation that you have learned the requisite skills at the school. The standard required has increased a great deal in recent years and is particularly high for Senior level.

Being an instructor requires a particular set of skills, not only must you have the right technical skills, it is also vital to have the "soft" skills of organisation, effective communication and a confidence-inspiring manner that allows the students to connect with you and trust your judgment. You also need to be able to put yourself in the student's position and understand their state of mind to be able to teach them effectively. Some of the very best pilots do not make very good instructors!

Making a living from paragliding is not easy. The work is seasonal in nature and involves a lot of weekends. The days

Instructor Ian assists student Lynn to get ready (Photo: www.sunsoar-paragliding.com)

themselves start early with obtaining forecasts, etc at 7.30am and often end with completing admin records at 9pm!

However, there is tremendous satisfaction in seeing your pupils progress to a good standard, and plenty of opportunity for flying, travel and meeting new people.

Coaching is supervising and helping pilots to perfect skills and tasks that they have already learned with an instructor. Coaching is voluntary and is a vital part of keeping the sport safe and helping new pilots feel welcomed into the club environment, and to progress after school.

To be a coach in the UK you should be reasonably experienced and be proposed by your club's chief coach. You must also attend a two day course which covers the skills you will need to master to help effectively.

Experienced pilots who give up some of their time to help coach new pilots (and some not so new) are a very important element of the sport, advising new pilots on the suitability of weather conditions, introducing them to new sites and offering the benefits of their experience to help pilots progress in their flying.

In clubs or associations without a strong coaching culture too many new pilots fresh from school find the challenges of paragliding without an instructor's guidance a bit overwhelming and sometimes even dangerous, and some find that their initial enthusiasm is damped after a few unsuccessful or frightening days out flying, and leave the sport.

Like instructing, coaching brings its own rewards in seeing your club grow and the standards improve as the more experienced pilots help the newer members.

Paramotoring 36

Photo: Skywalk GMBH)

In the 1980s as the sport progressed, a number of paraglider pilots who loved the freedom their sport gave them, but lived far from the hills or were often frustrated by the weather, sought the freedom to go where they wanted rather than where the wind dictated, – adding a back-pack motor was a fairly straightforward innovation, and a new sport was created.

Although paragliders were initially designed for un-powered soaring flight, it was inevitable that as hang gliding gave birth to microlighting, so paragliding would eventually lead to paramotoring.

The attraction of being able to fly from almost anywhere at any time is very appealing to many pilots.

There are two main paths that have been developed. Reinvention of the microlight "trike" configuration with a ram-air wing has been one method. Generally using specific wing configurations that are more akin to very early models with very large cell entries for easier ground control, they can often seat two people. This has some operating advantages, although their larger size and weight has generally meant that they demand considerable de-rigging or a trailer for transportation.

These machines are popular in the USA and some other countries, and had a big boost from their appearance in a James Bond movie a few years ago.

Unfortunately, they are not legal in the UK without expensive certification as a microlight wing, and because they are wheeled, the pilot must also hold a PPLM (Microlight licence). These two restrictions has meant that they are not particularly accessible and so they are still very rarely seen in Britain. Though the recent de-regulation of Sub-115kg microlights has meant that much of the onerous airworthiness criteria has been dropped for single seat trikes, and these are now available in increasing numbers, although at present the CAA microlight pilot's licence administered through the BMAA – (British microlight aircraft association) – is still required to fly one.

The second type is the backpack paramotor, which is foot launched just like a free-flight wing. This of course appeals very strongly to paraglider pilots because of its simplicity, small size and weight, and because it can often be used with their existing paraglider wing. As with a paraglider, a disadvantage is that you usually need to train solo, although much of the additional motor control can be demonstrated on the ground. The additional skills for ground handling and launching a PPG demand a reasonable degree of fitness and co-ordination.

For pilots who want to enjoy free flying, a paramotor provides a very flexible alternative to towing or long drives to the hill to get airborne. Paramotors can be used both for powered flight and unpowered soaring flight. Those with an air-start capability offer a distinct advantage to those pilots who may then choose to switch off and use lift in the usual way.

Back pack paramotors are the most popular variant and this section is principally concerned with this type.

An introduction to the equipment

The paramotor consists of a lightweight engine -commonly a 2 stroke, which offer excellent power to weight ratio, but there are now a number of 4 stroke engines on the market. A 4 stroke engine is usually smoother and quieter and certainly much more fuel efficient, but has less power for the weight.

The motor is driving a pusher propeller. This is mounted in a rigid frame of steel or aluminium. A fuel tank (up to a legal maximum of 10 litres) is also incorporated in the frame, while the propeller is shielded by a "cage" often covered in a mesh. This allows a free flow of air whilst protecting dangling lines and flung back arms from the spinning propeller.

Some smaller units use direct drive but most feature a reduction drive of some sort to efficiently match the rpm of the engine to the propeller. A long flexible throttle boom with a hand grip provides the pilot with engine controls, some wireless throttles are now on the market as well. The pilot's side of the frame has connection points for attaching the harness so that the whole unit can be worn as a backpack. Typical weight is around 14–35kg, depending on type.

The engines are chosen for lightness, good fuel consumption, reliability and suitable power output. The result is that the same few models are incorporated into many different paramotors. Typically, they are from 80cc up to around 300cc. A usable power output for a pilot who wishes to be able to launch comfortably from flat ground is around 15bhp, although some smaller units designed principally for sustaining flight may generate as little as 7bhp.

More important than engine size is the thrust generated by a paramotor, and this is dependent on matching the correct propeller type to the power of the engine at the right rpm. The prop choice is one of the major design factors in manufacturing a paramotor.

Designers typically test many props before settling on a final design. But thrust is only one consideration. It may be easy to increase it with a larger propeller, but this also has implications for the torque effect applied to the pilot and the noise level generated. If the propeller tips become supersonic the resulting increase in noise levels can be significant.

Many paramotors use a wooden propeller with a diameter of between 90 and 130cm. Depending on the diameter, rpm, and tip speed, two, three or four blades may be used in the quest to reduce noise or increase thrust.

Blades are commonly made of wood, with a variety of replacements being readily available at relatively cheap prices. Against this, one must accept that a wooden blade is going to suffer more easily from stone chips and will, by the nature of wood, be harder to maintain and keep in balance. Also, to maintain their strength, they have a thicker profile than composite blades. This produces more drag when spun through the air and higher levels of torque effect. Increasingly more popular, composite blades are inherently stronger, and can be manufactured in thinner and more radical swept shapes beneficial to thrust

and noise reduction. They will tolerate more abuse and can overcome many of the problems of wooden blades, BUT at a price. Most paramotor pilots will at some point be guilty of some propeller damage, so it's worth remembering that if replacement is necessary, a wooden prop is typically going to cost about half the price of a composite blade.

The frame and cage are frequently made from aluminum alloys, although stainless steel and steel alloys are just as suitable. Fibreglass or carbon fibre rod has also been used for the outer rim of the cage. The great advantage of being bendable is that it can be disassembled and packed into a small place. It may be less likely to sustain damage from being dropped than a metal rim, but being flexible the cage may not offer so much protection to a spinning propeller.

Most manufacturers offer a choice of size. The larger units with bigger engines and props give more thrust, but need

Paramotor trike (Photo: U-Turn GMBH)

a much larger and heavier cage. These may then have to be disassembled for transportation. The tiny ones may not be designed to get the heavier pilot off flat ground but are, of course, lighter and more compact.

Paramotors are started either with a recoil starter (pull handle), in the same way as a lawn mower or chainsaw. Or with an electric start. Because the compression is relatively high it is important that a motor with a pull start has a decompressor fitted, otherwise restarting in the air can be very difficult, if not impossible. A very useful feature on any unit (particularly for the soaring or fuel conscious pilot) is an air restart system. This can be a hand or kick start with an automatic de-compressor to allow an easier pull, or an electric start of some type. An electric start of course requires a battery and inevitably adds weight and price , and if your battery goes flat you are helpless.

The throttle control is typically a "squeeze for power" hand unit. These are initially rather awkward whilst ground handling, as the same hand is simultaneously controlling a brake, but with good training and practice, pilots soon master this technique. The throttle incorporates a kill switch so that the engine can be stopped at any time during the launch or flight if a problem occurs. A slip or stumble on landing can result in considerable damage if a rotating prop contacts the ground or the wing collapses onto the spinning prop. Landings are typically made "dead stick" with the engine off to avoid this risk.

Some designs features a centrifugal clutch, which means the running engine is disengaged from the propeller whilst the pilot is ground handling, landing, or even just putting the paramotor on his back. Once the wing is fully inflated and overhead, the throttle is applied, engaging

*Paramotor with J-bar connection points
(Photo: Northern Paragliding)*

*Paramotor with 'mid-point' connection points
(Photo: Northern Paragliding)*

the clutch and spinning the prop for launch.

Another important design factor is the connection of the harness to the risers of the wing. A well designed harness should allow the wing to relieve the pilot's shoulders of the additional weight.

There are three usual alternatives described here which all have their pros and cons.

The first method, using relatively high hang points at about head height, is the J bar. This is a curved metal extension of the paramotor frame which looks like an upside down letter "J". This extends up and over the pilot's shoulders. The risers are then physically attached to the top of J bar, while the harness is supported from the protruding ends. This type of set-up provides an excellent, if not almost remote, sense of stability. The inherent stability means the torque effect is less

Paramotor with spreader bars to allow low hang points (Photo: PAP Paramotors)

apparent but ability to steer by weight shift is significantly reduced. Another important consideration is that the controls will now be considerably higher up for the pilot to reach. In fact the operation of big ears may be impossible.

With higher than normal attachment points the pilot might not be able to reach the brakes at the keepers if they are released, hence lengthening of the brakes is necessary. This set-up is best suited to dedicated paramotoring use, particularly with powerful motors or larger propellers. Forward launching with "high" hang points can also be more challenging due to the extended arc the wing must be pulled up through.

Another method uses 'mid' hang points incorporated in the harness webbing, to which the risers are attached directly. These are similar to a paraglider harness, but with the hang points typically about 20cm higher, closer to shoulder-chest height to achieve the correct centre of gravity. To ensure the pilot's comfort and to provide the correct angle of thrust, the position of the hang points is adjustable. This type of harness requires no additional frame work to attach it to the motor. This set-up is simple; however, it still requires some lengthening of the brake lines, and it can make getting comfortably into the harness after launch a bit of a struggle. It is not very suitable for use with heavy machines, which can tilt the pilot and motor backwards in flight.

The third method uses a lower hang point at a similar height to a paraglider harness. Due to the extra weight of the motor trying to tip the pilot backwards, it is necessary to provide some additional method of moving the C of G backwards or forwards to provide the correct motor

Michel Carnet flying in Indonesia (Photo: Michel Carnet)

angle. To do this, one end of a pair of metal spreader bars is fixed to each side of the frame to support the motor's weight. The other end of the spreader bars protrudes forward below the pilot's arms to support the harness. The wing risers are then attached at an appropriate position along the spreader bar until the correct balance between motor and pilot is achieved. This solution has one particular advantage in that the position of the risers, brakes and big ears will be very similar to that of a paraglider harness, so the pilot has more direct feel and can use weightshift effectively. However, because there is less pendular stability than a high hang-point set up, the torque of the prop, especially at high revs, can be much more noticeable.

The effects of torque are covered in more detail later in this section.

Aerodynamic considerations

Weight

A paramotor full of fuel can add anything between 25-45kg to the payload carried by the wing. This raises a common question asked by pilots venturing into PPG: what weight is acceptable on their wing or what size wing should they consider using?

To answer that question we need first to understand how the recommended PG loadings are arrived at originally. Most manufacturers agree that the wing loadings for free flight are chosen to offer a reasonable range of pilot weights, while still providing the best sink-rate performance possible without sacrificing stability and recovery characteristics.

If you intend to use your paramotor simply as a means to "get up there" to thermal and free fly, then clearly it is an advantage if you can keep the total payload within the optimum free flight range to get the 'best performance'.

If, however, the intention is principally as a powered platform for taking off and cruising around the sky, then sink-rate becomes less important and a smaller wing may be a better choice by offering enhanced handling, speed and stability. As a rough guideline, a pilot who is placed in the top 30% of a wings weight range for PG will find that the addition of a motor provides a total weight that is usually well suited to the aerodynamic requirements for PPG flight.

Unfortunately, particularly for heavier motors, this total weight may exceed the recommended PG weight range. While it is current opinion that flying at an increased wing loading on a wing for paramotoring is advantageous, it is clearly a reasonable argument that disregarding the certified maximum is unwise.

This leaves many pilots in an awkward position; fortunately the growing interest in powered flight means more and more wings are now being tested with a higher certified upper weight range for use under power.

Increasingly power pilots are using purpose built wings and the weight ranges are not an issue on these models.

Most free-flight paraglider wings will accept power without too much problem, but there are a few models that have proven less suitable for this discipline. If you are considering powered flight, it is important that you seek expert, impartial advice from someone with broad experience. If you already own a free-flight wing and are considering adding a paramotor, it is well worth investigating whether the particular combination you are considering has already been tried (most have!).

Using the same wing for powered and un-powered flight requires some subtle variations in the application of brake input. Aside from the different safety considerations, you will often be launching and landing your PPG in a flat field with little or no wind. With the added weight and propeller effects to contend with, your techniques must be specifically tailored to the job in hand. Many "have a go" self taught pilots have tried and failed, resulting in broken props, damaged wings and a dented pride to boot.

Dedicated power wings. Because of the slightly different requirements of power pilots, most of those who fly regularly under power use a wing designed specifically for the job. Typically these use a reflexed profile for stability at speed and have a wider weight range. More details of these are given below.

Powered paragliding requires additional skills, and to achieve these, dedicated instruction is vital.

Most of these techniques will be taught during your training or conversion, and in time you will develop skills that will suit your particular PPG setup.

Powered flight practicalities

The main effect of flying with power is, of course, the ability to climb when there is no lift; but it is also important to understand that thrust also alters the behaviour of the wing in certain circumstances.

To understand the effect of thrust on a paramotor it is first necessary to cover a few practicalities.

Power to weight ratios

Wing-loading is an important consideration; powered paragliders are very slow aircraft, and in an effort to maximize speed, many dedicated power pilots may choose a small fast wing. This has a number of effects; the most immediately apparent is that a long hard run may be required in calm conditions and the climb rate may be relatively poor. Conversely, on landing the approach will be fast and require a good technique to land gently.

Some wings designed with powered use in mind, are fitted with trim devices that allow the wing to be flown at a range of angles of attack, (i.e trimmed back for T/O and landing and trimmed for speed for cruising).

The more powerful the thrust compared to the weight the easier the take off and climb out will be, so the choice of power unit is always a compromise between, available power, weight and matching this to the pilot weight and wing area.

Flying fast and with a higher wing-loading requires more thrust to maintain level flight.

This increases fuel consumption, and reduces flight duration.

A PPG pilot sitting upright with a big round cage on his back and with a significantly higher payload adds considerably more drag, reducing the glide and sink rate performance very noticeably. Quite a few paraglider pilots imagine that they can power up to altitude and then thermal as usual. This is certainly possible, but some are quite disappointed to find that the wing feels rather sluggish and unresponsive when the fan is switched off!

Your final choice of wing and motor size depends on the importance you give to speed, manoeuverability, response, and resistance to collapse from flying heavily loaded on a smaller wing, as opposed to a good power-off sink rate, easy launches and landings in light winds from flying on a more lightly loaded wing.

Reflexed wings

Reflexed airfoils are a very old solution to providing stability at speed in a tailless aircraft.

Put simply a reflexed airfoil is one that uses part of the rear of the foil for stability rather than lift production, this means a reduction in lifting performance, but increases in stability and higher airspeeds. The centre of pressure is closer to the leading edge of the wing, and the wing is less likely to pitch forwards into a very low angle of attack position, so frontal collapses or tucks are significantly less likely than with a traditional paraglider section.

Reflexed designs also alter the launching and turning characteristics of the wings, not always for the better. Launching simply requires good training and the right degree of pilot input to be successful, and designers have met the challenge of heavy steering at speed by incorporating a separate tip steering systems on may models that allow effective steering without heavy brake pressures.

If you intend to fly under power in wind or be flying through light chop, the reflex models offer a very big advantage in top speed and stability and are well worth considering, if your preferred flight mode is floating around at minimum revs and thermalling, or indeed using your wing for free-flying as well they are less attractive. Some pilots have formed the opinion that reflexed wings are safe to fly in strong turbulence as they are hard to collapse. This is not true, whilst they have greater stability they are still flexible wings supported by line tension, and if that tension is lost, say in a strong forward pitch or in turbulent air, they will collapse in exactly the same way as any other paraglider, and sometimes in quite a dramatic fashion.

Paramotor pilots fall into two main camps, the free-flyer who may wish to use a motor occasionally when the wind is very light. And those who those interest is primarily is in powered flight and who rarely if ever want to soar a ridge or core a thermal.

The first group are best served by choosing a free-flight wing that is capable of being used with a motor as well. Most gliders can be powered and a manufacturer will often have tested a model or two with trimmer risers and a higher payload for this purpose.

If you are a dedicated petrolhead expecting to fly under power in a wide variety of conditions, then it is better to choose one of the reflexed wings that has been designed specifically for powered flight.

Today almost all dedicated power wings are using a variation of the reflexed profile, as speed and stability are the main priorities for dedicated power flyers.

The dividing line between power orientated wings and free-flight wings is very similar to the split between microlight wings and hang-gliders a few decades ago, and if the use of trike undercarriages becomes more common allowing faster take off speeds, then smaller and faster power wings will surely become more common.

With a paramotor every flight can be a cross country! (Photo: Skywalk GMBH)

Understanding the aerodynamic effects of Thrust on PPG flight

The Paramotor throttle effectively governs both thrust and pitch (elevator) at the same time. This is because, unlike any other aircraft, the thrust line is far below the wing. The result is that, as thrust is applied, the pilot is "pushed" forward and the angle of attack increases, generating a climb. Due to the aerodynamic geometry of a PPG, this dual action is always present: you cannot add thrust without also producing the elevator force. (Although the addition of trimmers can slightly offset the effect).

The result: adding power increases the angle of attack and reduces airspeed.

The maximum speed of a powered paraglider is when the engine is switched off.

Typically, the increase in angle of attack experienced by a PPG in level flight is normally not enough to cause anything more dramatic than a small drop in airspeed. However, a very large amount of thrust from a powerful motor, or a sudden burst of power applied by the pilot can affect the aircraft's stability.

At any stage under power this increase in angle of attack must be taken into consideration when applying brake input. There will occasionally be circumstances where the amount of brake the pilot uses when gliding could be too much when under power. Brake input, when the wing is at a higher angle of attack than the PG pilot is used to, can cause instability, where parts of the wing may approach or experience a stall. This must be taken into consideration, particularly when making tight turns and adding power.

This is particularly important for the pilot who switches from powered to unpowered flight and back on the same wing to bear in mind.

With proper training and the correct equipment these variations in flying techniques will be taught to you when learning from an experienced and qualified instructor.

Torque

Sir Isaac Newton was the first person we know of to state the "equal and opposite reaction" law of motion. Unfortunately for him, he never had the opportunity to try it out on a paramotor. While the propeller spins one way, the rest of the aircraft will try and spin the other. Of course it cannot, because of the far greater mass of the pilot, but the effect is still felt as a tendency for the aircraft to turn in flight in the opposite direction to the propeller.

Large props, turning at high revs, can produce quite a noticeable effect. This problem can be reduced in a number of ways.

Wings that can utilise specially designed power risers with trimmers help enormously. These adjustable trimmers can be used to ensure dead straight flight or to adjust the wings rate of climb and speed at a particular throttle setting. Paramotors fitted with low hang-point spreader bars can also be adjusted to minimize the effect. If you do not have the luxury of the above, a simple alternative is to attach a diagonal torque strap across the front of your harness. This system is useful as it may allow you to alter the strap in flight. (A harness set for straight flight under power, will, of course, drift off track when the power is cut!) A little time spent adjusting your own setup on static hang points will often pay dividends in flight.

Electric flight

Petrol engines are noisy, thirsty and require a good deal of maintenance as they are effectively a box of explosions. By contrast an electric motor is quiet, and has far less moving parts. The only drawback in fact is that the energy mass of a battery is very poor compared to the energy mass of petrol, and a pilot can easily carry sufficient fuel for a 4 hour flight but even with the latest batteries, a 20 minute duration is good going for an electric paramotor. However this has not stopped enthusiasts, and there are several companies and scores of garden- shed enthusiasts building machines to try and capture the dream of quiet, clean and self-sustaining flight.

Skywalk's revolutionary electric paramotor in a harness, the E-Walk. (Photo: Skywalk GMBH)

The limiting factor is clearly battery performance , but with the massive interest in electric vehicles generally, there are billions of dollars, pounds and euros being spent on improved battery technology.

There is little doubt that in the next few years a new technology that is at the R&D stage now; like carbon nanotubes, oxygen batteries or hydrogen fuel cells will become a reality and with them the possibility of useful durations in electric flight.

Piloting considerations

Backpack paramotors are great fun to use and are certainly the most compact and portable powered aircraft on earth. However, like almost all designs, they are a compromise of many design criteria, and in addition to the complications of adding power to the aerodynamic equation we should also consider the effect on the piloting requirements.

Launch

A paramotor can be launched in the same two basic ways as an un-powered canopy – forward and reverse. It is generally done with the engine already warmed and running on tick-over.

If there is a little wind, then the reverse launch is a better bet, as the rotating prop and lines are kept away from each other until you are happy to turn round for take off. You also have a far better view and control of the canopy prior to committing yourself to takeoff. With heavier motors, a snatched launch in too strong a breeze can result in the pilot falling backwards, resulting in the aptly named "turtle" position. An expensive and embarrassing situation to be avoided. When reversing, 'cross brake' technique should be used, so that your brakes remain firmly in each hand for the entire launch. The alternative method of letting go of a brake while turning runs the real risk of a brake line being sucked into the prop. Scrabbling overhead for handles while trying to run and control your throttle is a recipe for failure.

Noise could frighten livestock!
(Photo: Backbone Paramotors)

For very light or zero wind conditions a forward (alpine) launch must be executed. Careful preparation of the wing in clean crescent, with all the lines untangled and free is critical. A poorly prepared launch, where the wing comes up asymmetrically, usually results in an aborted takeoff. This then requires the pilot to unclip, stop the motor, and often take it off in order to lay out the wing again. It will only take a few failed attempts like this to lead to exhaustion and frustration.

Take your time, do not let yourself be rushed. If necessary, stop for a few seconds and compose yourself before continuing.

In a forward launch the arms must be held out at the 10 to 2 position to hold the lines clear of the propeller cage. On larger machines this can often require a concerted amount of arm work. If you are not used to launching on flat ground, be aware that a paraglider may need a more committed pull to get it all the way overhead, as the tendency to drop back if you let off the pressure can be more marked. If your wing has speed trimmers, always check that they are correctly set for takeoff. Once again your choice of wing is important here, as some wings are distinctly better at flat field launching than others. The higher the hang-points, the more effort is required to get the wing to rotate up.

Once the pilot is running forward and satisfied with the wing's overhead flying position, full power can be applied to commit to the takeoff. To avoid any sudden torque effects care must be taken not to "blip" the throttle; power must be introduced swiftly but smoothly. You must be able to run fast enough to keep the wing solidly inflated and in control

until it is flying at its required takeoff speed. This part of the launch is the most energetic and the correct posture is important. The natural inclination is to lean forward, but if the position is too exaggerated the thrust will drive you down rather than along.

When you can feel the wing starting to provide lift, you must move to an upright running position with your shoulders back. This allows the propeller's thrust to take over and to push at the correct angle. In the next few paces the thrust should provide enough airspeed for the wing to lift you cleanly off the ground. On some wings a small dab of brakes at the critical moment of 'rotation' will help promote a swift departure from the ground. Use of techniques like these will depend on your wing and will be advised in your training. Do not retract your undercarriage until well clear of the ground. During the launch procedure the thumb should be poised over the kill switch to stop the prop spinning if anything goes wrong. Once fully airborne sit back into the harness and make a few post takeoff checks. Look and listen for anything that may indicate a problem.

For motors that produce torque steer, you may immediately feel the wing starting to fly slightly off the desired line. Whilst you can compensate to some degree with the brakes, it may not be possible to hold the wing perfectly straight. For this reason your launch "runway" should have adequate space to allow some deviation. Once you are happy that everything is as it should be, tuck in and make yourself comfortable for your flight.

In flight
Flying a paramotor is virtually the same as a canopy in free-flight, but with the distinct advantage that you will be able

to explore your horizon in any direction almost immediately

New paramotor pilots may find they have a tendency to treat the motor as something that might pack up at any moment, which is perhaps not a bad thing. You may witness experienced pilots turning downwind at almost zero altitude and then climbing away. However, this is not advised; always climb to a safe altitude before turning downwind, so that if you suffer an engine failure you have the option to turn into wind to land.

Flying under power does require a slightly different mindset, but the advantage of being able to fly more regularly in smaller windows of opportune weather makes using power to get up into the sky a very worthwhile skill to master.

Instability situations

A paramotor is really a light wind machine. Any paraglider is hard pressed to make much headway into wind, and a powered wing is no exception. For this reason they are not generally flown in strong wind conditions. However, it is perfectly possible to use the motor to put yourself above previously unreachable terrain: flying up a narrow valley, for example, or contacting high altitude wave, or viewing cloudbase from above! Of course turbulence may still be encountered and occasionally cause closures of the wing.

Because the motorised wing is likely to be more heavily loaded than in free flight it will retain a higher degree of stability. However, the additional weight, and the complication of thrust, may work against you in some situations, such as a spin. The best advice if conditions become rough is to escape the area as soon as possible, which may well mean a landing out.

In the event of non-critical asymmetric closures it is preferable to keep the power on whilst you clear the tuck if at all practical. In serious instability situations, however, it is better to cut the power. This is primarily to reduce the effects of thrust and torque, and if the wing is very out of shape it is possible that fabric or lines may get sucked into the prop. Tucks, etc should be dealt with in the same way as for free flight, by maintaining course and pumping out the collapse. But above all enjoy the flight and put faith in the mechanics on your back.

Respect your propeller

A prop at full revs may have tip speeds of over 600mph.. and at that speed the prop is effectively invisible.

This is obviously a very dangerous piece of equipment and both pilots and bystanders have been seriously injured by propellors, either directly with fingers chopped off, or indirectly by grit or bits of broken prop being flung outwards. Probably the most dangerous situation is that of a prop sucking in brake, a line or a piece of clothing. We appreciate the thrust of a propeller but often do not fully appreciate the suction of one pulling in the air from around the pilot.

Clothing and any loose objects MUST be securely fastened and unable to reach the propeller disc. Brakes must NEVER be released from your hands in flight unless they have been secured by poppers or some other secure means to the risers. (Even brakes with magnetic keepers have been sucked off by a propeller). It is very easy to simply drop a brake when you want to take a photo or adjust your harness or reach up for the big ears… If a prop at even low revs sucks that brake in, it will wind in the line and fabric of your wing in a fraction of a second and you will find yourself spiraling at the ground with no means of recovery.

This has already killed more than one pilot. Propellors demand your respect!

Noise

Because the groundspeed of a canopy is so slow, the noise from the motor lingers for some time. Though not noisy by aircraft or even microlight standards, because of its slow speed, the paramotor does have a very large "acoustic footprint". At the time of writing the Ministry of Transport has yet to impose a maximum noise level on these machines, but it is likely, (as is already the case with microlight aircraft in the UK) that a level will eventually be set. To minimise the noise for residents of your launch area it is important to vary your flight patterns and to avoid high revs for long periods at low altitudes. Research has shown that people are more annoyed by noise if they can see the aircraft! The very portability of the machine should make using a selection of different launch sites feasible. Noise affects the pilots too. If a radio and headset is not used then ear defenders are certainly a good idea for prolonged flights. Maintaining altitude at minimum revs is the most comfortable way to fly!

Landings

As a general rule landings should be made "dead stick" – with the power off. As you land, the weight of the unit being transferred to your shoulders can make keeping your footing more difficult. In the event of a slip or stumble, a dead stick landing avoids the obvious hazard of a spinning propeller. Good landings are essential, so ensure your landing area is suitable and that your approach is accurate. There is no excuse for losing the wind direction with a paramotor as you have the facility to examine the area

and fly a complete circuit to establish drift before entering your final leg.

Flying a heavily loaded wing requires a committed and well-timed flare. Unlike a paraglider it is not restricted to one approach for landing. So remember your final circuit checks, if you feel unsure, keep the power on and go around again. With practice you will be able to execute a perfect final approach with a paramotor into a flat field and achieve consistent landings.

Learning to fly a paramotor

What will a paramotoring training course consist of? The proposed syllabus below has been arrived at by the BHPA development and training panels, with some input from the British Microlight Aircraft Association (BMAA).

Whist it is being continuously refined, it is very likely to reflect the content of UK training courses for those with some paragliding background. The ab-initio (complete beginner) student who wishes to learn paramotoring will at present need to undertake a short period of un-powered paragliding training, either hill or winch based, and this is likely to remain the case.

If this is your situation, it is recommended that your paragliding tuition is tow (winch) based, as this is much more akin to the situations and effects that you will experience when you strap on a motor. Much hill flying is concerned with using lift and the peculiarities of flying in proximity to a slope; and useful skills like 360° turns and circuits are not a feature of early hill training, for example.

Theory

Show an appropriate understanding of the following topics;

1. The power unit

1.1.1. Configuration, including two stroke operation

1.1.2. Mixing fuel

1.1.3. Safety

1.1.4. Starting procedures

1.1.5. Power generated torque effects

1.1.6. Running in

1.1.7. Hang-points (effects of altering)

1.1.8. Weight checks

2. Power checks

1.2.1. Clearing the fuel supply of bubbles

1.2.2. Clear prop

1.2.3. Cut-off switch

1.2.4. Power on

3. Theory of flight

1.3.1. Thrust and drag

1.3.2. Forces in turns

1.3.3. Climbing and diving turns

1.3.4. Reduction drives

1.3.5. Propellor theory

4. Taking off

1.4.1. Choice of safe field including climb out clearance, ground conditions and turbulence generators

1.4.2 Assessment of conditions

1.4.3. Safe areas for onlookers

1.4.4 Noise nuisance

1.4.5 Torque effects

1.4.6 Methods of inflation

1.4.7. The run. Use of brakes

1.4.8. Emergency stopping (launch abort)

5. Flight

1.5.1 Torque effects

1.5.2 The micrometeorology likely to be found in XC situations. Valley winds, rotors etc.

1.5.3 Speed systems. The effects on a powered paraglider. Power on and power off situations.

1.5.4 Techniques for avoiding and recovering from tucks, stalls and spins.

1.5.5 Navigation exercise. The student will plan a 30km (total) flight either as an out and return with a pre-declared turn-point or as a flight to a declared goal.

6. Flying rules

1.6.1 Congested areas

1.6.2 Noise nuisance

1.6.3 Flying over water

7. Air law

1.7.1 Aeronautical charts.

1.7.2 Restricted and prohibited airspace

1.7.3 Line features, quadrangle rule.

1.7.4 VMC minima

1.7.5 CANP system

1.7.6 Radio considerations

8. Landing

1.8.1 Power on/off

1.8.2 Kill switch management

1.8.3 Light wind/high wind situations

1.8.4 Effects of weight on flying speed. Stall speed and flare.

Practical

Demonstrate the following in an effective/competent manner

1. Pre-flight

2.1.1 Canopy ground handling

2.1.2 Launch assisting

2.1.3 Pre take-off control of the paramotor

2.1.4 Post landing control of the paramotor

2.1.5 Parking the paramotor

2.   Flight

The student will perform the following tasks to the satisfaction of the instructor:

2.2.1   Three consecutive powered flights from a flat site with at least 100ft ground clearance with unassisted take off runs, smooth 90° turns to left and right and stand up landings.

2.2.2   Demonstrate a short field landing by landing within 40m of an imaginary 5m high construction.

2.2.3   Complete three landing within 10m of a defined spot in winds of less than 5mph.

2.2.4   Complete three landings within 10m of a defined spot in winds of more than 10mph.

2.2.5   Minimum of 10 paramotor flights logged including full deflation and inflation of wing between flights.

2.2.6   Demonstrate safe and effective use of rapid descent technique (not B riser stall)

2.2.7   Maintain directional control and show recovery from tucks of between 20 per cent and 30 per cent.

2.2.8   Carry out power-off landings to the satisfaction of the instructor from various heights some of which are over 500ft.

2.2.9   Show knowledge of forward and reverse launches and demonstrate them.

2.2.10   Complete a 30km (total) flight with a pre-declared goal.

Competence and experience

1.   Competence

The student will demonstrate competence of the following topics to the satisfaction of the instructor:

3.1.1   Consistently demonstrate safe airspeed control

3.1.2   Safely demonstrate slow flight awareness and discuss symptoms and dangers (deliberate stalls must be avoided)

3.1.3   Demonstrate an ability to fly co-ordinated 360° turns in both directions

3.1.4   Display the ability to fly safely with others maintaining a good look out complying with the Rules of the Air and exhibiting good airmanship. Demonstrate an ability to manoeuvre the paramotor safely, considerately and in accordance with air traffic rules.

2.   Experience

Prior to being certified as a paramotor pilot and/or flying outside direct visual range of the training field other than to execute specific training tasks, the student must satisfy the instructor regarding the following and, where required, furnish the appropriate evidence.

3.2.1   Passed the BHPA PPG exam

3.2.2   Must have successfully flown paramotors or paragliders or hang gliders or micro-lights on at least eight separate days within the previous nine months

3.2.3   Must have a minimum of five hours logged airtime on paragliders, hang gliders or micro-lights of which at least three hours must be on paramotors.

3.2.4   Satisfy the instructor that the pilot has correct attitude to continue a flying career both safely and competently

Training course

An actual training course is likely to conform to the following basic pattern.

At ground school you will be introduced to the actual equipment and learn about safety checks and procedures and watch the instructor demonstrate what a paramotor is capable of. This will include airfield discipline, the importance of correct clothing, (even simple things like long hair or a drawstring on a jacket can be drawn into a rotating prop), mechanical checks and dealing with spectators etc. If the school has a static simulator you may then have the opportunity to hang up in a paramotor and try it out, learning to respond to radio commands and just get the feel of the unit on your back. Launch is the critical phase of flying one of these machines and some time will be given over to practicing forward (alpine) launches. If the school is using a winch for pre-motorised flights you will then have an opportunity for low un-powered flights to get used to basic control of the wing, working up over a couple of days to towing up to a reasonable height and flying a good circuit with a dummy motor on your back. This stage can be reached almost straight away if you have some free-flying experience.

Mixed in with these exercises will be a fair bit of theory, covering much of the same ground as a free flight club pilot course with additional sections on air law and, of course, the use of power.

Very soon it will be time for your first paramotor flights and you will soon be buzzing around the field practising co-ordinated turns, dead stick (power off) landings, maintaining level flight etc. you will also cover subjects such as reducing noise nuisance, rapid descents (big

ears), dealing with small trucks, reverse launching and be able to demonstrate accurate landings. Once your instructor is satisfied that you have absorbed sufficient information and expertise, it is time for your 30km cross-country navigation exercise.

The "Navex" will mean you must decide on the suitability of the weather, calculate your approximate groundspeed and fuel consumption and be able to navigate either by compass bearing, ground features or even GPS to a prearranged goal. Very often this will mean flying an out and return pattern or perhaps a triangular course. It may mean avoiding airspace of some type. Your instructor may or may not follow you depending on his or her level of confidence! If you can successfully manage this task and convince your instructor that you are suitably competent and have a good safe attitude, it remains only to pass the theory exam paper, for which you should now be well prepared.

A non-pilot will take around nine days to achieve this level. Beware of anyone who seems keen to sell you a paramotor and tells you that you can be trained in much less time!!

For a pilot with experience in a related discipline – especially paragliding, this time could be as little as two or three days.

Foot launched powered aircraft (FLPA) Code of Practice

Preamble
This code of practice was originally written in mid 1996 as FLPA were being de-regulated. There has been some justified concern by other flyers that the unrestrained use of FLPA may jeopardise

other free flyers which is why this document was drafted.

Scope and authority

The Code of Practice is intended to give general guidance and unless stated its contents are not mandatory. However, it should be noted that where disputes arise which lead to legal action, non-compliance may be detrimental.

Mandatory requirement

All FLPA pilots should comply with the spirit and the letter of the General Exemption and all relevant Air Law. (Specifically this means carrying an airchart and avoiding controlled airspace, something that has sadly been poorly adhered to by some paramotor pilots)

Association requirements

In addition to mandatory requirements the BHPA may introduce regulations from time to time. Pilots should maintain their membership of one of the Association and keep up to date with existing and new regulations and guidance. If you are not a member of the BHPA you should join and obtain a pilot rating and acquire insurance. If you become involved in legal action in the future, proof of your skills, knowledge and pilot rating obtained via a recognised organisation will be an obvious advantage.

Taking off – general

Wherever possible FLPA should take off from a recognised and/or secure area. The ideal situation is an existing microlight airfield that has the appropriate Local Authority permissions.

When pilots take off from existing microlight areas they should familiarise themselves with and comply with local rules.

If the FLPA takes off from other areas, the following procedures should be taken

- The area should be secure from the possibility of animals and/or spectators being in an area of damage (note: a shattered propellor can scatter sharp shards of wood at high speed).

- Any spectators should be properly marshalled and any dogs should be firmly attached to a lead (they have been know to chase the FLPA when it starts to move).

- The take off strips should be closely inspected for possible trips and holes.

- Proper permission should be obtained from the owner of the land.

- Any neighbours should be warned of your future activities.

Taking off – planning approval

Unless the land is in a special zone such as a conservation area you can usually fly from a temporary take-off area on 28 days in any 12 months. If you fly on more than 28 days without Planning Approval the owner of the land may be served with enforcement order by the local authority and could be subject to a fine. Local authorities will generally include all of the land in one ownership in an enforcement order so don't try to argue that you are taking off from different fields and they each have a 28 day dispensation. The local authority may also have local byelaws that should not be contravened.

Taking off – nuisance

Even if you comply with the planning regulations you may fall foul of the law of nuisance. For a prosecution to take place, there must be evidence that the nuisance has occurred on a regular basis. A video of you taking off ten days in succession at 6am very close to a house could result in a large fine and the confiscation of your aircraft.

Taking off – hang gliding and paragliding sites

Don't – unless you have permission from the club.

Flying – general

If you take off from one place, vary your flight path to avoid annoying the general public.

In particular, powered paragliders flying against the wind will remain in view for a long period of time. If they fly higher to make less noise they will fly slower due to the wind gradient. If you are not making much headway it may be safer to land and get a lift back to base.

It should be noted that German research has shown that an aircraft is a greater source of annoyance if it can be seen.

Flying – hang gliding and paragliding sites

Even if you have taken off some distance away it will be very tempting to buzz your mates who are grounded on a hill top on a nil wind day. Don't.

A number of hang glider and paraglider clubs have introduced rules that generally exclude FLPA and in at least one case there is a self-declared exclusion zone round each site. FLPA pilots from the BHPA cannot be expected to be conversant with every rule introduced by clubs participating in other types of flying. However, where such a rule is known to exist it should be respected.

The general rule to be followed is "use your common sense and stay away".

Flying – livestock

Adherence to the General Exemption should mean that livestock is not disturbed. However, you should particularly avoid bird sanctuaries and riding stables. If you are taking off from a field you should check that there are no riders in the vicinity. If there are – wait.

Landing

For a variety of reasons you may decide to "land out". If you are landing on private land you should always find the landowner and tell him/her of your arrival. Courtesy takes five minutes of your time and invariably results in a pleasant experience. One pilot always carries a miniature bottle of scotch with him to offer to the landowner that is always accepted with amusement and gratitude (it's the thought that counts!).

It is worth noting that a forced landing due to exhausted fuel supplies is not generally accepted as a good reason to land where you like. (In fact for aeroplanes it is considered negligent operation, and therefore an offence by the CAA).

Display flying

Display flying should be undertaken only after seeking and being granted permission by a Display Evaluator appointed by the CAA. BMAA or BHPA head office will be able to give you the names of Display Evaluators.

Conclusion

Any breach of common sense or good manners is a breach of this code of practice. Please remember that the General Exemption has been issued on a temporary basis. This means that the CAA could very easily decide to impose full regulation on the sport..

Above all enjoy your sport, respect regulations, and this will help maintain our freedom to fly.

Passing your Exams 37

Most countries require their pilots to pass some form of written theory exam before qualifying as a pilot. There are several reasons for this – the most obvious to ensure that each pilot has sufficient knowledge to fly safely at the chosen level. Exams, when properly debriefed, also educate the pilot, allow the instructors to check their own thoroughness, strengths and weaknesses and, when collated by the national association, help pinpoint areas that require particular attention.

Preparation

It need not be a struggle to absorb the information that you need. Paragliding is something we do for fun and have an interest in and so the theoretical aspects can be related to real events or experiences. It may be hard to recall what cloud type occurs where, but recalling how the sky looked the day you first found yourself thousands of feet off the ground should not be too hard. Be aware of the level you are aiming at. It is not much use answering an advanced pilot question about the development of a thermal by saying "hot air rises". Equally, a student pilot level question about stability will not require a critique of design factors. Your instructor should brief you about what level to expect.

Taking the exam

● If you are not ready don't take it. Ask your instructor to ask a few similar questions first if you are not sure you are prepared. If it is a long exam, particularly for one of the higher levels, make sure that you are not tired, wet or hungry before you start. In other words, do not sit the exam straight after getting in from a day's flying.

● Make sure you have the correct equipment; some exams may require a calculator or a ruler.

● Read the instructions! In a multiple choice exam set recently the instructions clearly stated that one or more answers may be correct, but the majority of pilots still failed to tick more than one box, even though it transpired that they knew two options were right!

● Allow plenty of time. Make sure you have sufficient time to do the exam in the longest period allowed and some spare to go over it afterwards with your invigilator.

If the invigilator is a club volunteer or an instructor is staying on late to help you out, don't forget to buy them a beer!

In the UK the exams are set by the BHPA and are all multiple-choice papers. The topics you will need to know are:

Elementary Pilot (EP) level

- Rules of the air.
- CAA restrictions on when and where you can fly.
- How an aerofoil works.
- The stall.
- Airspeed groundspeed and windspeed.
- Identifying areas of lift and turbulence.
- Dealing with problems in flight.
- Basic weather and forecasts.

Sample questions for a student level exam:

1. A hang glider is circling in a thermal, you wish to use the same thermal. What rules apply?

   A You must circle in the same direction as him?

   B You have right of way as he is faster and more manoeuvrable than you?

   C The lower pilot has the right of way?

   D You must both circle to the left to reduce the risk of a collision?

2. You are flying downwind with an airspeed of 17mph, the wind is 18mph. What is your groundspeed?

   A 35mph

   B 1mph

   C 18mph

   D 17mph

Club Pilot (CP) level

All the topics for student pilot plus:

- Cloud types (including ground level).
- Basic air law.
- Principles of flight, lift/drag etc.
- Restrictions on other types of paragliding activity (eg power/towing/dual etc).
- Unstable situations, spins, stalls, tucks, etc.

Sample questions for a club pilot level exam

1. Define VMC when flying in Type G airspace at 5,000ft AMSL.

   A 5 nautical miles visibility, 1000ft clear of cloud vertically and horizontally.

   B Clear of cloud and in sight of the surface.

   C 1,000ft clear of cloud vertically and 1,500m horizontally with visibility of at least 5km.

   D Clear of cloud and in sight of the surface with visibility of at least 8km

2. A deep or parachutal stall can be caused:

   A By braking too deeply

   B When recovering from "B lining"

   C By pulling on both rear risers

   D By any of the above

Pilot (P) level

All the topics for club pilot plus:

- Reading an air chart (including abbreviations, symbols, scales, magnetic variations, etc).

- Temperature and pressure gradients and rates

- Aerodynamics and performance of a paraglider

- Instruments

Sample questions for pilot level exam

I What meteorological conditions could give rise to an inversion?

   A A high pressure area with extensive cloud cover during the night to trap convective heat

   B A prolonged period of high pressure when the air has become dirty with trapped dust and smoke particles

   C Warm air at altitude being pushed over colder air at ground level by an occluded front

   D An airmass being warmed as it is compressed by sinking in the centre of a high pressure area

2 The following symbol taken from an air chart shows:

   A A disused airfield with gliding activity.

   B A civil airfield with parachuting and winch cable activity

   C A civil airfield with microlight and paragliding activity.

   D A military airfield with winch cable and parachuting activity.

Advanced Pilot (AP) level

The topics for the advanced pilot paper are beyond the scope of this book, but it deals essentially with cross-country navigation skills.

38 Paragliding Equipment Design & Testing

Gliders

Manufacturers try to target the market with canopies they hope will sell a lot of units, and in order to do this they must first identify what their target market is, whilst all gliders seek to maximize the performance, this is tempered by the level of security and ease of use depending on the LTF class being aimed at.

The manufacturer will look at these requirements, see what his dealers have said (good and bad) about his last model and set to making improvements.

Most paragliders these days are evolved versions of earlier models. Only rarely does an innovation make a dramatic change.

All the major manufacturers now use CAD-CAM programmes to design and plot their fabric patterns and line lengths on a computer. It takes a matter of hours to plot, cut and sew together the first prototype.

After that the development is in the hands of the test pilots. How does it handle? Is it likely to pass the certification at the right

A laser plotter

level? Will it go faster without becoming too prone to collapse? There are a hundred questions that must be asked and answered by the pilots and designers. By contrast this can be a very lengthy process.

This procedure must be repeated to some extent with each size in the range, and eventually, when the design team is satisfied, a few dealers may be allowed to try the wings to get some feedback from the market.

If all is well (and everyone likes the name and the colour scheme!) the wing is sent for testing and the production line is geared up to produce them. Pilots sometimes ask why gliders cost so much when the materials must be no more than three or four hundred Euros at most, The simple answer is that this research, design and test procedure is so demanding and each model may sell only a few hundred example before it all starts again...

After being laser plotted, templates of the individual panels cut from some inert material such as mylar. The line lengths are also transferred onto a marking jig of some type, the materials are sourced and the paraglider is ready to go into production.

Panels from as many as 40 gliders may be cut at once, and each piece must be accounted for and put in the right place for sewing together. Stitching a paraglider is a skilled job, demanding great accuracy; catching just one stitch of a rib onto a top surface can ruin a glider. Once the envelope itself is assembled, complete with line hook-up points and reinforcement, the lines are attached, starting from the canopy and working down, until they are linked to the risers.

Some manufacturers simply pack the wings into the bag for the dealers to inspect; others inflate each wing individually; the majority check sample wings from each batch.

Quality control throughout the industry is very good as a rule, but it is worth noting that many gliders are built by sub-contract companies in the Far East, Eastern Europe or Sri-Lanka and the person sewing it is not known to the designers or dealers selling it. Mistakes can (and have) been made, and for this reason it is always advisable to inflate and thoroughly check every new wing before taking to the air.

Launching for a test flight, fully equipped with buoyancy aid, just in case (Photo: Swing Gliders)

Airworthiness classifications

Before any reputable dealer will sell a new paraglider, it will have passed an independent airworthiness test. This test is designed to ensure that the wing has no hidden vices, will react correctly to proper control inputs and is sufficiently strong.

Buying any paraglider without certification is not only likely to invalidate any insurance cover you may hold (including BHPA 3rd party cover) but it will also be virtually impossible to resell and could be bad for your health.

There have been two main bodies awarding airworthiness certificates. The German DHV (manufacturers association) which awarded the Guteseigel standard, and the EN European system. In 2009 the two have (after ten years of meetings!) been pretty well meshed into the LTF system that is recognized worldwide. Glider still appear with one or both of the CEN or LTF labels but these are now effectively the same.

Virtually all wings, harnesses, helmets and reserves are now certified with LTF or EN certification.

Load testing

The paraglider must successfully pass a load test with a payload equating to eight times the maximum placarded payload i.e. on a wing with a weight range of 80-100kg will need to withstand a load of 800kg without showing any structural damage. There is also a shock load test where the wing is suddenly loaded to 6G. This is done by "snatch" launching it with a tow line with a 6g weak link.

This is done by pulling the wing at speed, using a truck fitted with the appropriate weak link, load cells and monitoring equipment.

Description of the paraglider classes

Class	Description of flight characteristics	Description of pilot skills required
A	Paragliders with maximum passive safety and extremely forgiving flying characteristics. Gliders with good resistance to departures from normal flight.	Designed for all pilots including pilots under all levels of training.
B	Paragliders with good passive safety and forgiving flying characteristics. Gliders with some resistance to departures from normal flight.	Designed for all pilots including pilots under all levels of training. * NOTE *Quite a few designs are achieving B class although they are clearly quite dynamic in character. So this definition is widely considered inappropriate.*
C	Paragliders with moderate passive safety and with potentially dynamic reactions to turbulence and pilot errors. Recovery to normal flight may require precise pilot input.	Designed for pilots familiar with recovery techniques, who fly "actively" and regularly, and understand the implications of flying a glider with reduced passive safety.
D	Paragliders with demanding flying characteristics and potentially violent reactions to turbulence and pilot errors. Recovery to normal flight requires precise pilot input.	Designed for pilots well practised in recovery techniques, who fly very actively, have significant experience of flying in turbulent conditions, and who accept the implications of flying such a wing.

There is also a Dual (tandem) rating i.e. wings Suitable for tandem (2 person) flight.

Flight testing

Each canopy is flight tested at the top and bottom of its recommended weigh trange. Here are a variety of flight tests that are conducted , starting with take off and straight and level flight, and progressing through to spin, stall and tuck recovery. Each manouvre is graded by the pilot and the video evidence.

For example A glider that scores an A for the 55% asymmetric tuck with full speed bar applied; has demonstrated that it will self recover to normal flight having turned no more than 90°, recovered in less than 4 seconds and not dived or otherwise required any input in still air.

A "B" means that the recovery took longer than 4 seconds but less than 8 seconds and the turn may have been between 90° & 180°.

A "C" by contrast means the pilot has had to take corrective action to recover the glider to pilotable flight.

After the tests the glider is awarded a grade. If all the elements are A's except one element at one end of the weight range which is B then the glider is rated B. – In short the grade always reflects the "worst" value achieved.

Note : Whilst the choice of glider is very important, these tests are only an indicator of how they behave in relation to other models. Some pilots naively assume that because they have an A rated wing that I will self –recover if it collapses in turbulence. It may not!- Turbulence is chaotic airflow and by nature impossible to measure. All you can be sure of is that without a correct input a C rated wing will recover a lot more slowly! You

A glider is put through a full stall. (Photo: U-Turn GMBH)

Stall and recovery sequence. Pic: Bruce Goldsmith Design

may hear pilots refer to their gliders as "bombproof" or some similar misleading term.

Confidence in your kit is a good thing,- not least as doing nothing and letting the wing sort itself out can often be the best course of action. But it should be pointed out that any wing can collapse and lose height in rough air and pilots should exercise caution the conditions they choose to fly in and critically how close they get to the terrain.

Other tests!

There are other criteria as well, the distance of brake travel from activation to stall is specified, and the harness set up, with the distance from the seat to carabiners and how far the carabiners are apart is also a specific value. There is a comprehensive document available on line from the paragliding manufacturers association with all the up to date details for those who would like to know more about airworthiness testing.

Airworthiness issues and debates about classifying top end competition wings still rages.

This is the area that drives many innovations, but it also features pilots willing to fly fast and in close quarters in powerful conditions, and the accident rate has in recent years caused concerns, particularly as some of the gliders in use have had questionable stability.

The whole question of certifying paramotor wings is currently in a state of change and everything from harness protection to reserve stability is still being explored. Although the sport is over 30 years old, we are all still learning.

Harnesses

Harnesses are also load tested and the back protection systems also require a further test to be certified. These tests involve placing a 50Kg dummy in the harness and dropping it onto a flat surface from 165cm height, the maximum load to the dummy load sensors cannot exceed 38g for 3 milliseconds or 50g for one millisecond . This sounds like a massive shock, but is apparently what a healthy person should be able to tolerate without sustaining permanent injury.

(As a matter of interest if you land on your feet, bend your knees and roll from a drop height of 165cm you should be able to sustain a g force of less than 2.5g!!) – which sound a lot more comfortable. For this reason the parachute landing fall technique is still taught at BHPA training schools.

Some harnesses do not have back protection fitted, or it is not up to this standard. Unless you are a specialist user (a climber for example), then it is strongly recommend that you purchase harness with a certified level of protection.

Harnesses must also pass a load test, and conform to the height and spacing of hang-point criteria. A glider certification usually requires the harness hang-points to be set 42cm apart (38cm in the case of small gliders and pilots). If this distance is set much greater or less the recovery of the wing may be affected.

There is more information on harness protection and the pro's and cons' of different systems in the chapter on buying your equipment.

Reserve Parachutes

The present LTF system for testing reserve parachutes requires a maxium sink rate in still air of no more than 5.4m/sec with the maximum payload indicated by the manufacturer.

This arrived at by calculation and by pulling the reserve to measure it's coefficient of drag. It is worth pointing out that in a real life deployment situation there may be lifting or sinking air, the paraglider canopy may affect the performance of the reserve by dragging it in one direction or the reserve may oscillate for some reason. So this standard is only an indicator of performance. Reserve design has not changed all that much over the years and so some new systems are still sold with the original certification. You may come across Gutesigel (DHV) or EN rated systems. The EN demanded a sink rate of 5.5msec but the older DHV Gutesiegel only required a sink rate of 6.8m/sec. For this reason if your system is only DHV certified the recommendation is that it is used at no more than 75% of the maximum placarded weight limit.

In live tests performed at the test facility Air Turquoise in Switzerland, in 2009 with a weight dropped from a paraglider *(so still not at all realistic)* the actual sink rate results were frequently worse than this standard for many models, (though a few come out very well). These tests were not much liked by some manufacturers and there were some valid objections to how they were performed, but the fact is, it does highlight that testing such a thing is difficult to do accurately. The good news is that almost all actual deployments in emergencies have good results, – probably due to the fact that very few pilots are flying at the maximum payload anyway, and perhaps also to the possibility that some pilots do hit the ground harder but get away with it.

Reserves should be repacked at least annually and again if they have become damp. otherwise the deployment time may be much longer.

Reserves are "lifed" at 10 years so any system that is older than that *(though it should still work)* cannot be relied on to be able to withstand a shock opening , and should be replaced.

Top: Air turquoise reserve tests
(Photo: Sup'Air)

Above: Sup'Air's harness test rig; linked to accelerometers it can measure the amount of G that a pilot will be subjecetd to in an impact, thereby allowing them to design protection systems to minimise injury
(Photo: Sup'Air)

Pushing the Limits 39

or...

Licking the sticky bit of the flight envelope!

(Or other exciting things you can do with your paraglider).

SIV

Many pilots are, very wisely, a little concerned about how they will react if their canopy should suffer a major collapse, or if they should find themselves in a spin or deep stall situation. Undertaking more radical manoeuvres like spirals, B lines, or wingovers can also be quite a daunting prospect, but these are skills that may one day be required to get out of trouble.

Pilots may have read the test pilot's reports on their wings, but there is really no substitute for trying it yourself, to discover the true limits of your paraglider's flight envelope.

SIV (Simulation d'Incidents de Vol) courses have been designed to allow pilots to become better acquainted with these situations in a (relatively) controlled environment, and hopefully, in doing so, making them safer and more confident pilots.

Typically such courses are run by highly experienced instructors. They take place at venues where there is plenty of altitude to play with and where manoeuvres can be practised with radio communication over water with a rescue boat on hand.

Pilots are unlikely to benefit much from an SIV course until they have a pretty good level of familiarity with

their equipment. For this reason it is not ideal to do a course like this if you have less than 10 hours or so airtime, or have just changed glider. Nervous pilots are unlikely to get the best out of this kind of course.

SIV courses offer the opportunity to explore the limits of your glider in a safe environment

Synopsis of a typical SIV course

Initial briefing: This will cover the theory of the manoeuvres to be attempted and why they are important. *(If your instructor cannot give a convincing reason why you need to know something, then it probably is not worth doing- this applies to all courses).*

The briefing should also include a discussion of your own experience, why you wish to do this course and the option to quit the manoeuvre programme if you are uncomfortable.

Introduction to the equipment and procedures:

1   How to deal with water landings and getting into the boat.

2   The radio protocols that will be used, including commands, what to do if communication is lost and supplying waterproof containers for radios, etc.

3   Checking your reserve deployment system, and ensuring you know how and when to use it.

Flying

A good SIV course will start gently, and a briefing will precede each manoeuvre. A typical programme will include:

1   Asymmetric tucks of steadily increasing degrees of severity. Both sides should be collapsed and recovery technique.

2   As above, but with the speed system applied.

3   Exploring the glider's envelope. Turn reversal and gentle wingovers. Exploring the edge of the speed range. Recovery from incipient stall.

4   "Get down quick" manoeuvres like spirals and B lines, and appropriate recovery.

5   Searching for, identifying, and recovering from the onset of a spin. This is done by making steadily more radical turns from a steadily decreasing airspeed. It will also cover what to do next if it all goes horribly wrong… how to deal with a full spin, when to deploy a reserve, etc.

6   Other manoeuvres, such as symmetrical tucks and searching for deep stall with rear risers and recovery.

7   Reserve deployment (see below).

You should be cautioned against "cascading" manoeuvres into one another, as this can cause unexpected behaviour of the wing.

Each manoeuvre will be watched by the instructor, who will coach you on the radio and after completion you will receive a de-briefing on how it went, and points to help you next time.

In the past some pilots (and instructors) have amused themselves by advocating manoeuvres that have no real value other than looking radical, such as holding in spins or repeated dynamic full stalls. As these situations never happen in reality, their only use is in training for Acro display flying.

For most pilots the additional risks involved in attempting them are unnecessary and unwise. Even on an SIV

course with a boat, etc, falling into your canopy and getting gift-wrapped is likely to seriously injure you.

One radical situation that some feel is useful, (and others an unnecessary risk) is a practice deployment of your reserve. You do not learn much except how it feels, but as many pilots are reluctant to chuck it out, even when things do look bad, on balance a practice deployment that teaches you to trust your system is probably a good thing.

During the course you will learn to "feel" "the onset of a stall or spin, to react calmly and correctly to collapses, and be secure in your ability to lose height quickly.

There is little point in doing a manoeuvre just once, the primary object of SIV training is to learn to prevent and recover

Pilot's eye view of a spiral dive (Photo: U-Turn)

from unstable situations, and to do this you must be reasonably familiar with them. To go on a course like this and have "done" a spin for example is almost worthless. Far better to have identified an incipient spin and successfully recovered from it several times. Repetitive practice is the key to all these tasks.

A real eye-opener to many pilots is the difference between a typical first time buyer's wing and higher rated wings. The high aspect ratio and faster wings are, interestingly, often easier to control during less severe asymmetric tucks, and will usually wingover much better, due to improved energy retention, but the behaviour in a spin, or if most of the wing is lost in a severe asymmetric, can be much more radical.

The first time wings tend to self- recover in smooth conditions if the pilot is not sure what to do and does nothing. With some higher-level wings, the situation can deteriorate very quickly if the pilot is not quick and decisive in his actions.

It follows that if you have ambitions to fly a glider which requires pilot input to recover from unstable situations (LTF C or equivalent), then an SIV course is probably the best way to acquire these skills.

When your SIV course is completed, you should be more confident in your ability to deal with unexpected situations, and should be a better pilot for it.

Expedition and Safari Flying

The beauty of a paraglider is its portability. Moving a sailplane, a microlight or even a hang-glider to a remote location can be a major logistical challenge.

Taking a paraglider with you on holiday is as simple as carrying it to the airport.

Some pilots have been quick to capitalise on this aspect of the sport, and paragliders have been flown in Antarctica, from mountains on every continent, in deserts and over jungles.

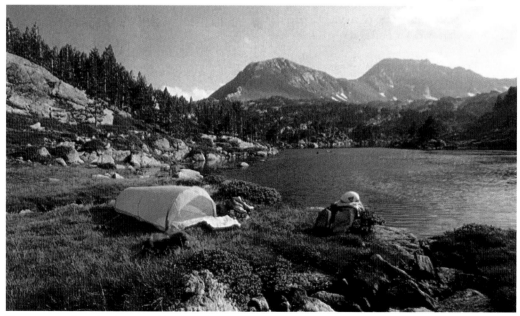

The essesnce of travel with a paraglider. One of Pierre Bouilloux's bivouac sites during his traverse of the Pyrenees (Photo: Sup'Air)

Of course flying the Himalayas, or the Great Rift valley requires a little more planning than your local hill, and all the advice given in Chapter 33 *"Flying in new environments"* is even more applicable.

You may need to carry spares such as line material and repair tape. For long trips you will need food and bivouac gear like tents or stoves, and of course you will need maps and probably a GPS. Naturally you will need a harness and wing capable of carrying all this.

In recent years some manufacturers and pilots have come up with wings and harnesses that are specifically tailored to portability and ease of use in extreme situations.

Very lightweight expedition paragliders are available that can be packed very small for climbing and long carry-ups. Harnesses are also available in a huge variety of styles that include those with no seat plate at all for fly-down use only, and those with massive storage space for

Pic: Ozone Gliders

Expect a warm welcome when you drop in by paraglider. Children from a small Himalayan near Manali in India (Photo: Neil Cruickshank)

all your kit. The French harness company Sup-air (whose founder Pierre Bouilloux is one of the original bivouac flyers) even produce a purpose-built tent that fits in your pocket and weighs in at less than 1kg.

There is a kind of sub culture of ultra-light gear users that is steadily becoming more popular as pilots venture further afield and as the mainstream equipment gradually gets more sophisticated, but also heavier and bulkier.

Innovations from outside the sport like satellite phones, lightweight digital movie cameras, solar powered battery chargers and of course GPS systems, have all made flying in remote parts of the world just a bit easier and more accessible.

Expedition flying does require a different mindset, as, despite all these toys, essentially you will be cutting yourself off from the infrastructure of prepared launch areas and help from others. This is a big step, and you will be pioneering in the true sense. Clearly it carries increased risks, but this is an element of the sport that encapsulates the feeling that attracts many into flying in the first place: total self-reliance and complete freedom.

Whether you are flying dunes in the Sahara or glaciers in Siberia, flying in unknown territory is an experience that you never forget. The look of incredulity on the faces of the local people who have probably never seen anything like a paraglider is an experience in itself.

Expedition flyers are unanimous in their discovery that some of the world's poorest and most isolated people are among the most generous of spirit and welcoming of strangers. Paragliding certainly gives you a talking point when you drop in.

Speed flying

Speed flying is a new twist on the origins of the sport: using a very small paraglider a pilot can sacrifice his sink rate and glide performance for speed. This has three advantages, the kit is very small and light, you can safely fly in stronger conditions and it looks really cool. The downside is that you cannot soar in lift, flights are short, and your take off and landings are very fast. Speed flying is therefore well suited to big mountains and fast launches where there is little lift anyway. Winter resorts with big snow covered slopes for ski launching and lifts to the top are perfect.

Some skiers have found that using a very severe slope with 100ft+ vertical rock faces or other drops that used to be too extreme to ski down are now accessible if they combine skiing and flying, the wings for this kind of speed flying can be the size of a large kite at just 8-10sq metres. A variation is the larger wings of 12- 18m that are simply smaller and faster than a regular wing and can still be foot launched and landed. Some mountaineers, conscious of the fact that descending can be at least as hazardous as ascending big peaks have already used speed wings to make a quick get away from major Himalayan peaks.

On November 19th 2009 Stuart Holmes flew his Gin Yak speed wing from the summit of Ama Dablam in the Himalayas descending over 4500m (about 15,000ft) in ten minutes. Saving himself at least a day and half's descent.

Acro Flying

One of the reasons that we fly is that we enjoy testing our own limits. Another strong reason is that we all have an exhibitionist tendency to a greater or lesser degree. Certainly we all enjoy the praise and approval of our flying colleagues. To some with competitive instincts this is manifested in a desire to enter competitions, and this has been a driving force in the improving standards of our equipment.

For a few pilots, the most interesting area of flight is in aerobatic flying. Paragliders are quite possibly the least conventionally aerobatic of all aircraft, in the sense that they can be collapsed and alter shape in mid air in difficult-to-predict ways. But for aerobatic pilots this is simply another challenge, and the discipline of Acro flying has steadily attracted more pilots over the years. Acro flying is a mixture of the technical and the artistic and is – to pilots and the public alike – fascinating to watch.

©2002 Red Bull - www.redbull-vertigo.c●

Acro competitions are held in various locations which have similar requirements to SIV courses, as the chance of a catastrophic failure and the need to deploy a reserve is reasonably high compared to most flying situations. They are typically flown from mountain sites overlooking lakes, but can also be winch launched (though this will give limited altitude), and there have been a number of pilots who have launched by "D-bagging" from a helicopter or balloon..

A typical Acro sequence will involve a number of manoeuvres, which are linked into one another to give a display sequence. This is marked in competitions by a panel of judges who give points for difficulty and presentation.

Elements of an Acro display may include:

Spins

Where the canopy is rotating horizontally through a vertical axis. If the centre of rotation is outside the wing, the canopy can be kept fully inflated.

Helicopters

A variation of the spin, where the axis of rotation is inside the wing-span, so that effectively part of the wing is flying backwards. Depending on the internal pressure in the wing this can cause the portion flying backwards to collapse and fold under (rather like a big-ear in reverse). This can further tighten the spin.

SAT

Invented by the flyers of the interestingly named Safety Acro Team, this figure takes its name from their team initials. It is hard to describe accurately, even after having watched it done in slow motion! The glider is descending in a spiral somewhat like a regular spiral dive, but with the centre of rotation between the pilot and wing. The pilot is therefore rotating in the opposite direction to the glider. This manoeuvre is unlike anything found in any other form of aerobatic aviation!

Spirals

Linked 360° turns where the centrifugal force throws the pilot out at 90° to the wing. The nose-down attitude of the wing and fast rotation mean that height is lost very rapidly (the flight path is similar to the thread on a drill bit). This manoeuvre generates massive speed and therefore energy, which can then be converted into a wingover or other figure.

When continued to ground level (when a wing tip or hand touches the ground), this is known as a 'death spiral'.

Wingovers

When a glider has excess energy, either from a series of pitching movements, or from linked turns, a hard control input can generate a high banked turn. Turns of more than 90° are known as wingovers, and Acro pilots frequently link wingovers into one another, achieving angles of bank of 140° or more, where their bodies are completely above the wing, which remains fully inflated and flying normally.

Close syncro flying (Photo: U-Turn)

Loops (Tumbles)

The logical extension of the wingover is a loop, and given sufficient energy the pilot can achieve a positive loop (ie with lines tight all the way over). If there is not quite enough energy to pull a full "G" all the way over, the lines may go slack as the pilot free- falls for a moment until the loading is resumed.

Ther are are number of other figures that the Acro pilots may incorporate into their routine such as the Mc Twist or the Misty Flip…

Accuracy

The old favourite with the crowds is trying to land on a specific spot. This is a skill in itself, and in Acro comps the spot is frequently placed on a beach, or even on a floating pontoon, so that the pilots can make stylish approaches in relative safety. Spiralling until one wing-tip touches the water before levelling up on a final approach is a real crowd pleaser, and demands commitment and perfect timing.

Synchro

What could be more thrilling than watching a pilot doing a superb Acro routine? The answer is watching two or more pilots doing them in

Close formation flying (Photo: U-Turn)

synchronisation. This is, of course, more of a display than a competition, and demands excellent communication and teamwork. Flying a manoeuvre like a spiral dive or wingover in close proximity to another pilot also demands a high degree of trust in each others abilities!

Stacks

It is a short step from Synchro to stacking, ie linking canopies and pilots together in some way. This is already a favourite activity among sport parachutists, and Acro teams like the Rebels already incorporate it into their routines..

Testing new wings

If competitions and aerobatics are not exciting enough for you, there is always being a test pilot! (In fact many top Acro flyers and competitors are designers and test pilots by profession)

Testing new canopies falls into two categories. There are professional pilots who work for the testing authorities and whose job is to allocate ratings to production wings.

Each manufacturer also has development test pilots whose remit is to work with the other members of the design team to refine the prototype craft into saleable products. Tasks can vary from trying to remove creases from the leading edge by endless launching, landing and trimming the wing to checking the recovery characteristics in a stall and making modifications to the design. Much initial design work is now done with computer aided design programmes, but there is still no substitute for getting the craft into the air. The process of designing and testing a new wing is covered in Chapter 38.

©2002 Red Bull - www.redbull-vertigo.

©2001 www.redbull-vertigo.com

40 The Future

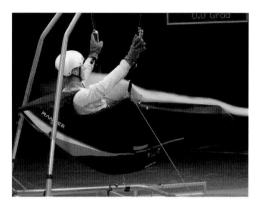

Aerodynamic testing in a wind tunnel : Pic Skywalk GBh

At the time of writing (January 2015), the top performance canopies are offering a sink rate of around 0.8m per second This is similar to the wings of the last two or three years, but the real improvement has come at the top end of the speed range: 50kph + top speeds and glide performance of 12: 1 is now achievable and on these machines cross-country flights are becoming more and more commonplace. The world open distance record is currently 502.2km, and even more notably, the distance and average speed being achieved in international competition tasks is still climbing steadily. Perhaps the most important achievement, however, is that the wings aimed at the recreational pilots are also capable of long XC flights, and the safety and security offered by them far superior to that available just a few years ago.

Interestingly, in real terms the price of paragliders and equipment has reduced steadily over the last few years as well; there has never been a better time to get involved!

Over the last few years prototypes have been flown that are swept forward, contain spanwise battens, have air intakes on the underside of the wing, valved entries, ever more sealed cells, and most noticeably the introduction of thin plastic rods, to helping form a well- defined leading edge. There is a trend for an ever-decreasing number of lines.

Harnesses have evolved enormously, ever more efficient air and foam spinal protection systems has been a major change in the last ten years, enclosed pod type harnesses are now becoming much more common and on the instrument side, the revolution in navigation caused by the accessibility of GPS data has had a major impact.

What of the future? Paragliding is a now a mature sport with a history of over 30 years, it is no longer growing in most European nations though there is continuing interest in new markets. The sport will need to continue to become ever safer, and more accessible (as it has been doing) to keep growing and to remain attractive to a wide range of people.

It will never be a huge mass-appeal sport, as most people are not that keen on throwing themselves off mountains into space. And modern society is becoming ever more risk averse. But as we continue to buy sites and work with local communities and landowners it will become more firmly established.

The biggest threat to paragliding is the insurance situation. Insurers are worried by the prospect of big payouts to injured people, and are shunning many activities that involve risk. A few high profile claims could make the sport uninsurable.

In the UK the trend is no longer for the hardened enthusiast who racks up thousands of hours and spends almost every weekend out on the hills, but for pilots who enjoy their sport by flying on a few of the best days of the year at home, and taking two or three week's holiday a year flying in the Alps, or perhaps somewhere warm like Portugal, Greece or Morocco. Spring and autumn have become the favourite times for flying trips to destinations like this, or winter for combining skiing and flying or travelling to the southern hemisphere.

This is the same pattern for many sports, from scuba diving to windsurfing, and of course has always been the norm for skiing. With our busy lives, our sports and hobbies have to fit in with a million other things.

Sports go in and out of fashion in our culture, and paragliding has certainly had its meteoric rise, but it has now settled to a more sustainable level,. The continuing development of the new and visually appealing discipline of Acro flying, and especially the accessibility of

The Sup air BASE cut away reserve system in operation, the discarded main canopy deploys the reserve canopy automatically

paramotoring continues to attract new pilots.

Flying is one of mankind's oldest dreams, yet sport flying just for fun has always been very inaccessible. You needed time, money and expertise to get airborne, making it impractical for many people.

Paragliding makes flying accessible to a huge range of people. After all, a flying machine you can carry with you wherever you travel, or store under your bed, is a dream come true for most of us.

41 Information

National associations – Useful web addresses

British Hang-Gliding and Paragliding Association (BHPA)
The British Hang Gliding and Paragliding
Association Ltd
8 Merus Court
Meridian Business Park
Leicester
LE19 1RJ
United Kingdom

Telephone: 0116 289 4316
Fax: 0116 281 4949
Email:office@bhpa.co.uk
www.bhpa.co.uk

United States Hang-gliding & Paragliding Association
www.ushga.org

FFVL (French Association)
www.ffvl.fr

DHV (German Association)
www.dhv.de

Australian Federation
www.hgfa.asn.au

New Zealand
www.nzhgpa.org.nz

Canada
www.hpac.ca

Korea
www.kpga.or.kr

Italy
www.fivl.it

Denmark
www.danskdrageflyverunion.dk

Sweden
www.paragliding.se

Switzerland
www.shv-fsvl.ch

Weather Information

UK weather forecasts
www.bbc.co.uk/weather

Actual weather at UK launch sites:
www.wendywindlblows.com
(subscription service)

Aviation weather, UK (log in required)
secure.metoffice.gov.uk/logon.jsp

RASP (UK)
rasp.inn.leedsmet.ac.uk/

XC Weather
xcweather.co.uk

International weather forecasts

Accuweather
www.accuweather.com

Meteoblue
Meteoblue.com

Other Useful Information

FAI (Federation Aeronautique Internationale)
www.fai.org
www.fai.org/hang_gliding/paragliding

Paragliding world Cup data inc pilot rankings
www.pwca.org

UK Air chart updates
www.caa.co.uk/dap

DHV (Glider certification data)
www.dhv.de

Information, specs etc of gliders.
www.para2000.org/wings/index.html

Further Reading

Skywings Magazine (BHPA publication)
Subscriptions: BHPA office.
Editor: Joe Schofield, skywings@bhpa.co

Pilot Handbook
Mark Dale

Paramotoring From the Ground Up
Noel Whittal

Paramotoring the Essential Guide
Dean Eldridge

Meteorology and Flight
Tom Bradbury

Understanding Flying Weather
Derek Piggott

flybubble

We want to help you fly

We offer training for all levels of pilots.

Build confidence and gain skills so you get the best out of your time in the air.

Focused on your success

Our website is filled with articles to help you fly better.

Our videos share essential skills and safety techniques.

Our mailing list offers regular news, flying articles, reviews and tips to help you progress.

Looking for the best value?

Don't buy something because it's the cheapest and end up with the wrong kit. This can be an expensive mistake!

We use our expertise as instructors to match your skills with equipment which is perfectly suited to you.

We have the widest range of top brands so we can recommend the best choice.

Try our demo wings

Advance	
Gin	
Nova	
Niviuk	
Ozone	
Skywalk	
Sup'Air	

Nothing beats a test flight of a new wing! We offer harness and helmet fittings too.

A great selection - in stock!

	Aircotec
	ASI
	Flytec
	Flymaster
	Naviter
	Syride

And that's just the instrument range ...

Your enthusiastic experts

We regularly review new gear while we fly cross country. That's why we are able to give you the best advice, based on real experience with the latest designs.

So if you value great service, visit **flybubble.com** or give us a call!

FlySpain

FlySpain

Europe's favourite flying centre
Full time BHPA School

The perfect environment to learn, reliable sunny weather, great instructors, a safe environment and great flying.... what better way to learn all year round!

Post club pilot course for soaring, thermalling and XC Build up your hours in southern Spain's friendliest flying area.

The web site says it all - **www.flyspain.co.uk**

Anlgodanles, Andalucia ,Spain

Email: info@flyspain.co.uk **Tel:** 0208 144 2087 **Mobile:** +34 651 736 718

BHPA REGISTERED SCHOOL

Fly Spain acredited by the British Hang Gliding & Paragliding Association

Paragliding

training in Wales
training in France
training in Morocco

paragliders
paramotors
speedwings

Webshop : School
www.paraglide.co.uk

UK main dealers

Glossary of terms

"A" line
Line to the leading edge of the wing

ACPULS
Now defunct European airworthiness testing body

Aerodynamics
The study of moving air

Aerofoil
The shape of a section through a wing

AFNOR
Previous European airworthiness body.

Airspeed
The speed of the aircraft through the air

Alto-
Prefix for cloud types, those between 8,000ft & 18,000 ft altitude.

Angle of attack
The angle at which the airflow meets the wing

Aspect ratio
The ratio of the span to the average chord (width) of the wing

ATZ
Aerodrome traffic zone

Brake
Control used to alter the speed or direction of the wing

"B" line stall
A manoeuvre to disrupt the smooth flow over a wing by pulling down the "B" lines

CEN
(Often just EN European standards agency : see LTF)

Chord
Straight line distance from the leading edge to the trailing edge at any given point on the span.

Cirro-
prefix of a cloud type meaning above 18,000ft.

Cirrus
Very high ice clouds

Cumulus
A "heaped" cloud found above thermals

Drag ailerons
The correct term for the control system of the paraglider

Dyneema
A type of line material

Flare
The action of applying full brake hard to slow down on landing.

FLARM
A type of transponder (qv) that displays the position of any nearby aircraft which are also equipped with a transponder.

Glide ratio
Ratio of distance travelled horizontally to the height lost

GPS
(Global Positioning System) – a hand held navigational instrument

Groundspeed
The speed of the aircraft over the ground

Keeper
A ring or pulley sewn to the rear riser to retain the control line

Kevlar
A type of line material

Lift
Either the upward force created by the action of the aerofoil, or air that is rising faster than the wing is sinking

Lapse rate
The rate of temperature decrease with height

Maillon rapide
Trade name of the steel links used to connect the lines to the risers and sometimes the risers to the harness

MATZ
Military aerodrome traffic zone

Min(imum) sink rate
The canopy's slowest rate of descent

Pitch
Rotation of an aircraft through lateral axis (nose up or down)

PLF
Parachute landing fall

Polyester
Type of canopy fabric

RASP (Regional Atmospheric Soaring Prediction)
This is a forecast of the likely thermal strength. Very useful to Cross-country pilots.

Rip-stop nylon
Type of canopy fabric

Riser
Webbing connecting the harness to the lines

Roll
Rotation of an aircraft through its longitudinal axis (banking)

Sink
Descending air

Stall
Point at which the airflow over the wing breaks away an there is no longer sufficient lift to support the aircraft

Thermal
Bubble of a column of rising air

Wind gradient
Reduction in wind speed near the ground due to friction

Conversions

1 knot	=	**1.15 mph**
1 mph	=	**1.609 kph**
1 kph	=	**0.622 mph**
1 kg	=	**2.204 lbs**
1,000ft	=	**305 metres**
1000 metres	=	**3,280 ft**

Index

accelerator systems 3, 19-20, 25, 42, 81, 94, 127-128, 129, 175

accidents 11, 14, 33, 36, 40, 44, 56, 102, 113-114, 182, 185-186, 190, 194, 199, 236

Acro 177, 206, 241, 245-249, 251

active flying 42, 83-84, 170

advanced pilot 45, 229, 231

aerofoil 10, 17, 22-23, 25, 27, 31, 170, 176, 230, 261-262

AFNOR 261

air chart 143, 191, 231, 253

air law 3, 5, 39, 54, 92, 108, 130, 135-145, 191, 224, 226-227, 230

Air Navigation Order 12, 40, 142

airspace 13, 63, 69, 107-108, 110, 135-141, 143, 145, 158, 161-163, 165-167, 169, 224, 226-227, 230

airspeed 20, 22-23, 25, 28, 30-32, 38-39, 48, 79, 81-82, 90, 99, 168-170, 173-175, 191, 216, 218, 221, 225, 230, 240, 261

airways 136, 139

airworthiness 10-11, 33, 55, 60, 104, 111, 113, 115, 117, 182, 210, 233-234, 236, 261

alcohol 12, 131, 195

alpine flying 103

alpine launch 3, 64, 74, 92, 191, 197

Alps 8, 44, 91, 94, 110, 149, 192, 198, 202, 206, 251

altimeter 62, 108, 110, 136, 143-144, 154, 165-167

altitude 9, 12-13, 15, 25, 29, 36, 44-45, 50, 54, 79, 82-83, 86, 105, 107-110, 120, 122, 132, 135, 138-139, 141-144, 148, 151, 153, 156, 158, 160-161, 165-166, 174-175, 177, 181, 191, 202, 216, 222-223, 231, 239, 245, 261

anabatic flow 201

angle of attack 23-30, 90, 121, 127, 129, 170-171, 174, 216, 218, 261

annual inspection 43

anti-collision rules 39, 123, 132-135

aspect ratio 28, 30-31, 242, 261

asymmetric tuck 42, 83, 117, 172, 235, 240, 242

ATZ 139-140, 144-145, 166, 261

back protection 96, 98, 111, 182, 236, 237

barograph 108

Bennett, Bill 8

big ears 19, 42, 84, 129, 174-177, 213-214, 222, 226

bird sanctuaries 141, 228

bivouac 242-244

"B" line stall 84, 176, 181, 261

BMAA 210, 223, 228

bottom landing 52, 86

brakes 25-26, 29-30, 63, 65, 69-73, 75-76, 82, 85, 88-90, 104, 123, 125, 127-129, 132, 170-174, 176, 179, 191, 195-199, 212-216, 218, 220-222, 224, 236, 261

British Hang-Gliding and Paragliding Association (BHPA) 3, 5, 11, 33-34, 36-37, 39, 42-43, 45, 58, 81, 83-84, 92-93, 131, 134, 137, 182-183, 190, 193-195, 206-207, 223, 225, 227-229, 234, 237, 252-253

CAA 45, 110, 191, 210, 228, 230

canopy control 44, 90, 126

care of the canopy 120

cells 16-18, 25, 63, 65, 68, 119-120, 172, 175-176, 180, 234, 250

CEN 60, 102, 104, 106, 112, 114, 116, 194, 234, 261

centre of pressure 27, 216

certification 21, 55, 60, 97, 103, 106, 112-117, 210, 232, 234, 237, 253

clothing 15, 57, 111, 222, 226

clouds 54, 56, 108, 124, 135-136, 146-155, 158, 160-162, 165, 181, 201-202, 222, 229-231, 261
    alto 148, 150, 261
    cirrus 148, 150-151, 261
    cumulus 54, 56, 124, 148-151, 153-154, 161, 165, 261
    lenticular 56, 150, 155
    nimbus 56, 148, 150-151, 158, 181
    stratus 148, 150

club pilot 9, 40, 43, 45, 91, 226, 230-231

compass 108, 163-164, 166-167, 226

competitions 3, 9, 34, 108-109, 114-115, 117, 127, 129, 160, 163, 165, 168, 182, 188, 204-206, 236, 245, 249, 250 control area *139*

controlled airspace *108, 136-137, 139, 141, 143, 145, 161, 169, 227*

controls *24-26, 32-33, 35, 38, 63, 65, 69-72, 75-77, 83, 85, 88-89, 126, 129, 170, 172-174, 176-177, 179, 187, 198-199, 210, 213*

cross country flying *152, 158-167*

CTA *139, 166*

Daily Inspection *61*

danger area *139-141, 166*

deafness *12*

death spiral *247*

deep stall *83, 113, 174, 176, 191, 239, 240*

depression *150-152*

design *3, 7-11, 16, 18, 20, 27-28, 31, 85, 97-98, 102-106, 112-115, 117, 130, 137, 142, 147, 168, 176, 209, 211-213, 215-219, 229, 232-233, 237, 239, 249*

DHV *99, 106, 112-113, 116-117, 234, 237, 252-253*

Dickenson, John *7*

drugs *12, 43, 131, 186, 195*

Elementary Pilot *230*

emergency procedures *3, 178-184*

exams *3, 34, 91-92, 207, 229*

fabrics *9, 18*

first aid *182-184*

fitness *35, 36, 210*

flare *88-90, 126, 178, 223-224, 261*

flight planning *44, 52, 77-78, 80, 92, 178-179, 202*

flying abroad *14-15, 44, 93, 200*

flying suit *14-15, 111*

Foehn *202*

foot launched *8, 191-192, 210, 226, 245*

footwear *15*

forecasts *146-148, 154, 158, 165, 205, 208, 230, 253, 262*

form drag *27*

forward launch *3, 67, 74, 191, 213, 221*

free-fall *9, 192*

front risers *65, 68-69, 72-73, 75, 127, 175*

fronts *150-152, 157*
    cold *150-152*
    occluded *150, 231*
    warm *150-152*

front tuck *172*

full stall *173-174, 181, 235, 241*

glide angle *29, 85-86*

glide ratio *29, 168, 261*

GPS *108-110, 137, 162-164, 205, 226, 243-244, 250, 261*

ground handling *19, 26, 36, 38, 42, 72, 75-76, 80, 128, 197, 210, 212, 224*

groundspeed *82, 89, 107, 109, 160-161, 163-164, 192, 223, 226, 230, 261*

gusts *50, 55, 126, 151, 170-172, 180*

Hang-gliding *7-11, 33-34, 104, 145, 163, 252*

harness *15, 17, 19-20, 37-38, 57, 61, 63, 67, 75, 89, 96-102, 104, 107, 111, 115, 118-121, 127-128, 131, 178-180, 182, 185, 194, 199, 210, 213-214, 218, 221-222, 234, 236-238, 243-244, 250, 262*

helmet *12, 20-21, 57, 61, 63, 102-103, 107, 111, 131, 182, 184, 194, 234*

high pressure *105, 143, 154, 231*

induced drag *18, 27-28, 127*

inflation *9, 17, 65, 70, 196, 224-225*

instability *3, 18, 25-26, 42, 55, 83, 170, 182, 188, 191, 218, 222*

instructor *3-6, 12-14, 20, 32-45, 75, 77-81, 83-84, 86, 88, 90, 92, 94, 102, 113-114, 168, 172, 176, 182-183, 185, 190, 193-194, 196, 198-199, 207-208, 218, 225-226, 229, 239-241*
    ratings *207*

insurance *14-15, 33-34, 40, 61, 130-131, 182, 194-195, 199, 200, 227, 234, 250*

jetstream *150*

keeper *19, 25, 61, 68, 179, 213, 222, 261*

kites *7, 72, 189-190, 192, 245*

landing *3, 12, 15, 26, 35, 37-42, 44, 49-54, 56-57, 77, 79-83, 85-90, 92, 94, 98-100, 102, 120-121, 124-126, 129-130, 142-144, 162, 164, 175, 178-180, 188, 191, 194, 196-199, 201-205, 212, 215-216, 222-226, 228, 237, 240, 244, 249, 261-262*

lapse rate *153-154, 158, 262*

launching *3, 5, 7-8, 19, 35-37, 39, 42, 44-45, 60, 62-76, 78-81, 85, 89, 92, 94, 96, 98-99, 110, 125-126, 130-131, 142, 147, 162, 164-166, 189-192, 194-197, 199-204, 210-213, 215-216, 220-221, 223-226, 233-234, 244-245, 249, 253*

   problems *3, 74-76*

leading edge *16-19, 22, 24, 62, 64, 75-76, 118-119, 121, 127, 171, 173, 178, 203, 216, 249-250, 261*

lift *9-10, 22-30, 39-42, 44-50, 53, 56, 68, 79, 81-83, 86-87, 90, 94, 103, 106-108, 110, 122-125, 127, 132-133, 141, 147, 149-150, 154-158, 160-162, 164-166, 168-169, 173-175, 177, 179, 181, 188, 190, 192, 201-202, 204, 210, 215-216, 221, 223, 230, 237, 244, 262*

lines *17-19, 23, 25, 27, 45, 55, 60-63, 65, 67-70, 74, 76, 89, 112-113, 118, 120-121, 126-128, 171-172, 174-176, 178-180, 191, 210, 213, 220-222, 233, 239-240, 248, 250, 261-262*

loops *177, 248*

low pressure *27, 47, 143-144*

manufacturers *9-11, 29, 31, 43, 60, 104, 106, 111, 113-116, 131, 176, 193-194, 206, 211, 214, 217, 232-234, 236-238, 243, 249*

MATZ *140, 143, 166, 262*

minimum sink rate *24, 29, 45, 168-169, 262*

mountain flying *44, 201*

Moyes, Bill *8*

navigation *108-110, 134, 137, 141-142, 163, 224, 226, 231, 250, 261*

Neumark, Walter *8*

NOTAM *141, 142, 165*

paramotoring *3, 143, 209-228, 251, 253*

parascending *8*

parasitic drag *27-28, 51*

performance *5, 8-11, 16-19, 23, 28-31, 42, 52, 101, 106, 111-114, 117, 158, 160-161, 163, 168-169, 174, 185, 188, 205, 214-216, 219, 231-232, 237, 244, 250*

phonetic alphabet *145*

Pilot Rating *3, 33, 207, 227*

Pilot Rating System (PRS) *3, 33, 45, 83-84*

planform *17, 30*

polar curve *3, 168-169*

power lines *49-50, 54, 181*

pre-flight checks *3, 38, 43, 60-64, 67, 94, 121, 165, 178*

pressure altitude *144*

profile drag *27*

Purcell, Tom Junior *7*

QFE *144, 166-167*

QNH *144-145*

radios *12, 14-15, 20, 39, 41, 44, 63, 77, 79, 83, 92, 109-110, 136, 140-141, 144-146, 148, 162, 165-167, 188, 190, 223-224, 226, 239, 240-241*

ram-air *8, 9, 209*

rate of descent *10, 262*

rear risers *19, 72, 83, 89-90, 126-127, 174, 178-179, 230, 240, 261*

rear riser steering *83*

reserve parachute *20, 38, 42, 61, 96, 103-104, 121, 172, 182, 188, 237*

responsibility *13-14, 33, 35, 39, 133-134, 138, 198, 207*

reverse launch *3, 26, 36, 40, 42, 44, 63, 67- 76, 89, 92, 94, 126, 196-197, 220, 225-226*

ridge soaring *41, 45, 55, 105, 123, 144*

risers *17, 19, 61, 63, 65, 68-69, 71-72, 75-76, 83, 89-90, 97, 104, 120, 126-128, 174-176, 178-180, 197-198, 213-214, 217-218, 222, 225, 230, 233, 240, 261-262*

Rogallo, Francis *7*

rotor *47-49, 124, 156, 172, 179, 202, 224*

Ryan Aircraft *7*

sailplanes *11, 28, 56, 134, 141, 166-167*

SAT *246*

sea breeze *44, 111, 152, 157*

sink rate *24, 29, 30, 45, 87, 103-104, 106, 111, 123, 168-169, 174-175, 194, 216, 237, 238, 244, 250, 262*

SIV *117, 239-240, 241-242, 245*

skis *3, 36, 189-192*

soaring *3, 6, 8, 13, 34, 36, 40-41, 44-45, 47-49, 53, 55, 81, 83, 90, 92, 95, 105, 111, 115, 122-126, 133-134, 137, 143-144, 147, 155, 189, 192-193, 209-210, 212, 262*

speed bar *128-129, 169, 176-177, 235*

spins *42, 121, 172, 174, 218, 224, 230, 241, 246*

spiral dive *84, 175, 181, 198, 241, 246, 249*

stability *9-10, 17-18, 31, 81, 104, 111, 117, 213-218, 222, 229, 236*

stall *10, 24-26, 28, 30-31, 42, 53, 55, 73, 81-84, 89-90, 105, 113, 121, 126, 168, 170, 172-176, 181, 190-191, 196, 199, 218, 224-225, 230, 235-236, 239-241, 249, 262*

standard pressure setting *144, 165*

tandem *3, 19, 30, 35, 36, 44, 72, 90, 97, 102, 113, 127, 186, 193-199, 234*

thermalling *34-35, 108, 133, 135, 174-175, 193, 216*

thermals *9, 11, 34-35, 44-45, 49-50, 53-54, 56, 83, 87, 107-108, 114, 123-124, 132-135, 147, 149-154, 158, 160-162, 165-167, 169-172, 174-175, 193, 200-201, 205-206, 214, 216-217, 229-230, 262*

top landing *41, 94, 124-125, 179, 196, 198-199*

torque effect *211, 213, 221, 224*

towing *8, 45, 189, 191, 210, 226, 230*

trailing edge *17, 19, 24-27, 55, 65, 68, 75, 118-119, 174, 178, 181, 261*

trainee instructor *207*

training *5-6, 8-9, 11-12, 15, 20, 27, 33-38, 40, 42-45, 55, 58, 77, 79-81, 83, 85, 91-93, 95, 111, 115, 117, 140-141, 143, 165-166, 182-183, 186, 188, 194, 196, 198-199, 207, 212, 215-216, 218, 221, 223, 225-226, 234, 237, 241*

tree landings *180*

trimmers *19, 30, 127, 218, 221*

tuck *18, 23-24, 26, 42, 46, 58, 74, 83, 94, 114, 117, 161, 170-177, 216, 221-222, 224-225, 230, 235, 240, 242*

tumbling *47, 177, 197, 248*

turbulence *14, 27-28, 42, 44, 46-47, 53, 55-56, 58, 75, 103, 111, 123-124, 127, 147, 149-150, 156, 158, 161, 170-173, 176, 178-179, 181, 188, 196, 216, 222, 224, 230, 234-235*

turns *26, 39-42, 44, 79-81, 83, 85-87, 105, 122-124, 126, 174-175, 192, 218, 223-226, 240, 246-247*
   360° *42, 44, 71, 83, 162, 174-175, 192, 223, 225, 246*

valley wind *44, 53, 87, 201, 224*

variometer *29, 107-108, 111, 124*

venturi *49, 51, 53, 201*

Visual Meteorological Conditions (VMC) *135, 136, 139, 143, 165-166, 224, 230*

vortices *27-28, 161*

water landing *98, 179, 240*

wave *9, 56, 122-124, 147, 150, 155-157, 180-181, 202, 222*

weather *3, 5-6, 13, 15, 31, 34-39, 42-44, 50, 54, 56, 63, 80, 92-94, 110, 143, 146-157, 170, 179, 185-186, 201, 203, 205, 208-209, 222, 226, 230, 253*

Williams, Gerald *8*

wind *13, 15, 19, 29, 31-32, 34, 36-37, 39, 42-53, 55-56, 63-65, 67-72, 74-76, 80-83, 85-90, 99, 111, 118, 122-126, 128, 133, 146-148, 150-152, 155-158, 160-163, 165-169, 174-177, 179-182, 190-192, 196-197, 199-202, 209, 215-217, 220-225, 228, 230, 250, 253, 262*
   direction *45, 47, 88, 150, 155, 158, 162, 179, 223*
   gradient *50-52, 88, 228, 262*
   speed indicator *55*
   strength *48, 52-53, 55, 147, 156, 202*

wing-over *177*

Wright brothers *7*

yaw *25*